Formula Funding of Public Services

Public services account for a major segment of most economies. With an increasingly aware public, governments are seeking to find more systematic and transparent approaches towards allocating public funds, in the form of mathematical funding formulae. The philosophy, design and economic consequences of funding formulae have become key policy issues worldwide. Examples include the increased use of pupil case payment methods in schooling, increasingly elaborate capitation payment mechanisms in health care, and the specification of vouchers for users of services in fields as diverse as personal social services and universities.

Peter C. Smith presents a comprehensive introduction to the theory and practice underlying the use of formulae as a basis for funding public services. *Formula Funding of Public Services* discusses the objectives of public finance systems, and the role of formulae funding within those systems, as well as introducing a general economic model with which to analyse the formula funding problem. The author also examines a series of case studies and illuminates how the theory can be turned into practice. Special attention is given to the issues of budgetary risk in formula funding, and of integrating incentives for service quality into the funding mechanism. Throughout, the author gives many examples of operational funding mechanisms, as well as examining priorities for future work, most notably the need to integrate the funding of public services with performance criteria.

Formula Funding of Public Services draws on the author's wide experience of designing formulae and advising governments on their implementation, and brings together the economic, statistical and political issues underlying formula funding.

Peter C. Smith is Professor of Economics and Director of the Centre for Health Economics at the University of York.

Routledge studies in business organizations and networks

Formula Funding of Public Services

Peter C. Smith

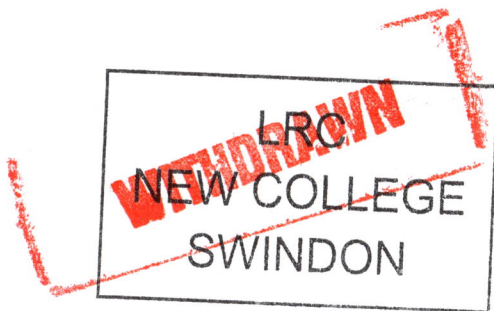

Routledge
Taylor & Francis Group

LONDON AND NEW YORK

First published 2007   2017001807
by Routledge
2 Park Square, Milton Park, Abingdon, Oxon OX14 4RN

Simultaneously published in the USA and Canada
by Routledge
711 Third Avenue, New York, NY 10017

Routledge is an imprint of the Taylor & Francis Group, an informa business

First issued in paperback 2012

Typeset in Times by Wearset Ltd, Boldon, Tyne and Wear

British Library Cataloguing in Publication Data
A catalogue record for this book is available from the British Library

Library of Congress Cataloging in Publication Data
A catalog record for this book has been requested

ISBN13: 978-0-415-51152-0 (pbk)
ISBN13: 978-0-415-36289-4 (hbk)
ISBN13: 978-0-203-01302-1 (ebk)

Contents

Figures

Tables

Boxes

Preface

Public services account for a major segment of most economies, and there is growing importance attached to the outcomes they secure. As a result, citizens and their representatives are showing heightened concern that tax payments may not be being used to best effect, and governments are increasingly seeking assurance that the methods they use to pay for public services are not wasting taxpayers' money. In particular they wish to be assured that the funds paid to local governments and public service providers are in line with policy intentions, and are encouraging the cost-effective provision of public services.

As a result, there has been a desire to move away from traditional methods of paying for local public services, such as historical precedent or political patronage. Instead, governments and other payers are seeking to place greater emphasis on making approaches towards allocating public funds more transparent and systematic, in the form of mathematical funding formulae. Examples include the increased use of pupil case payment methods in schooling, increasingly elaborate capitation payment mechanisms in health care (particularly in countries relying on social health insurance), and the specification of vouchers for users of services in fields as diverse as personal social services and schooling.

A cynic might argue that this trend reflects the desperation of governments trying to devolve to the technical domain increasingly fraught political debates over funding decisions. There may be an element of truth in this view. But equally many governments clearly do wish to place their funding methods on more solid technical foundations. At the very least, in order to retain support for the taxation necessary to sustain the public services, governments may wish to demonstrate to the public that tax revenues are being distributed systematically, in accordance with voters' preferences.

The trend towards formulaic funding mechanisms has been given added impetus by dramatic improvements in the scope and timeliness of data sources measuring the inputs, activities and outcomes of the public services. These informational developments have opened up spectacular opportunities to apply scientific approaches to the funding of local services. Moreover, many new statistical and econometric techniques are emerging that enable models to be placed on a more scientifically secure foundation.

Yet, notwithstanding the increased demand for scientific funding mechanisms, and the rapid improvements in analytic potential, the state of current methodology for the design of funding formulae is – with a few exceptions – very rudimentary and frequently analytically unsatisfactory. Although supposedly scientific, many formulae in use are frankly unfit for their stated purpose, and may be perpetuating the inefficiencies and inequalities they purport to address.

This book summarizes the current 'state of the formula funding art'. It covers the most important analytic issues relevant to the development of funding formulae, and seeks to offer guidelines for best practice. The book is intended to be practical. It covers theoretical issues to the extent that they illuminate the practical design of funding mechanisms. However, it is not feasible to do justice to the entire research literature relevant to the finance of public services. Instead, the reader is referred to more specialist texts where relevant. Given my own preoccupations, many of the examples are taken from UK public services, and there is an emphasis on health care. However, I have sought throughout the book to draw out the implications for other countries, and for services beyond health care.

The book is aimed at those directly charged with designing and implementing funding mechanisms. It presents a framework for thinking about the formula funding approach, summarizes some of the more important statistical approaches towards designing such formulae, and describes possible extensions to current methods. However, it is important that the political context of formula funding is kept in mind, so the book includes a discussion of the political economy of formula funding. A full description of the contents is given in Chapter 1.

Peter C. Smith
University of York
December 2005

Acknowledgements

The book is the fruit of over ten years working on the design of funding formulae in a variety of public services. It therefore reflects the contributions of many colleagues in universities, government departments and international agencies whose wisdom informs many of the observations made in the book, but whom I may regrettably sometimes fail to acknowledge directly. I should however like to make special mention of my colleagues Roy Carr-Hill and Nigel Rice, without whose qualities much of this work would have never come to fruition, and who jointly authored much of the material on which Chapter 5 is based. I should also like to thank co-authors Katharina Hauck and Rebecca Shaw, with whom I jointly wrote much of Chapter 4, and Nick York (Chapter 7). Vanessa Windass provided invaluable secretarial support, and Rob Langham at Routledge offered help and advice throughout. Finally, and most importantly, I should like to thank Sally and Lily for their forbearance during what has not always been the smoothest of projects.

I am grateful to colleagues in the Management Department at the University of St Andrews for providing a quiet haven during preparation of the manuscript, and to participants at conferences and workshops organized by the Royal Statistical Society, the American Statistical Association, the World Bank, the World Health Organization, the International Monetary Fund, the Spanish Health Economics Association, the Chilean Health Insurance Fund (FONASA) and many academic seminars. The preparation of the book was funded by Economic and Social Research Council research fellowship R000271253.

Chapter 4 is based on material that has previously appeared in *Health Economics* (Hauck *et al.*, 2002) and the *Oxford Review of Economic Policy* (Smith, P.C., 2003).

Chapter 5 is based on material that appeared in the *Journal of the Royal Statistical Society, Series A* (Smith *et al.*, 2001).

A shorter version of Chapter 7 appeared in *Health Affairs* (Smith and York, 2004). The material was originally prepared with Nick York for the meeting *Improving quality of health care in the United States and the United Kingdom: strategies for change and action* held at the Pennyhill Park Conference Centre, 11–13 July 2003, organized jointly by the Commonwealth Fund and the Nuffield Trust.

1 Setting the scene

1.1 Introduction

Most government expenditure is geographically specific. This is manifest in the vast number of local institutions that arrange the financing, regulation and provision of public services, such as local governments, courts, schools and hospitals, and the natural preference of service users to secure access to public services locally. The major exceptions to this localism are a small number of national public goods, such as defence and international relations, and some (but not all) systems of welfare payments. Yet even these programmes can have important local dimensions, for example in the form of the choice of location for a military airport.

It can be argued that – because local people enjoy the benefit of local public services – they should be funded solely through local taxes and charges. Indeed this was the dominant principle underlying early systems of local government in the UK, most notably the provisions of the Poor Law of 1602, which for over 200 years placed the financial responsibility for poor relief on local parishes. However, this principle became unsustainable. A central concern was the coincidence of high spending needs and low taxable resources that occurred in the poorest jurisdictions. This gave rise to pressures for needy citizens to emigrate to more generous parishes, and an incentive for parishes to stint on poor relief, in order to discourage such emigration (Keith-Lucas, 1980).

As a result, a series of reforms in the nineteenth century created the precursors of modern local government, in Britain, Europe and elsewhere. A central feature of the reformed systems was a desire to effect financial transfers from richer, low needs areas to poorer, high needs areas in order that certain minimal standards could be secured everywhere. In England, such transfers were effected through a range of central government grants-in-aid to local governments. Bennett (1982) cites examples from the nineteenth century in fields as diverse as prisons, police, roads, schools, sanitation and housing.

Thus, even when public expenditure is undertaken locally, national or regional government has a crucial role in financing and influencing the nature of local public services, through its financial equalization role. An extensive literature has now developed in the field of fiscal federalism, which seeks to model the economics of grants-in-aid from central to local government (Oates, 1999). Many of the principles of fiscal federalism often apply even when the local organizational unit is not a tier of government, but rather some other administrative unit (such as a welfare benefit office) or a local service provider (such as a university). The role of public finance in local public services is discussed in more detail in Chapter 2.

The remainder of this chapter sets the scene for the book. I first seek to clarify terminology and then outline the various forms of funding mechanism found in most systems of local public services. The chapter then introduces the notion of formula funding, and discusses the broad arguments for its use. The chapter ends with a brief description of some landmarks in formula funding of UK public services, and an outline of the remainder of the book.

1.2 The flow of funds in public services

In order to secure clarity about the terminology used in the book, Figure 1.1 offers a conceptual framework for the flow of funds implicit in the finance of local public services. The prime source of central government funds is taxation, paid in a variety of forms by citizens and businesses. This creates a pool of revenue (A) available to the government, which must decide how it will allocate the funds to support locally delivered public service programmes, either wholly or in part.

The central government might pay local providers directly (E), as for example in the US Medicare programme of health care for older people. However, national governments usually devolve purchasing powers to lower tiers of government, such as states, regions or various forms of local government or local administration. Throughout, I usually refer to these devolved administrations as local government. They are to a greater or lesser extent financed by grants-in-aid from the central government funding mechanism (C).

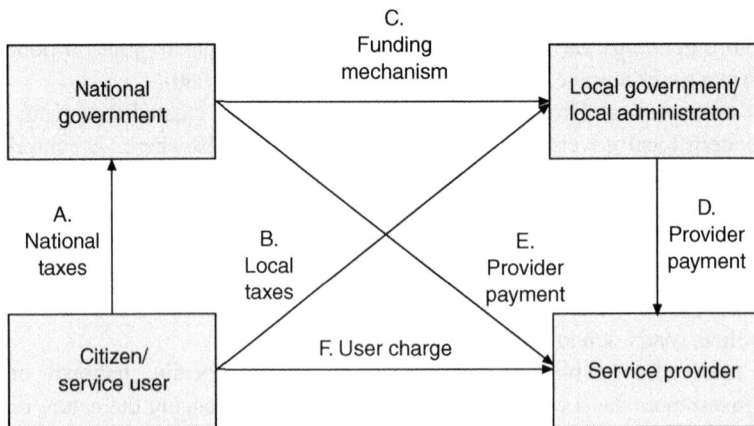

Figure 1.1 The flow of funds in public services.

Local governments may be solely reliant on national funds, but are often able to augment their revenue with local taxes (B). They then purchase services from providers (D). In some circumstances, the distinction between purchaser and provider may be unclear (for example, schools are often directly provided by local governments). However, even where there is no explicit payment mechanism, local governments must in principle purchase their services from vertically integrated providers. Finally, the service user might be required to pay a charge to the local government or directly to the service provider (F).

In practice, the flow of funds may be more complex than this schema suggests. For example, regional local governments might in turn devolve some purchasing powers to municipalities, or police authorities might devolve funding to local operational units. There are also other potential sources of funds, such as commercial municipal businesses. However, in essence, the six flows shown in Figure 1.1 represent the most important conduits of finance found in most public sectors. Indeed, the funding of many public services can be much simpler than this general schema, for example, when there are no local taxes or user charges.

This book is centrally concerned with just two of the funding flows represented in Figure 1.1: the mechanism for funding local governments from national revenues (C); and the mechanism that local governments use for paying providers (D). In addition, by addressing flow D, the book will implicitly address situations in which national governments pay local providers directly (E), without reference to a local intermediary payer. At whatever level of government, I shall refer to the disburser of funds as the payer, whether the payment is made to a lower tier of government or to a provider. The payer's problem is to design a payment mechanism that secures its policy objectives. Flows other than C and D in the diagram are referred to only when they are material to this policy problem.

Under flow C, the recipient of funds is an intermediate tier of administration, acting as a local purchaser of services (for example, a local government, a housing association, a district health authority). Indeed, in the extreme, the recipient could be an individual, who receives cash (for example, the cash payments made to some social care users in the Netherlands) or a voucher (for example, university students in England) with which to purchase public services. Under flow D, the recipient of funds is a provider of services (for example, a university, a hospital, a social services day centre). The ownership of the provider is largely immaterial – it could be a for-profit commercial undertaking, a not-for-profit foundation, a stand-alone public organization, or a wholly owned part of the purchaser organization. However, when designing the funding mechanism, the payer may need to take account of the ownership of providers, and the market in which they operate.

1.3 Types of funding mechanism

Determining the level and distribution of local financial allocations is often very challenging for payers. First, it is a difficult technical exercise to determine where public money is best spent. Second, any funding mechanism introduces powerful incentives for local organizations, and it is important to ensure they are in line with the payer's intentions. Third, the political ramifications of any geographical funding choice can be acute, particularly when parliamentary representatives are elected on a geographical basis. And finally, a national government requires reassurance that public expenditure is being spent locally in line with intentions, yet monitoring the effectiveness and efficiency of local spending is often a difficult undertaking.

There are numerous ways in which a payer could determine the allocation of public funds. At its crudest, the distribution could be based on political patronage, perhaps rewarding localities according to their political support in the past, or their importance for future elections. Although few payers would admit openly to engaging in such patronage, there is ample evidence to suggest that to some extent it informs many allocation systems that are supposedly nonpartisan. The US literature is replete with the practice of pork barrel politics, whereby certain parts of the federal budget are 'earmarked' for local projects in order to secure an acceptance in the legislature of the government's budgetary proposals (Mueller, 2003).

Another approach in widespread use is to distribute public funds according to historical precedent. Politically, it has the great attraction that it minimizes disruption to existing public services, and avoids potentially large swings from year to year inherent in other allocation mechanisms. Its popularity is manifest in the way that more systematic approaches to distribution are frequently abated by 'damping' mechanisms that seek to reduce the magnitude of year-on-year financial losses and gains to localities. However, sole reliance on such methods would leave a payer hostage to history, and powerless to react to changed circumstances or to implement new policies.

A third possibility is to allocate funds according to bids submitted by localities, or to make allocations contingent on some measure of local performance. In principle, this approach has much to commend it. If undertaken properly, it could ensure that public funds were spent in line with national policy intentions, in a cost-effective manner. Its major weakness is that it usually entails large transaction costs, in the form of central scrutiny and policing, and the preparation of bids by localities. It also makes local budgets contingent on the quality of local management, and so may lead to large geographical inequalities. Moreover, even if funds are allocated with scrupulous probity, unsuccessful localities may nevertheless perceive that the allocations have been made according to patronage rather than the quality of bids, leading to a further potential for perceived unfairness.

Finally, financial allocations could be made according to how much localities actually spend. In many circumstances, this approach contradicts principles of good public finance, as it is likely to encourage spending in excess of efficient levels. However, it was in England, the basis for most nineteenth-century forms of central grants-in-aid from central to local government, and its continued importance can be observed in many systems of matching grants (Bennett, 1982).

In practice, most systems of financing local public service institutions use a mix of all four types of mechanism to allocate funds from central to local institutions. However, a fifth approach – allocation by mathematical formula – is increasingly becoming the favoured approach to determining local financial allocations. It can be defined in broad terms as the use of mechanical rules to determine the level of public funds a devolved organization should receive for delivering a specified public service. The next section expands on the concept of formula funding.

1.4　What is formula funding?

The essence of formula funding is that the payer specifies in advance mathematical rules that determine the magnitude of the funding received by a devolved entity in a certain period, and that there are no provisions to change the allocation rules after the budgetary period. The rules might be very simple (for example, a fixed amount of *per capita* funding *per annum*) or very complex (see the example in Box 1.1). They might also be to some extent augmented by other funding mechanisms (for example, additional specific grants from the national government, or local taxes). However, the overarching objective of formula funding is to contribute to the creation of a budget for the local entity with which it is expected to fulfil its duties, in the form of the provision or purchase of public services.

There are two broad approaches to formula funding, discussed in detail in Chapter 3. The first reimburses the local entity (local government or service provider) on the basis of some measure of local activity, typically a count of the number of service users. Such case payment mechanisms are widespread in education (counts of pupils) and health care (counts of patients), and they are especially relevant when an unambiguous indicator of a service user's need for the service can be established. However, they can be vulnerable to perverse incentives to create unwarranted or inappropriate service utilization. Case payment methods give rise to a variable budget for the local entity, based on recorded activity.

The other approach to formula funding is to reimburse according to the *expected* level of local activity. Typically, this takes a measure of the size and characteristics of a locality's population, and infers the expected level of local service expenditure without reference to actual local service use. Because these methods are based on population counts, they have become known as capitation funding methods. They circumvent some of the perverse incentives inherent in case payment, but their effectiveness depends on how successfully the payer can adjust the capitation payments to account for variations in population characteristics. This 'risk adjustment' problem forms the core of Chapter 5 on empirical methods. In general, capitation methods give rise to a fixed budget for the recipient of funds.

Whatever the chosen mechanism, four institutional aspects must be in place for formula funding to take effect in its purest form. First, the delivery of the public service must be to some extent devolved. At one extreme the devolved

Box 1.1 Example of a funding formula: the calculation of Formula Spending
Shares for Social Services for Older People, England, 2003/04

Basic amount

£337.77

Top-ups

AGE TOP-UP
HOUSEHOLD AND SUPPORTED RESIDENTS AGED 75 TO 84 *divided by*
HOUSEHOLD AND SUPPORTED RESIDENTS AGED 65 AND OVER,
rounded to 4 decimal places and *multiplied by* £324.35; *plus*
HOUSEHOLD AND SUPPORTED RESIDENTS AGED 85 AND OVER
divided by **HOUSEHOLD AND SUPPORTED RESIDENTS AGED 65 AND
OVER**, rounded to 4 decimal places and multiplied by £1,093.92; *minus*
£179.15

DEPRIVATION TOP-UP
£238.39 *multiplied by* **PENSIONERS IN RENTED ACCOMMODATION**; *plus*
£344.29 *multiplied by* **ELDERLY WITH LIMITING LONG-TERM
ILLNESS;** *plus*
£480.09 *multiplied by* **ELDERLY ON INCOME SUPPORT/INCOME BASED
JOBSEEKER'S ALLOWANCE**; *plus*
£287.81 *multiplied by* **PENSIONERS LIVING ALONE**; *plus*
£954.60 *multiplied by* **ELDERLY ON ATTENDANCE ALLOWANCE OR
DISABILITY LIVING ALLOWANCE**; *plus*
£516.23 *multiplied by* **PENSIONERS NOT IN A COUPLE AND NOT HEAD
OF HOUSEHOLD**; *minus*
£430.65

The full formula used to calculate the *Social Services for Older People* element is:
(a) **HOUSEHOLD AND SUPPORTED RESIDENTS AGED 65 AND OVER**
multiplied by the result of:

OLDER PEOPLE PSS BASIC AMOUNT; *plus*
OLDER PEOPLE PSS AGE TOP-UP; *plus*
OLDER PEOPLE PSS DEPRIVATION TOP-UP;

(b) The result of (a) is *multiplied by* **LOW INCOME ADJUSTMENT**;
(c) The result of (b) is *multiplied by* **SPARSITY ADJUSTMENT**;
(d) The result of (c) is *multiplied by* **AREA COST ADJUSTMENT FOR
OLDER PEOPLE PSS**;
(e) The result of (d) is then *multiplied by* the **SCALING FACTOR** for the *Social
Services for Older People* sub-block.

Source: Office of the Deputy Prime Minister, 2003.

entities might still be very large governmental organizations, in the form, say, of the Chinese provinces (typical population of 100 million). At the other extreme, the devolved entities might be individual citizens in receipt of vouchers to spend on specified services. Whatever their form, the devolved entities are then responsible for using the funds they receive either to purchase or provide the intended public services, or to devolve the funding to more local institutions.

Second, there must be adequate data, available on a consistent basis across all local organizations, to which can be applied a mechanical formula that determines the level of funding to be allocated to those organizations. The data should of course be verifiable and timely. Also, the formulaic rules should be specified *ex ante*, so that there are no immediate provisions for altering the consequent level of funding. The possibility of *ex post* adjustments to the rules suggests that formula funding budgets are being moderated by considerations of historical spending or political patronage.

Third, there must be some explicit performance criteria against which the performance of the devolved entity is to be judged. It is meaningless to devolve funds without some statement as to what use they are to be put. However, the chosen performance criteria might range from the very rudimentary (for example, assurance that services are delivered with some basic adherence to quality standards), to the extraordinarily complex (see the general practitioner performance measurement example in Chapter 7).

Finally, there must exist some incentive to adhere to the financial allocation implied by the formula. Formula funding is a mere ritual if the recipients of public finances can with impunity ignore the allocations implied by the limits. Sanctions and rewards may take many forms. And they might apply to an organization, to a team, or to an individual manager. For example, local governments that spend in excess of their assumed spending limits may be required to fund the excess from local taxes. Or a head teacher might face dismissal if a school's financial allocation is persistently exceeded. Or a for-profit provider might be threatened with bankruptcy if it fails to secure enough business. There is no requirement that the sanctions should be as 'hard' as these examples, but there must be some incentive for recipients of formula finance to take notice of their allocations.

Formula funding is becoming the dominant mechanism for devolving public finances. Smith (2003) estimates that annually at least £150 billion of UK public expenditure is devolved in this way, and Louis *et al.* (2003) suggest an equivalent figure of $250 billion for federal spending in the United States. Table 1.1 shows some of the major programmes of public expenditure in England for which some sort of formula funding is the dominant method of allocating resources from government departments to local institutions.

1.5 The arguments for formula funding

The main driving force behind formula funding is the desire of payers, such as national and local governments, to limit the magnitude of aggregate expenditure, to share that limited expenditure in an optimal fashion, to transmit objectives to

Table 1.1 Some major national systems of devolved finance, England, 2002/03

Programme	£million
Local government	
(Payer: Office of Deputy Prime Minister)	
Education	22,503
Personal Social Services	9,231
Police	3,577
Fire	1,521
Highway Maintenance	1,955
Other services	8,961
Capital Financing	2,014
Housing	
(Payer: Office of Deputy Prime Minister)	
Housing corporation capital	940
Local government capital	1,325
Local government rents subsidy	4,322
Health authorities	
(Payer: Department of Health)	
Hospital and community	33,782
Prescribing	6,220
HIV/AIDS	362
Primary care	3,890
University funding	
(Payer: Higher Education Funding Council)	
Teaching	3,268
Research	940
Further education	
(Payer: Learning and Skills Council)	
Adult	3,932
Youth	2,570

Source: Smith, 2003.

devolved entities and to give them appropriate incentives. The detailed rationale is set out in Chapter 2. In summary, some of the more important reasons advanced in favour of a formulaic approach towards sharing out limited resources are as follows:

• Formula funding offers the payer a widely accepted mechanism for setting budgets for devolved organizations. Devolution has become a cornerstone of modern public service management, seeking to promote local managerial entrepreneurship, autonomy and financial discipline (Osborne and Gaebler, 1992). Most other methods of budget-setting offer greater scope for game-playing and perverse incentives. Moreover, by facilitating devolution, formula funding can greatly reduce the information and monitoring demands on the payer, and thereby reduce agency costs.

- Formula funding permits resources to be directed where they will secure most benefit. For example, if certain schools receive more than their 'fair' share of finance per pupil, they will be able to offer a better education than other areas. However, assuming decreasing marginal returns to expenditure, that additional finance may secure larger educational benefits if it were directed at less well financed schools. That is, funding on an equal footing can lead to an efficient allocation of resources.
- A well-designed formula allows finance to flow to providers in proportion to the services provided. If public sector providers are not recompensed for the relative needs of their users (for example, if schools were not properly compensated for pupils with special educational needs), they might seek to 'cream skim' only the less needy clients, making it difficult for more disadvantaged citizens to secure the public services to which they are entitled.
- Formula funding facilitates the separation of purchaser and provider, allowing the creation of competitive provider markets or quasi-markets (Bartlett *et al.*, 1998). This may increase efficiency of supply (perhaps by opening up provision of services to the independent sector) and increase the potential for choice of provider among service users.
- Formula funding is an essential tool for addressing equity issues, such as offering equal access to services, or securing equal outcomes, which are often invoked as important policy objectives for public services. The systematic rules embodied in formula funding are needed to make such criteria operational.
- Although other budgeting mechanisms – such as bidding for funds, continuation of past expenditure or political patronage – may appear to be simpler to implement in the short run, in the longer term they often generate enormous political pressures and precedents that are difficult to defuse. The use of formulae allows explicit presentation of the criteria for funding, which enables the various parties to enter into an informed dialogue. Also, by tying the hands of officials and politicians, it can reduce the scope for special pleading.
- More generally, the distributor of funds wishes to be seen to be fair and non-partisan. A formula appears to treat all in the same way, and if it can be shown to have been derived in a reasonable (or fair) fashion the recipients of funds are more likely to accept the outcome. That is, the *procedure* for deriving an allocation of funds often has a vital importance over and above any consideration of the *outcome* of the allocation.

These arguments reflect considerations of efficiency, equity and politics. Equity concerns have played a particularly strong role in formula funding in the United Kingdom. In other systems, such as competitive health insurance, efficiency concerns dominate (Van de Ven and Ellis, 2000). However, another interpretation of the current pre-eminence of formula funding in many public service systems is that it offers a solution to the political difficulties associated with the allocation of public finances, and that promoting efficiency and equity may be a secondary consideration (Glennerster *et al.*, 2000). This book examines formula funding mainly from an economic and statistical perspective. However, it seeks throughout to recognize the political context within which formula funding is implemented.

1.6 Some formula funding landmarks in the UK

Although the use of formula funding of public services is becoming increasingly widespread, it is far from a recent phenomenon. Bennett (1980) and McLean (2005) discuss the development of grants-in-aid in the reformed local government system of nineteenth-century England. At first, most central grants were 'matching', in the sense that they reimbursed local authorities for a proportion of the expenditure they incurred. This approach economized on data collection, and merely required audit of the probity of local expenditure. It also stimulated expenditure on services that local government would otherwise under-provide. However, in most other respects it led to many undesirable outcomes, most notably by failing to direct national finance to the areas most in need – indeed, it tended to encourage spending in wealthy areas, which enjoyed the lions share of the subsidies implicit in the matching scheme. It was this concern that led to a search for more satisfactory formulae for allocating national finance.

Foster *et al.* (1980) give a highly readable account of the early attempts to model spending need more satisfactorily, and allocate central grants accordingly. In 1888 there was an early government proposal to allocate some grant according to a count of 'indoor pauperism' (the numbers resident in work-houses). This would have been an early form of case payment for service users. However, it was rejected on the grounds that the number of 'indoor paupers' was not always a good indicator of spending need, as some authorities implemented relief for poor largely outside the workhouse. Indeed, if it had been implemented, the formula may have discouraged more cost-effective forms of poor relief than the workhouse, or attempts to prevent the need for poor relief arising. This type of critique is still a central concern of policy makers today, and is discussed in detail in Chapter 3.

The early debates summarized by Foster *et al.* (1980) emphasize the principle that grants should enable local authorities to deliver some national standard level of service at some standard rate of local taxation. This principle informed the proposals of successive official enquiries, such as the 1914 Kempe Committee of the House of Commons and the 1920 Royal Commission on Local Taxation. However, lofty ideals were often tempered by severe data limitations, and the first attempt in earnest at implementing a needs-based formula was the 1929 Local Government Act. This introduced a baroque attempt to allocate central grant according to objective measures of local needs and taxable resources. The formula is summarized algebraically by Foster *et al.* (1980) as in Box 1.2. The formula is mainly of historical interest, and the reader should not dwell on the impenetrable algebra, as it does not appear to be based on a coherent model of service needs. However it indicates that the intention was to allocate grant according to population, weighted for: children under five; unemployment rates; a measure of population sparsity; and taxable resources.

Box 1.2 Needs-based formula, English Local Government, 1929 Local Government Act

The 1929 formula distributed the grant according to the weighted population of a local authority (P_w). The weighted population was calculated by first adjusting the actual population (P) by the following two factors

(a) the number of children under 5 (C)
(b) the rateable value (tax base) per head V.

(a) and (b) determined the intermediate weighted population P_w^1 in the following way:

$$\text{Let} \quad w_c = 20\frac{C}{P} - 1 \geq 0$$

$$w_v = 1 - \frac{V}{£10} \geq 0$$

Then $P_w^1 = P(1 + w_c + w_v)$

To get the weighted population for grant purposes, the intermediate weighted population was adjusted for unemployment and, for counties, by a sparsity measure in the following way:

Let U_m = unemployed males
$\quad U_f$ = unemployed females
$\quad U$ = $U_m + 0.1U_f$ averaged over the three years preceding the grant period
$\quad P^a$ = average population over the three years preceding the grant period
$\quad R$ = number of miles of road.

$$\text{Then, if} \quad \frac{U}{P^a} > \frac{1.5}{100}$$

$$w_u' = 10\left(\frac{U}{P^a} - \frac{1.5}{100}\right)$$

$$\text{And} \quad w_s = 1 - \frac{P}{200R} \quad \text{if} \quad \frac{P}{R} < 100$$

$$w_s = 50\frac{R}{P} \quad \text{if} \quad \frac{P}{R} \geq 100$$

The weighted population was then equal to

$$P_w = P_w^1(1 + w_u' + w_s) = P(1 + w_c + w_v)(1 + w_u' + w_s)$$

Source: Foster *et al.*, 1980: 197–198.

Although the exact formulation of the 1929 mechanism is difficult to defend, the use of a mathematical structure set the tone for the future pattern of grants-in-aid in the UK. Subsequent developments have been largely concerned with enhancements to measurement and estimation methodology rather than the underlying principles of seeking to develop a mathematical formula that compensates local areas for differences in needs and resources.

A particular landmark in UK formula funding was the recommendation of the Resource Allocation Working Party (RAWP) for allocating National Health Service funds to English regions (Department of Health and Social Security, 1976). At that time, English National Health Service (NHS) funds were allocated mainly according to historical precedent, leading to a very large imbalance in favour of London and the south-east of England (Mays and Bevan, 1987). The intention of the RAWP was to allocate funds so as to allow geographical regions to offer NHS patients 'equal opportunity of access [to health care] for those at equal risk'. It recommended distributing finance on the basis of population, weighted according to two fundamental criteria: first, adjustments were made for perceived differences in the *need* for health care; and second, account was taken of the unavoidable geographical differences in *costs* of providing services. Details are given in Box 1.3.

The RAWP recommendations were implemented in 1976, and phased in gradually over a 15-year period. They took formula funding in the UK to a new level of intellectual coherence and sophistication, and have been highly influential internationally. However, they were hampered by a shortage of adequate data, and there was no empirical justification for the assumption of a one-to-one relationship between mortality rates and the need for health care expenditure. Therefore, when the opportunity emerged to move to a more empirically based formula in 1991, the RAWP system was superseded (Royston *et al.*, 1992).

Bennett (1980) describes the analogous history in the English local government domain. Although some sort of formula was used from 1917 to distribute national grants-in-aid, it was not until 1958 that a coherent system was introduced, in the form of the 'needs and resources' equalization grants. These sought systematically to compensate local governments for variations in their spending needs and their taxable resources, and represented a major advance in the coherence of local government funding. The intention was to give all local governments the opportunity to deliver a standard level of services while levying a standard local tax rate. Since then, the system of grants to English local governments has been through a number of incarnations, but these general principles remain intact.

Two particular features of the historical development of English funding formulae should be highlighted. First, notwithstanding the 1929 example in Box 1.2, there has been a steady increase in the complexity of the formulae, to the extent that by 1990 the grants to English local governments required the measurement of over 100 indicators of spending need. And second, there has been increased reliance on statistical methods to determine the contents and the nature of the formulae. This increased technical complexity reflects a growing desire to ensure that grant distribution should faithfully reflect the payer's policy inten-

Box 1.3 Summary of the Resource Allocation Working Party (RAWP) recommendations

---

Per capita need was calculated by first disaggregating the population by age and sex. The different expected health care utilization of each demographic group was approximated, its the national average *per capita* hospital bed utilization. These were in turn adjusted by a series of standardized mortality ratios (SMR). The SMR is defined as the number of *observed* deaths in an area as a percentage of the *expected* deaths in the area, given its demographic profile. It was used by RAWP as an index of an area's relative morbidity, and therefore as a proxy for medical need over and above demographic considerations.

RAWP also broke down health care into a small number of broad categories of conditions, and the index of relative need for care for each category was determined by applying the condition-specific SMR to the population of an area. This process generated a notional total use of bed days by the population in an area, assuming utilization conformed to the national average, after adjusting for local need, as indicated by the SMRs. Algebraically, the equation can be represented as follows:

$$RA_i = \sum_j SMR_{ij} \left(\sum_k BEDS_{jk} POP_{ik} \right)$$

where RA_i is the financial allocation to area i; SMR_{ij} is the SMR of condition j in area i; $BEDS_{jk}$ is the national number of bed days required by age/sex group k diagnosed with condition j; and POP_{ik} is the population in area i in age/sex group k.

The final stage was to apply an 'area cost adjustment' to all budgets to reflect the large variations in input prices, especially pay, among the regions.

---

tions, and has placed ever-growing technical demands on the design of funding mechanisms. This book is intended to help those charged with that task.

Although England has often been one of the first countries to experiment with new approaches to formula funding, analogous developments can be found in almost all other developed countries and many lower income countries, and some accessible historical summaries for local government funding can be found for countries such as Australia (McLean, 2004) and the United States (Louis *et al.*, 2003). In the UK the Department of the Environment, Transport and the Regions commissioned a comparison of local government grant distribution methods in 19 OECD countries (PricewaterhouseCoopers, 2000), and Rice and Smith (2001a) compare formulaic methods used specifically in health care

1.7 This book

This book sets out the economic, statistical and political background to formula funding, and discusses its strengths and limitations in a variety of settings. The contents are directed at the analyst, academic or policy maker seeking an understanding of the theoretical, empirical and implementation issues associated with the topic. Throughout, the main emphasis is on the practical policy problem of seeking an efficient and equitable funding mechanism that – to the extent that is practicable – answers the needs of the payer. The book therefore refers to a diverse range of relevant academic literatures, such as the economics of fiscal federalism, multilevel econometric modelling and the political economy of budgeting. However, these are discussed only to the extent that they are relevant to the practical formula funding problem. Where appropriate, the reader interested in a more comprehensive or theoretical treatment of these related literatures is referred to the relevant texts.

The next chapter introduces the institutional background to the funding by formula of public services, placing the topic in the broader context of public finance. A variety of theoretical economic models have been developed to explain the scope and behaviour of modern public services. These include extensive literatures in the fiscal federalism, principal/agent and public choice traditions. Each of these literatures can help shed light on the rationale for and design of funding mechanisms.

Chapter 3 then examines in detail the elements of formula funding. It describes the two broad methods of capitation payments and case payments, and explains the important function of risk adjustment, which seeks to adjust the level of payment according to the characteristics of the citizen or service user. The chapter introduces the crucial notion of a 'legitimate' influence on local expenditure (which should in principle be reimbursed by the payer), and contrasts it with the many illegitimate influences on expenditure that should be ignored by the funding formula.

Chapter 4 places the formula funding problem within a theoretical framework. It focuses on the individual production function, which traces the link between the level of public services consumed by an individual and the outcomes achieved. The model indicates the different levels of payment that should be directed towards an individual depending on the payer's objectives. The intention is to highlight the crucial role of the payer's equity and efficiency objectives in the design of the payment mechanism.

Some empirical approaches to the design of capitation payments are described in Chapter 5. Statistical methods have become increasingly central to the design of funding mechanisms, but the limitations of the data available to the analyst are a crucial consideration in determining the methods to be used. The chapter first describes approaches used in American health care that in many respects represent the apotheosis of capitation methods based on individual level data. However, for many public services, use of such data is infeasible, or would lead to unacceptable perverse incentives. As a result, many payers rely on area-wide data rather than individual level data as the basis for their funding mechanisms, even though this introduces considerable analytic complexities. The chapter discusses why these arise, and how they might be might be addressed, using examples from English local government and health care.

Public service expenditure needs are intrinsically uncertain, and a particular problem that arises in any funding mechanism is therefore budgetary risk. The behaviour of the system might be crucially dependent on how that expenditure risk is distributed between the national payer, the locality, the provider and the user. Chapter 6 therefore discusses the various sources of expenditure risk, their potentially adverse consequences, and the implications for the design of funding formulae.

A weakness in most public service funding mechanisms has been a lack of explicit attention to the quality of services provided. Without countervailing instruments, most payment mechanisms have few direct incentives for providers to supply the quality of public services required by the payer. This has been a particular concern in health care, where it has become clear that indirect incentives (such as market forces or professional regulation) have been inadequate to secure the desired levels of clinical quality. Chapter 7 therefore describes an ambitious initiative in UK health care, under which explicit incentives to improve quality, in the form of about 150 performance indicators, are embedded in the funding formula for general practitioner payment.

The bulk of the book emphasizes technical considerations. However, the essence of formula funding is that it seeks systematically to resolve competing claims for limited resources. It is therefore a profoundly political undertaking. Chapter 8 outlines some of the important political considerations that often preoccupy the payer, and that inevitably play a central role in the design of funding formulae. The discussion highlights the multitude of choices usually available to the payer that lie outside the technical domain, facilitating pursuit of covert as well as explicit objectives. The chapter also suggests that in many cases the development of funding formulae can be seen as the resolution of a bargaining process between the various stakeholders, rather than a purely technical reflection of the payer's intentions.

Chapter 9 summarizes the state of the art. It picks out three priorities for improvement: linking the funding mechanism to the performance standards required of public service organizations; understanding the incentives inherent in formula funding; and correcting the information weaknesses in the funding mechanism. It concludes that – although there has been considerable progress in the design of funding formulae – many systems currently in use fail to reflect properly the payer's intentions, and do not consider the broader regulatory system within which public services operate. If anything, as the scope and timeliness of available data improve, these debates become more important. Moreover, there will always be crucial tensions in the design of funding formulae, for example between simplicity and sensitivity to local needs, or between the accuracy of payments and the creation of perverse incentives for providers.

Notwithstanding these difficulties, it is in my view essential that the search for improved funding mechanisms continues. Public services offer enormous scope for improving public welfare, by correcting market failures and protecting disadvantaged populations. However, the public support for public services also relies crucially on assurance that taxes are being spent wisely. An important element of such reassurance is the fair and efficient distribution of funds between localities and between providers. The rest of this book offers some guidance on how that goal might be pursued.

2 Formula funding within a public finance framework

2.1 Introduction

There is a huge body of academic literature examining the role of public services and public finance in the modern economy. Among many other topics, it examines the optimal nature and volume of public services, the arguments for and against decentralization, the appropriate sources and levels of taxation, and the role of contracts between purchasers and providers. In this short book it is not feasible to do justice to a fraction of this wide-ranging and important material, and much must be taken for granted. This chapter therefore summarizes only those parts of the literature directly relevant to the practice of formula funding. In doing so for the most part I assume:

- the national government is charged with the overall stewardship of public services, and has a set of objectives for them. It has taken a policy decision on the desired magnitude and nature of public services;
- the delivery of public services is devolved to a system of local government, or local administration, that is responsible for detailed implementation and enjoys a certain degree of local autonomy. It may deliver services directly, or purchase them from local providers;
- local governments may enjoy some freedom to set their own priorities, local taxes, or user charges, within a framework determined by the national government;
- the national government seeks a funding mechanism for local governments that secures its objectives with respect to public services;
- local governments seek a funding mechanism for local providers that promotes national and local objectives.

For most of the book I assume such an institutional framework is in place and that the payer's objectives can be articulated. The implications of that framework for funding mechanisms are then examined. However, to set the scene, this chapter first examines the rationale for decentralization of services, and the separation of the purchasing and providing functions that has become an accepted feature of most public sectors. It then examines in general terms the types of payment mechanism that are used for public services. In this context, it is important to recognize that the precise *method* of paying for local services may have important incentive effects for the recipients of funds, over and above the *level* of funding. The chapter concludes with a discussion of the policy objectives that are addressed by formula funding under two broad headings: efficiency criteria and equity criteria. Detailed design issues of formulaic methods are not discussed in this chapter – they are deferred to Chapter 3

2.2 The institutional framework for local services

This book is concerned with the flow of funds from national payers to local governments, and from local governments to public service providers. This section sketches the institutional framework underlying such flows, and some of the relevant economic models. It first considers the fiscal federalism tradition, and then examines the relevance of the principal/agent literature to devolved public services. Finally, it briefly notes the distinctive public choice perspective on public services.

2.2.1 Public services in the absence of local government

Consider first a national government that seeks to provide a public service without the use of intermediate payers in the form of local governments or other local administrations. In these circumstances, there will be no local scrutiny of public services, so demand for services will arise solely from the actions of individual citizens and the providers who advise them. Assuming there are no user charges, the provision of services in excess of socially optimal levels will result, and in the absence of countervailing instruments major departures from the payer's objectives will arise. The national payer may therefore usually draw up very explicit and extensive criteria for a user's entitlement that must be satisfied before a provider can be reimbursed.

Such principles form the basis of many national systems of welfare benefits. Extensive and very detailed rules of entitlement are drawn up by the national government to define who secures access to welfare payments, and the magnitude of that entitlement. Local benefit administration offices are charged merely with mechanically carrying out national government rules. Similar principles underlie a number of health care systems, such as US Medicare and some systems of social health insurance. Citizens can seek out any approved provider and – providing the service requested lies within a specified 'basket' of health services – the payer will reimburse the provider according to a fixed national tariff of fees. Although some systems of social health insurance (such as Japan) are based on local insurers that are nominally responsible for managing local demand, in practice they traditionally reimburse the invoices of local providers passively according to a fixed national fee schedule.

The difficulties associated with such national systems of public services, delivered without the mediation of an active local regulator, are manifest. Local service users and providers have no incentive to moderate demand, and it is often difficult to check whether the intentions of the payer are being honoured. In short, there is an informational difficulty that can only be properly addressed by a local organization, given the role of actively purchasing services and managing demand within a predetermined budget. For example, many traditional systems of social health insurance are experiencing problems of cost escalation, and some – such as the Netherlands, Germany, Belgium and Israel – have introduced competition between insurers in an attempt to make collective purchasing of health care less passive than has traditionally been the case (Van de Ven and Ellis, 2000).

2.2.2 Local government in the absence of a national payer

Local government (or at the very least local administration with strong discretionary powers) is therefore needed to deliver local public services because of the informational advantages it enjoys over the centre in understanding the demand for and supply of local public goods. Such information is often in the form of soft, tacit local intelligence. It is often adduced as a fundamental reason for decentralized decision making, as it can never be conveyed with any reliability to the centre. Of course, by decentralizing decision making the centre may lose some power of control, but that is generally considered a necessary price to pay for improved local decision making.

However, consider a system of local government, funded in its entirety by local taxes, that seeks to deliver public services with no intervention from a national government. In general, such autonomous local governments will experience great variations in cost functions, tax bases and local preferences. Indeed, high demands for services and poor tax bases are likely to coincide, leading to enormous variations in the standards of local services and local tax rates. For example, without some central subsidy, the costs of delivering some standard package of services would be borne in their entirety by the local area. Suppose that the sole source of revenue was a local tax base, such as local property values. Then, assuming no revenue from any other source, the local tax rate would be given by the ratio of expenditure needs to the size of the tax base. In general, therefore, the tax rates imposed on identical citizens living in different areas in order to secure a standard package of public services would vary substantially depending on (a) the local area needs and (b) the tax revenue base of the area.

To illustrate, Table 2.1 shows regional variations in tax bases and spending needs in English local government. The first column shows the national government's estimate of the average expenditure per household needed to secure a 'standard' level of services, and the second column the per capita local tax base (residential property values) as a percentage of the national average. Notice the negative correlation between the two. The third column shows the percentage of the level of standard spending the regions could deliver if there were no intergovernmental grants. Conversely, the final column shows the local tax that would have to be levied as a percentage of the national average if the region were to spend at the national government's standard level and there were no intergovernmental grants.

Table 2.1 Local government expenditure and tax base, English regions, 2005/06

Region	Standard spending per household (£)	Tax base as % national average per capita	Spending with standard tax (as % of standard)	Tax with standard spending (% national average tax)
South West	3,083	104	117.6	85.1
South East	2,920	111	124.1	80.6
London	4,054	111	89.4	111.9
Eastern	3,182	105	113.9	87.8
East Midlands	3,625	92	100.0	100.0
West Midlands	3,975	92	91.2	109.7
Yorkshire and Humber	4,017	90	90.2	110.9
North East	4,378	86	82.8	120.8
North West	4,101	91	88.4	113.2
England	3,624	100	100.0	100.0

Notice in particular the large variations in tax rates that would arise if all regions sought to spend at the standard level, ranging from 19 per cent below the national average tax in the wealthy south east to 21 per cent above the national average in the poor north east. Furthermore, variations between local governments *within* the regions would be even greater. It was such variations that led to the nineteenth-century interventions of the UK national government described in Chapter 1, and they have remained a central driving force behind the large programmes of grants from national to local government seen in all developed economies. The central purpose of formula funding is to make such grant programmes operational.

It should be noted at this point that there has traditionally been a strong dissenting view about the need for intergovernmental transfers in the fiscal federalism literature, and there are some who argue that the heterogeneity between areas implicit in a system of pure (fragmented) local government is not a cause for concern. The Tiebout model of local government (Tiebout, 1956) suggests that citizens might migrate to the locality most closely offering their preferred mix of public services, tax rates and housing costs, and that financial transfers between localities may not therefore be required. For example, if taxes are raised from a local property tax, high levels of local taxes (or inferior local services) might be reflected in lower property values. Some or all of a deprived area's disadvantage may therefore be compensated in the form of lower housing costs (Oates, 1969).

In practice, the influence of the extreme *laissez faire* approach implied by the Tiebout perspective has been small outside academic circles. However, the model does highlight some important issues. In particular, there is strong evidence that variations in the quality of local services, such as schools and policing, are reflected in local house price variations (Leech and Campos, 2003; Gibbons, 2004). More specifically, the *expected* future level of local taxes and the quality of local services may be capitalized in a locality's house prices. If those expectations are changed, for example by a new grant-in-aid that seeks to compensate a rural area for low service levels, then there is a windfall gain to local property owners – not necessarily the payer's intended consequence. This sort of insight is one reason why policy makers should be cautious about making major unanticipated changes to payment regimes. It also emphasizes the need for clear thinking about who might be the ultimate beneficiaries of new financing arrangements.

2.2.3 The rationale for intergovernmental transfers

Setting aside the Tiebout critique, the fiscal federalism literature sets out the numerous arguments for financial grants-in-aid from central to local government. The broad assumption underlying the literature is that powers should be decentralized to the most local tier of government consistent with satisfying national equity and efficiency criteria. Within that framework, this section very briefly summarizes the main arguments for grants-in-aid. The standard texts, such as King (1984), should be consulted for a more comprehensive treatment.

Most fundamentally, grants to local government can help secure the national payer's policy objectives, and therefore contribute to an efficient allocation of resources within the public services. Fragmented local government will in general lead to greatly varying services, standards, taxes, user charges and outcomes. The issues of national efficiency and equity objectives are considered more fully below in Sections 2.4 and 2.5. However, it is important to keep in mind that properly designed grants are often a necessary (but not sufficient) condition for those objectives to be achieved. For example, a grant system can be designed to give local governments the means to deliver a standard level of service, but there can be no guarantee that the funds will be spent as intended. If the payer wants that standard to be achieved in practice, it may need to augment the grant system with regulatory devices such as performance monitoring.

Local governments are to some extent inter-dependent. The services provided by one jurisdiction affect citizens from another. For example in health care there may be public health interventions, such as childhood vaccination programmes, that will ultimately yield benefits for the whole country. Likewise, there may be some circumstances when – without central intervention – the actions of local governments may collectively create important adverse macroeconomic effects. Such interdependencies (generally referred to as 'spillovers' in the fiscal federalism literature) suggest an important role for a national government grants. There is generally an assumption that most types of spillover effects lead to underprovision of services, so expenditure must be stimulated by positive matching grants-in-aid. However, there may be circumstances when it is in the interests of the national government to depress local expenditure by withdrawing grant in proportion to local expenditure. Notice that the unwanted performance variations brought about by fragmented local government leads to inequity between jurisdictions that can be thought of as a special class of spillover effect.

Where local governments rely on mobile tax bases, such as sales taxes, a particular concern that has arisen is the potential for provision of services below optimal levels because jurisdictions compete for that tax base by under-cutting the tax rates of their neighbouring jurisdictions. For example, local governments might try to attract taxable businesses by offering low property taxes, and consequently low levels of public services (Wilson, 1999). Where this is a concern, grants-in-aid can be designed to compensate for variations in local tax bases. However, such grants effectively make local governments indifferent to their tax bases, which may not be desirable if a policy intention is to stimulate the development of local enterprises. An alternative approach to addressing tax competition may therefore be to offer matching grants to stimulate expenditure.

In an analogous fashion, in some public services – such as long-term care for older people – local areas may perversely have an incentive to perform *poorly* if to do so deters immigration of citizens who may be a burden on local public services. This leads to a form of adverse 'service level competition' in public services. In health care, such competition has become known as a 'race to the bottom' in the quality of service provided, as insurers seek to deter patients for whom they are not adequately reimbursed by the finance system (Glied, 2000). Even if a locality provides services to a high standard, in order to deter in-migration of expensive users, it may not want to see such quality widely reported.

There is in such circumstances a clear role for national government grants to neutralize adverse incentives. Yet, equally, if the grant compensates for disadvantage that is within the control of the jurisdiction, then different types of perverse incentives might arise. For example, there is in one sense a case for basing grants to police forces on local crime rates, an obvious and relevant measure of service needs. Yet to do so offers no longer-term incentive to the police force to prevent crime – indeed it creates a 'moral hazard' incentive to maximize the local level of reported crime. In such circumstances payers may find it necessary to repudiate the use of 'obvious' measures of need when allocating funds.

It is also the case that inter-jurisdictional competition can be favourable. For example, a system of 'yardstick competition' between jurisdictions might promote accountability by indicating to regulators or local voters whether a local government is performing well (Shleifer, 1985). The UK has been especially active in stimulating such quasi-competition between local governments, for example, in the form of a high profile 'comprehensive performance assessment' published annually for every local authority by the Audit Commission (2005a). In these circumstances, if properly designed, a good grant mechanism can place all jurisdictions on a level playing field so as to render such comparison more meaningful.

2.2.4 The principal/agent viewpoint

In the economics literature, the relationship between the payer and recipient of funds is characterized as a principal/agent relationship (Prendergast, 1999). In the context of this book, the principal might be the national government, and the agent the local government. Local government might then in turn become a principal, in its dealings with agents in the form of providers of public services. Within the principal/agent framework, the role of the funding mechanism is to maximize the 'payoff' to the principal in the knowledge of the agent's behavioural response. In designing the payment mechanism, the payer has to recognize that it lacks full information on local circumstances, and that local agents may not hold the same objectives as the payer. This gives rise to an *agency cost* – the reduction in the principal's payoff caused by information weaknesses and divergences in objectives. The principal will seek to devise managerial, informational, budgetary and payment systems to mitigate the cost of agency, taking account of the direct costs of implementing such systems, which we can call *transaction costs*. The principal then wishes to choose a payment system that maximizes achievement of its objectives, while minimizing agency and transaction costs.

In effect, the economist's principal/agent model examines the nature of the contract that a principal puts in place with its agents in order to secure its objectives, assuming the agent does not necessarily precisely share those objectives, or may have additional objectives it wishes to pursue. Central to the contract is the payment mechanism, which embodies a set of financial incentives for the agent. The agent must be given these incentives in order to exert an appropriate level of effort, in line with the principal's objectives. However, the principal does not know with any certainty how much of the observed outcomes are attributable to the agent's effort, and how much to uncontrollable external influences. It therefore cannot reliably contract either on the basis of the actions of or the outcomes secured by an agent. In short, there are substantial problems with both hidden action (on the part of the agent) and hidden information (the agent's contribution to outcomes) (Milgrom and Roberts, 1992). The design of the payment mechanism should acknowledge both divergent objectives (between principal and agent) and informational weaknesses.

An emerging theme in the fiscal federalism literature is the application of principal/agent modelling to the relationship between central and local government. There is of course an important issue here regarding the legitimate autonomy and discretion of local governments as agents in a federal state, and there must often be scope for local variations in preferences regarding public services. But it is nevertheless the case that ultimate accountability for the state of public services usually lies with the national government, so the principal/agent viewpoint certainly has some relevance.

For example, Gilbert and Picard (1996) assume that central governments are less well informed than local government about two crucial aspects of local services: local production costs and local preferences. They argue that – if central government had full information on production costs – then full centralization is optimal, while the reverse is the case if the central government had full information on local preferences (including the values attached to spillovers). Ambiguity arises when (as is usually the case) there is imperfect information on both costs and preferences. If information on costs improves, then the scope for exploitation by local providers decreases, so central government is in a good position to exercise its prime role of accommodating spillover effects. If on the other hand information on costs is poor (or spillovers not important) then decentralization is preferred because of the better knowledge of local governments about the efficiency of local providers.

Laffont (2000) examines an important class of problem in which decentralization increases the probability of collusion between local purchasers and providers. This risk is especially important in health care, where there is an ever-present danger of local purchasers being 'captured' by powerful providers. Again, a key element of his model is the bounded rationality of the centre in capturing and processing information about localities – in short, the information requirements of effective centralization may be costly. As is frequently the case in this domain, economic analysis offers no clear-cut policy prescription. The informational advantages of delegation have to be weighed against the potential efficiency costs of collusion. Furthermore, whether local or central governments are more vulnerable to provider 'capture' is a matter for debate.

The principal/agent viewpoint implies that – in theory – the principal's objectives might be best served by designing bespoke funding mechanisms, or contracts, that are specific to each agent's characteristics. In practice, such bespoke design is rarely implemented, perhaps because it is technically infeasible, but more likely because the payer must be seen to be treating agents even-handedly, by offering a uniform financial regime to all agents. One of the purposes of formula funding is to offer a single payment mechanism that applies to all local organizations.

2.2.5 A public choice perspective

The nature of the payer's objectives is central to the principal/agent literature. A naïve view might be that the national government payer is a selfless servant of the people, implementing programmes that maximize some noble concept of social welfare. A more jaundiced view – as expressed in the public choice literature – is that national and local governments are self-serving entities, pursuing the interests of citizens only when it serves their own interests.

Some of the earliest public choice models derive from the work of Niskanen (1968) who developed the notion of self-interested 'bureaucrats' subverting the public services to their own ends. He hypothesized that the bureaucrat was interested in maximizing an agency's budget, and would therefore use its monopoly power to expand public service output beyond socially preferred levels. The relevance of this view has been hotly disputed, and it is of course likely to be more relevant in some settings than others. However, it has been highly influential among politicians and others seeking to secure control of public services. The public choice viewpoint has been one of the driving forces behind efforts to improve the accountability of local services, and to reduce the information asymmetry between politicians, citizens and local agencies, using instruments such as public performance reporting.

Many variants of the public choice perspective have been put forward. A particularly enduring example has been the 'flypaper' model of local expenditure. This suggests that – instead of acting as general subsidies to local citizens – grants to local governments 'stick' to the functions of the agency in receipt, once again leading to budgets in excess of those that are socially optimal or those intended by the payer (Hamilton, 1983).

Seabright (1996) examines the distribution of powers between central, regional and local governments from a public choice perspective. The advantage of decentralization is that it brings electoral power closer to local people, and so may more closely align local preferences with local services. The advantage of centralization is that it permits better coordination of public goods, most notably when the choices of one locality have spillover effects for other localities. Seabright's model presumes that governments at all levels are interested in re-election, and that the probability of re-election is determined by the level of welfare enjoyed by the population. National (or regional) governments are interested only in those lower level areas that are marginal to their expected re-election (a sort of 'jurisdictional' median voter model). The existence of positive spillovers from one locality's services to another's welfare increases the case for centralization. However, this must be traded off against a lack of accountability in jurisdictions that are not critical to the central government's re-election.

There is in Seabright's model an implication that aggregate spending will usually be higher under centralization, because the central government takes into account the positive spillover benefits from higher spending. Centralization also increases the willingness to transfer resources from rich to poor areas, therefore benefiting disadvantaged localities. However, Seabright's analysis suggests that centralization might benefit some localities more than others, most notably the 'pivotal' electoral battlegrounds. This prediction suggests that national governments may seek to skew any system of formula funding of local government towards electorally important local governments.

Decentralization supported by central grants may also offer localities an incentive to act strategically in misrepresenting their true needs and preferences. Levaggi and Smith (1994) give an example of the nature of a game in which the locality increases its spending beyond its preferred level in order to attract higher government grant. Barrow (1986) shows how the competition between jurisdictions for a fixed central grant can induce spending in excess of efficient levels. In the same vein, Besley and Coate (2003) present a model of political economy in which localities have an incentive to elect representatives with high spending preferences to national legislatures. In such cases, information asymmetry may lead to local expenditure that is higher than socially optimal levels, as localities seek to persuade the central payer that they have high spending needs.

Finally, in the provider market, there may be considerable scope for what Krueger (1974) refers to as 'rent-seeking', the process whereby providers compete to appropriate the producer surpluses created by regulated market structures. When individuals can gain from government policies, they have an incentive to expend resources up to the expected value of that gain in order to secure their private benefits, potentially imposing substantial losses on society in the process. Under this view, whenever the government undertakes initiatives – such as formula funding innovations – the possibility of wealth transfers is created. This triggers rent-seeking activity that dissipates some or all of the potential gains of the intervention, thus to some extent thwarting the government's initial intentions.

Public choice perspectives can be crucial to understanding some aspects of formula funding of public services. However, for most of the book I presume that governments at all levels are seeking to act in the public interest. Within this framework, the following sections examine in more detail the economic arguments for using formulae as the basis for funding decisions.

2.3 Types of grant-in-aid

King (1984) summarizes the types of grants-in-aid from central payers to local governments according to two broad criteria:

* specific or general: the funding might be conditional on some specific conditions being fulfilled, or might be general (unconditional on any specific actions);
* lump sum or matching: the funding might be unrelated to local expenditure, or might match it wholly or in part.

These are now briefly considered in turn.

2.3.1 General or specific grants

General grants are the simplest to design. They offer financial support to localities irrespective of what services are provided. Of course, if they are matching grants, the amount received will be dependent on the aggregate level of expenditure, but there is no direct incentive for a local organization to favour one type of service at the expense of another. General grants therefore promote local autonomy, but offer little detailed control to the payer.

In contrast, the receipt of specific grants is conditional on certain types of service or levels of performance being delivered. When local governments are multi-purpose, the payer might often be concerned that the funds intended for one function are diverted by localities to other services. For example, there has been a persistent concern in English health care that localities divert the parts of the budget intended to support mental health services to the acute sector. In such circumstances, a payer may want to 'ring fence' the funding for the disadvantaged service.

Making grants-in-aid conditional has become very popular with payers wishing to 'micro-manage' local organizations. However, as well as protecting vulnerable services, ring fencing can give rise to unintended incentives and potentially adverse outcomes. For example, it may make infeasible informational demands on the payer, and make it difficult for localities to manage the risk inherent in public services by transferring expenditure between budgetary headings (see Chapter 6). In effect, ring fencing is a centralizing instrument that can nullify many of the advantages of decentralization.

Furthermore, the use of specific grants can lead to a wide variety of gaming responses, whereby localities either manipulate information to ensure they qualify for the specific funding, or distort service provision in order to satisfy the rules for receipt of funding. Specific grants therefore imply a need for more careful audit and validation than general matching finance.

A particular type of conditional grant is to reimburse according to some measure of local activity, as embodied in the case payment system described in detail in Chapter 3. For example, a school might be paid in part according to the number of pupils enrolled, or a care home according to the number of people in care. Rather than stimulate expenditure *per se*, such case payment can encourage providers to seek out service users, and therefore reduces the incentive to constrain access to services implicit in the block budget.

2.3.2 Lump-sum or matching grants

The most basic method of funding devolved organizations is to allocate a lump-sum (or block) annual budget. The methods of capitation funding described in detail in Chapter 3 usually result in a block budget, and makes the level of funding independent of local service activity. In systems of local government with autonomous sources of local taxation, a lump-sum transfer is in effect a subsidy to local incomes. It is purely redistributive between localities, and has no effect on the prices of local services. In principle, therefore, it should lead to an allocatively efficient outcome, if local decision making truly reflects local preferences. Lump-sum funding also offers strong incentives for local efficiency, as the organization seeks to satisfy performance standards within a fixed budget. Furthermore, lump-sum funding eliminates expenditure risk for the payer.

However, the public choice perspective suggests that local decision making may sometimes not function properly, perhaps being captured by interest groups, such as local bureaucrats or user representatives. In particular, widespread reports of the flypaper effect in local government suggest that lump-sum grants do not function merely as subsidies to local income, but stimulate expenditure in the services to which they refer (Barnett *et al.*, 1991).

Moreover, lump-sum grants imply a strong incentive for the devolved entity to skimp on both the quantity and quality of service provision. To be effective, therefore, they must often be implemented alongside other regulatory mechanisms to assure that the budget is being spent in line with intentions. These might include quality criteria specified as a condition of payment, performance reporting requirements, local democratic scrutiny, independent inspection and other systems of accountability.

In the absence of other funding sources, lump-sum funding of public services places a great burden on accurate estimates of local spending needs, and can expose the local entity to high levels of expenditure risk if demanding performance requirements are specified by the payer. This is discussed further in Chapter 6. The risk arises from two main sources: the failure of the budget accurately to reflect expected local expenditure requirements, and unexpected local variations from assumed levels in either demand or input prices. The potential for this latter form of risk increases markedly as the size of the devolved organization decreases. It is probably not material for large urban local governments delivering a broad range of services. Yet budgetary risk may be a dominant consideration for (say) a small primary school delivering a single service.

An alternative mode of payment is matching finance, under which the payer agrees to reimburse all or some proportion of the expenditure reported by the local organization. This approach of general matching funding effectively reduces the local price of providing services, and can therefore be used to stimulate general levels of service provision when they would otherwise be underprovided, perhaps because of spillover effects. However, if not used with care, matching funding may encourage provision in excess of policy intentions, for example, in the form of 'gold-plated' services for users.

From an equity perspective, matching funding can also be useful when seeking to compensate for variations in tax-raising power among localities. For example, the increase in tax rates required to raise an additional unit of expenditure can vary substantially between jurisdictions, depending on the nature of the taxable resources. If the *per capita* tax base (say property values) in jurisdiction i is B_i, and the *per capita* level of expenditure required to deliver some standard service is X_i, then the required local tax rate r_i is equal to X_i/B_i. A block grant equal to G_i can be allocated to each locality so as to equalize the tax rate in all areas to r, such that $r = (X_i + G_i)/B_i$ (of course G_i could be negative).

However, although such a block grant equalizes the tax rate r at the standard level of service, it does not eliminate variations in the marginal tax effort required to finance additional expenditure, should the locality wish to vary from the standard. With no matching grant, the marginal tax effort is equal to $(\partial r/\partial X) = (1/B_i)$. That is, the tax increase required to finance a given increase in *per capita* expenditure is inversely proportional to the local *per capita* tax base. To neutralize this inequality, an expenditure matching grant specific to jurisdiction i, with matching rate proportional to $1/B_i$, can be deployed. Likewise, if the interest is in equalizing tax increases for a given *percentage* increase in expenditure, the matching rate for jurisdiction i must be amended to be proportional to X_i/B_i.

Perhaps the most ubiquitous example of matching funding in payment mechanisms is the widespread practice of 'damping' the swings in budgets implied by the pure use of capitation funding or case payments. Such damping uses historical spending as part of a local organization's budgetary allocation, and has a number of virtues, such as reducing managerial and political turbulence in the public service. However, in the extreme, damping mechanisms merely become reimbursement of historical expenditure. The extent to which damping should abate the budgetary implications of pure funding formulae is a key policy judgement (rather than a technical judgement) for the payer, and is discussed further in Chapter 9.

A similar form of matching finance is applied by payers that nominally use lump-sum budgets if they periodically 'rescue' budget holders that exceed their financial allocations, by writing off their accumulated deficits. Financial relief of local governments in financial distress has been historically quite prevalent in some countries, notwithstanding the clearly dysfunctional consequences of such policies. If a payer has a reputation for rescuing devolved organizations, their budgets effectively become soft, as they recognize that at least some of any excess expenditure may be reimbursed.

2.3.3 Mixed grant systems

In practice many payers tend to use mixed payment systems. For example, an element of cost sharing between payer and recipient can be secured by augmenting a block grant alongside some matching reimbursement. And some case payment systems include an element of 'cost-sharing' with the provider if service costs exceed some threshold, implying an element of matching finance. Moreover, different parts of a public service might be reimbursed in different ways. In particular, many systems that pay for capital investment employ different principles to revenue finance, sometimes according to very detailed estimates of local capital costs. The ubiquity of mixed payment systems suggests that they are in practice most likely to meet best the requirements of payers, because they soften the stark incentives inherent in pure block or matching finance regimes.

Compared to the single systems of reimbursement, however, mixed systems may require fine judgements on the extent of reliance on each of the different mechanisms. For example, it has long been recognized that health care providers should be funded according to a mixed system. But the precise nature of the optimal mix has yet to be resolved (Newhouse, 1994). It is moreover likely to be different depending on the type of health care under scrutiny (emergency, elective, long term, psychiatric or maternity).

While in principle there are many possible ways of constructing the pure and mixed payment mechanisms outlined above, in pursuit of the payer's objectives, the use of mathematic formulae to determine the magnitude and mode of payment is becoming increasingly widespread. The essence of the formulaic approach is that it codifies the budgetary entitlement of each recipient in advance, on the basis of objective, verifiable data. The devolved entities can therefore make operational decisions in full knowledge of the revenue implications. Furthermore, there is usually an implication that the devolved organizations are in some sense treated even-handedly by the formula.

2.3.4 The provider market

The discussion above has discussed mainly the relationship between national and local government. However, the principal/agent viewpoint is especially germane for the flow of funds from payer (whether national or local) to public service provider. Increasingly, public services are relying on explicit contracts between payers and providers that specify the level of service expected, and the rules of reimbursement. Formula funding mechanisms have a central role to play in making such contracts operational (Milgrom and Roberts, 1992).

It is nevertheless the case that – for most public services – it is infeasible to specify in advance in a single contract all the required conditions of performance. That is, contracts are necessarily incomplete. Payers must therefore to some extent rely on extra-contractual mechanisms to assure quality. For example, Chalkley and Malcolmson (1998) show how, in the absence of verifiable quality measures, contracts for purchasing health care can nevertheless be designed to take advantage of the natural professional 'altruism' of doctors in wanting to do the best for patients, even when not given explicit incentives to do so. The need for detailed quality specifications is thereby to some extent obviated.

The use of a diversity of providers opens up the opportunity to create a competitive market for public service provision, either in the form of a 'quasi-market' of public service providers, or a more genuine market of mixed public, not-for-profit and for-profit providers, for example as found in many systems of social care (Le Grand and Bartlett, 1993). There are many virtues and perils associated with markets in public service provision. The efficiency benefits of providers competing for business are manifest, and become more obvious as contracts can be specified more completely. Equally, so long as contracts remain incomplete, there are risks associated with a sole reliance on markets, and it is likely that some form of careful regulation will always be necessary in public service markets.

Quasi-markets have been a particularly important feature of the UK public services as they make a transition from a vertically integrated public sector, in which local governments both purchased and delivered public services, towards a separation of purchasing and provision. An example was the quasi-market in the National Health Service, under which health authorities became purchasers of health care from the hospitals and other providers they had previously owned (Le Grand *et al.*, 1999). The providers remained public sector organizations, but were given their own boards of management, and could provide services to a range of public sector purchasers. Recent policy moves have sought to make the provider market more heterogeneous, embracing other not-for-profit and commercial enterprises, leading to the sort of market that has always existed in countries that rely on social health insurance (Saltman *et al.*, 2004).

A particular form of 'pseudo-market' in public services is created by the public reporting of achieved levels of performance, particularly when service users have the power to switch providers. For example, examination pass rates are published for English schools, in order to stimulate overall improvement and help parents choose schools for their children (West and Pennell, 2000). The intention is that the threat of 'exit' by parents might encourage schools to secure improved performance. Such public reporting has much to commend it, and is probably an intrinsic element of the improved accountability demanded of public services. However, it is worth noting that the publication of exam success rates can give rise to perverse outcomes unless results are carefully adjusted for the relative difficulty of the task faced by different schools, in the form of pupil ability. This 'risk adjustment' problem is analogous to the task of designing a risk-adjusted funding formula, discussed at length in Chapter 5.

In a similar vein, there has been extensive experience of public reporting of performance in US health care, but hitherto it has had little impact on patient behaviour (Marshall *et al.*, 2003). Indeed, Dranove *et al.* (2003) suggest that the celebrated system of report cards for individual heart surgeons in New York state may have led to worse outcomes for patients than would otherwise have been the case. They offer evidence that – because of the risk adjustment system in use – surgeons in New York appear to be undertaking fewer operations on high risk patients who could benefit from treatment, and more operations on low risk patients for whom the health benefits are more questionable.

An alternative form of public reporting seeks to promote the accountability of local providers to their electorates (or to the national government) by publishing comparisons of general performance measures of comparable organizations. This might be especially important when no realistic choice of provider exists. An example is the set of 'police monitors' prepared by the UK Home Office, which seek to compare the performance of police forces to similar forces along a number of dimensions (Home Office, 2003). The intention is that such information should improve the ability of voters or their elected representatives to exercise 'voice', and hold local providers to account. Of course, such yardstick competition is truly meaningful only when the local organizations under scrutiny are fairly funded to secure the chosen performance criteria.

2.4 The efficiency rationale for formula funding

Formulaic methods may have an important role to play in making operational the public finance models described above. This section therefore describes in some detail the efficiency arguments for formula funding (as opposed to other funding mechanisms), while Section 2.5 examines the equity rationale for formula funding.

Economic efficiency has a number of connotations. The two most fundamental notions are allocative efficiency (the extent to which allocations of resources are in line with society's preferences) and managerial efficiency (the extent to which agencies perform specified functions at least resource costs). Formula funding is intended to address both aspects of efficiency. First, it seeks to align incentives and resource allocations with the payer's intentions; second, it seeks to promote efficient management among local organizations. This section briefly elaborates on some of the more important efficiency objectives underlying most formula funding mechanisms.

No coherent system of financial transfers can be developed without first establishing clear objectives for the financial regime. Once objectives have been set, the fundamental efficiency argument for implementing formula funding is that – if properly designed – it allows the payer to implement an optimal allocation of finance in line with those objectives. Any deviation from such a formula implies a reduction in the effectiveness with which funds are used, and therefore a loss of efficiency. For example, if objectives are set in terms of service outputs – such as maximizing school examination results – the formula should be designed to secure that objective at a national level, subject to an aggregate budget constraint. This implies designing allocations such that the marginal benefit (marginal improvement in exam results) for an extra unit of expenditure is equal in all jurisdictions. Any departure from this criterion leads to a loss in total examination success. Of course the key empirical challenge then becomes one of successfully designing a formula in line with that objective.

It could be argued that an optimal allocation could be secured through means other than formula funding. For example, one could envisage an iterative mechanism under which the national government makes incremental changes to local budgets each year in the light of where it feels the funds are best spent (increasing budgets where the marginal benefit appears to be high, and reducing them where it seems low). Apart from requiring an indefinite time horizon over which to converge to an optimal allocation, such methods are vulnerable to gaming on the part of the devolved jurisdictions. For example, they may have an incentive to underperform in order to imply that they would benefit from increased funding. In contrast, well-designed formulae can secure an instantaneous solution, and can be designed so that they are not susceptible to such gaming.

A central concern of many payers is the extent to which their mechanisms for financing local organizations rely on data provided by those same localities. Under many circumstances, such data may be vulnerable to manipulation or create perverse incentives. For example, the measure of indoor pauperism described in Chapter 1 as the proposed basis for an early measure of need for local government services was rejected (a) because the count of 'indoor' paupers was vulnerable to fraud and (b) it may have encouraged unnecessary use of the workhouse (in order to raise numbers of indoor paupers, the proposed basis for payment). Even in systems in which such responses are rare, a suspicion that they exist may undermine the credibility of the funding mechanism. Many of the most creative systems of formula funding therefore seek deliberately to avoid the use of such data, so reducing the danger of moral hazard in the actions and reporting of local institutions.

It is important to note that funding formulae are more than reimbursement mechanisms. Carefully designed, they can allow the payer to put in place financial incentives for localities to respond in line with the payer's objectives. This may often involve a judicious mix of instruments (fixed budget, case payments and cost sharing). For example, if tax competition is inducing localities to under-provide certain services, this might be addressed by augmenting a fixed budget regime with a certain proportion of case payments. If a pure case payment system is inhibiting access for some high needs service users, then it might be augmented by a degree of cost sharing between payer and locality above some cost threshold. Such mechanisms are far more likely to be effective if specified explicitly *ex ante*, by means of a formula, than if addressed arbitrarily on a case-by-case basis.

Formula funding seeks to accommodate the information asymmetry between the payer and the locality. It offers an estimate of the expected local expenditure needed to deliver a standard level of service. This expenditure estimate forms the budget for the local organization. The locality may then be free to adjust the centre's estimate, either by varying local taxes or user charges, or by varying the type of provision from the assumed standard. The use of formulae can allow the centre to develop estimates of local spending that rely only on objective indicators of relative needs, and that are therefore independent of special plead-ing or gaming on the part of the local organization. Formula funding can there-fore offer practical means of managing the information asymmetry implicit in the relations between centre and locality.

The payer can also reduce the need for detailed scrutiny of the case for funding localities, or the accuracy of information provided. The locality does not need to make a case to the centre, and is freed to concentrate on delivering local services. Furthermore, and perhaps most importantly, it has no incentive to distort behaviour in order to suggest a need for more funding. Thus, formula funding can economize on agency costs, both at the centre and at the locality. Of course, in practice, even under a formula funding system, localities are likely to make representations to the centre about the accuracy or fairness of the formula. However, special pleading is likely to be less profitable and more easily rebutted if a well-designed formula is in place. Transaction costs may also therefore be reduced.

Implicit in these arguments is the belief that the use of formulae economizes on the analysis, audit and oversight required at the centre to construct budgets. Almost any other method, such as basing budgets on bids by localities or histor-ical precedent, has great potential for adverse responses on the part of localities, in the form of distorted information or gaming behaviour. Such responses were endemic to planning systems in the former Soviet Union, where the setting of budgets incrementally 'from the achieved level' led to widespread incentives for chronic underperformance in devolved institutions. Had the central authorities been able to set budgets that were at least partly independent of historical prece-dent, they may have been able to overcome many of these problems.

Formula funding can also have important implications for managerial effi-ciency, as it leads to the creation of clearly defined local budgets. Budgets are a central feature of most systems of public service delivery, and are associated with numerous incentives to local efficiency. The setting of clear budgets (whether fixed or variable) offers local organizations freedom to respond to local circumstances, to innovate, and to seek out economies, in line with the prescriptions of the new public management (Osborne and Gaebler, 1992). The use of mathematical formulae is the foremost means of enabling the centre to set a robust budgetary regime.

2.5 The equity rationale for formula funding

Many systems of formula funding seek to promote some concept of equity. The pursuit of equity might be valued for its own sake, or it might be valued because it secures acceptance for the redistribution implicit in the assignment of government revenues to pay for public services. Central governments raise most of their revenue through national taxes, levied at some standard rate across the country, and they therefore usually try to redistribute these revenues in a fashion that appears fair and in line with concepts of natural justice.

It is usual to divide equity concerns into the two broad Aristotlean principles of horizontal and vertical equity. A concern with horizontal equity suggests equal treatment of equals, while a concern with vertical equity suggests that those who are in more need (however that need is defined) should in some sense be treated proportionately differently (Rice, N. and Smith, P.C., 2001). Chapter 4 examines in detail the implications of adopting different equity criteria. This section offers some general observations on using funding formulae to address equity issues. It is concerned mainly with the distribution from the national payer to local governments, although the principles are equally valid for paying providers, such as schools.

Systems of formula funding are often accompanied by objectives expressing the payer's concern with equity, such as wishing 'to overcome territorial inequalities in social and health conditions' (Mapelli, 1998) or wishing 'to secure equal opportunity of access to those at equal risk' (Department of Health and Social Security, 1976). However, careful scrutiny suggests that the stated principles are often vague or even misleading. For example, is it really the case that the English NHS seeks to offer equal opportunity of access to health care? If so, it raises profound questions (for example) of how people living in rural areas are to be guaranteed the access to hospital and ambulance services enjoyed by those living in conurbations without very heavy expenditure on rural facilities. In general, the equity concerns of payers can appear to be a jumble of horizontal and vertical principles, addressing both access to and outcomes achieved by public services.

When put into operation, most of the high-minded equity principles translate into a more tractable policy objective of enabling all local jurisdictions to deliver some 'standard' package of services. As stated, this criterion usually ducks the issue of what that standard might be. In practice, the standard is often interpreted as the national average level of services, given a local area's social, economic and geographical circumstances. This interpretation allows for the possibility (for example) that rural areas may have lower levels of service than their urban counterparts. In compensation, it may be the case that citizens in rural areas can be offered lower local taxes, or the lower level of service may be reflected in lower property prices and rents. Therefore, implicit in many equity criteria is the understanding that equity will be pursued 'up to a point', but that it must to some extent be moderated by considerations of cost and efficiency.

The standard package might be defined in terms of expenditure (for example, a certain level of spending on each citizen in need of services), process (a stated service entitlement for citizens with specified needs) or outcome (a stated level of outcome to be secured for all users). However the standard is defined, when applied to a locality it implies a certain level of expected expenditure, which I term the area's 'spending need'. This will of course depend on the geographical, demographic, social and economic characteristics of the area. The characteristics to be taken into account in calculating an area's expected expenditure will be determined by data availability and society's ethical preferences, as discussed further in Chapter 5. We can define the public service expenditure needs of a locality as the expected costs of delivering the standard package of services, given the characteristics of the local population (or service users), and assuming a given level of productive efficiency. The economist's usual approach towards inferring such costs is to develop a cost function, and many of the empirical techniques of formula funding implicitly use cost function methodology.

We have already noted how – in the absence of some central redistribution of revenues – large inequalities in tax rates, levels of service and user charges will arise. Central grants-in-aid seek to reduce such inequalities, and an explicit statement of the standard package of services is usually essential in order to specify the necessary grant distribution mechanism. Where the local government has the freedom to vary local tax rates, the definition of the standard should include a statement on the standard levels of local taxation, as well as the level of service offered. A carefully designed formula can then make operational the redistribution of finance and services required by the payer.

Note also that, if the local government has some discretion over the nature of local services, the objective is to enable local governments the *opportunity* to deliver a standard level of service at a standard local tax rate. Local democracy may then give local jurisdictions freedom to vary some elements of the package of services or the local tax rate. It will then usually be the case that – if a locality chooses to vary the package – the entire burden of any extra expenditure falls on the locality, in the form of additional local tax or user charges. The level of discretion enjoyed by localities is of course a fundamental matter of national political choice of great importance. It is, however, for the most part beyond the remit of this book.

In contrast, if the service under consideration is a central government responsibility, merely delivered by local administrative offices (such as the English NHS), or if the concern is with paying providers, the nature of the local tax base is immaterial, and the main emphasis of formula funding is on devising a measure of local spending needs only. The objective is to allocate funds so as to allow the local agent to deliver the standard level of service.

Where the local provider has discretion to vary charges to users, or raise income from voluntary donations, the equity criterion is easily augmented in principle to embrace the principle of allowing the local organization to deliver the standard level of service while implementing some standard charging regime. However, although easily stated, this criterion may be difficult to make operational. For example, the 'standard' charging regime may include exemptions from charges for low income users, so an estimate of the proportion of users qualifying for exemption may be needed. Moreover, the application of a charging regime may affect the level of demand for local services. The practical difficulty of incorporating user charges into the equity criterion should therefore not be underestimated.

The principles underlying the pursuit of the equitable funding of public services can be illustrated, as in Figure 2.1. This shows the production functions OP_1 and OP_2 of two jurisdictions, in terms of the level of services achieved, perhaps for example in the form of securing a given level of examination pass rates in primary education. Area 2 requires more expenditure effort to achieve the given standard S than area 1, perhaps because it has a higher proportion of pupils from disadvantaged families. Thus, if the service is a central government responsibility, the funding received by each jurisdiction will simply be determined by the chosen standard, in this case leading to funding allocations X_1 and X_2.

Consider now the case of a service delivered by local government and funded by a local tax. Suppose the equity criterion is one of securing a given service standard for a standard tax rate. The policy interest is in equalizing the local tax rate required to secure the service standard. The expenditure axis must therefore be relabelled, and the production function expressed in terms of the tax rate, as in Figure 2.2. The shape of the production functions will in part be affected by the size of the local tax base. In this example, compared to Figure 2.1, the dif-

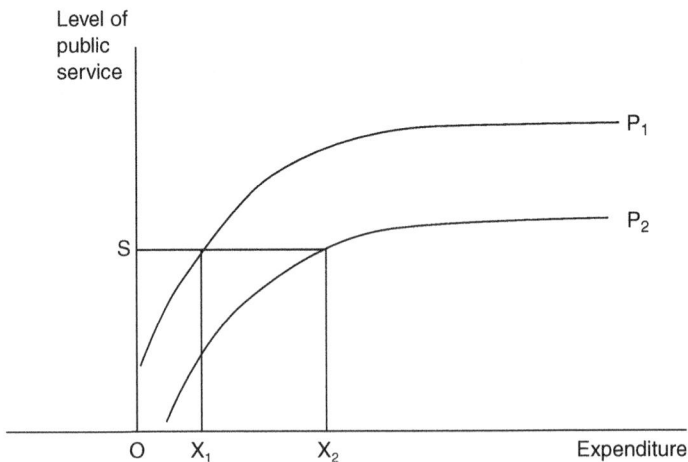

Figure 2.1 Expenditure required to secure equal level of service in two jurisdictions.

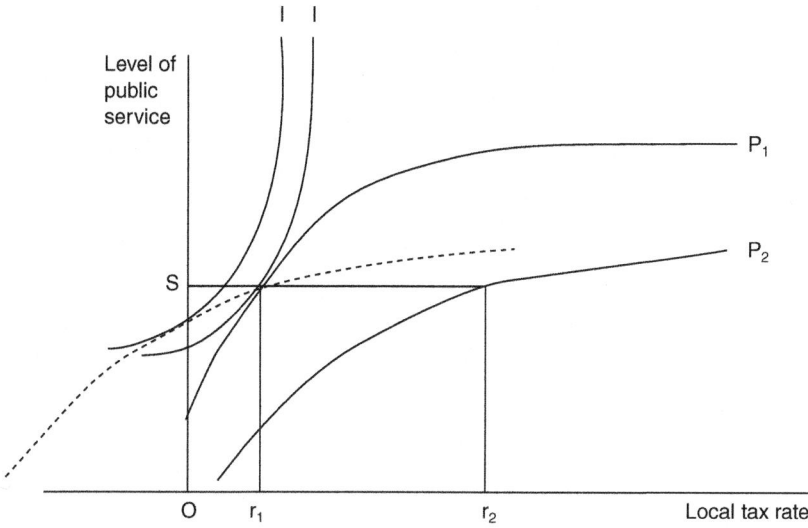

Figure 2.2 Tax subsidy required to secure equal level of service and equal tax rates in two jurisdictions.

ference between the jurisdictions has been accentuated because I assume the disadvantaged jurisdiction also has a poorer tax base. Then the required transfer to jurisdiction 2 (relative to jurisdiction 1) is calculated by moving the curve OP_2 to the left until it passes through the required service standard S and tax rate r_1. In the diagram, this requires a leftward shift equal to r_1r_2, suggesting the need of a subsidy of local taxes in the disadvantaged jurisdiction from central grants by that amount.

It is worth noting that neither jurisdiction might choose to implement the chosen central standard. For example, if in Figure 2.2 we introduce indifference curves II for a representative voter, we find that jurisdiction 1 will choose provision at about the standard level of public service, while jurisdiction 2 would choose a lower level than the standard. Note that – in this case – the representative voter is better off in jurisdiction 2. There is of course no suggestion that this illustration is at all general. However, it does suggests that in principle a more suitable criterion for determining the level of grant in aid might be one of securing a standard level of *utility* for the representative voter. Of course, making this criterion operational is more difficult than choosing a standard level of service (indeed it is probably infeasible in many circumstances).

2.6 Discussion

This chapter has sought to indicate the role of formula funding mechanisms within traditional economic theories of decentralized public services. It has argued that decentralization is an inevitable characteristic of the delivery of public services, given the needs of citizens to secure access to geographically convenient services, and the inevitable information asymmetry between central and local authorities.

That being the case, formula funding in principle offers a powerful tool for securing a payer's efficiency and equity objectives. When undertaken well, it can offer the payer a secure means of setting local budgets in line with those objectives. Moreover, by relying on independent sources of data, formula funding can reduce the incentive for local agencies either to misrepresent local circumstances, or otherwise to distort behaviour to secure favourable treatment by the payment mechanism.

However, a payment mechanism consistent with good practice is a necessary but not sufficient requirement for addressing the payer's objectives. Even though local governments are given budgets adequate to address the payer's equity and efficiency objectives, there is no guarantee that the funds will be used to that end. Indeed, from a principal/agent viewpoint, it is quite plausible to argue that they will not be. Additional regulatory instruments will therefore usually be needed alongside the funding mechanism to ensure the payer's objectives are met. In short, a formula funding mechanism should be seen within the broader 'contract' between principal (payer) and agent (local organization).

Moreover, notwithstanding the powerful potential of a formulaic approach to funding, poorly designed formulae may fail to secure the payer's objectives. Poor design may arise from a weak theoretical framework, poor data or inadequate statistical methodology. For example, I shall discuss in later chapters how many systems of formula funding fail adequately to address the payer's concern with reducing barriers to service access among vulnerable populations. This is because the formulae are based on empirical examinations of *current* expenditure patterns. Empirical approaches are therefore fundamentally unsatisfactory if there exist aspects of need that are currently not being met by the public services.

In short, formulaic approaches to setting grants-in-aid for local governments, or for reimbursing public service providers, offer a potentially valuable tool for making operational the payment mechanisms recommended in the public finance literature. However, to do so they need to be designed carefully, using data sources to their best effect, and avoiding perverse incentives. The following chapters offer guidance on how his might be achieved.

3 The elements of formula funding

3.1 Introduction

This chapter describes the various types of formula funding mechanisms commonly used. It starts by highlighting the analogy between local public services and insurance risk pools, and then describes two broad approaches towards designing funding formulae. In the capitation approach, an estimate is made of the *expected* level of activity local services would experience if they were to deliver some standard level of service to their local population. In the case payment approach, local services are reimbursed according to some measure of the *actual* level of activity. The chapter then considers three fundamental issues relevant to all systems of formula funding: the practical implications of data limitations; what constitutes a 'legitimate' source of expenditure variation; and the role of supply side influences on funding levels. The insurance analogy highlights a central consideration in designing funding mechanisms – how risk is shared between the payer and the budget holder. Although discussed in this chapter, the issue of risk sharing is treated in more detail in Chapter 6.

3.2 Local government as a risk pool

Most public services are *personal* services, in the sense that the main beneficiary is an individual or household user, rather than the population as a whole. Such services – in the form of education, health care, social security and personal social services – form the bulk of public sector expenditure. There are of course other public services such as fire, policing and transportation that may offer more collective benefits to society. Moreover, some personal services, such as education, may yield benefits to the broader population. However, with some straightforward re-orientation, the principles I set out below can be applied to these services also.

If there were no public services, individuals would have to pay privately for alternative provision by competitive markets, or forego the service. The defining characteristic of public services is that – for a number of reasons – markets do not yield a socially desired outcome. Society therefore chooses to aggregate the needs of individuals into entities, such as local governments, that arrange for the collective purchase of those services.

In insurance terminology, a local government can in many respects be thought of as a *risk pool* for public services. The expenditure risks of a defined population group are aggregated. Financial contributions derive from collective payment mechanisms, such as national or local taxation. In principle, membership of the risk pool entitles the citizen to a defined basket of public service benefits when the need arises. In this context, need can be defined as satisfying the service entitlement criteria determined by the local government.

In the absence of user charges, government financing of public services has the effect of making citizens' contributions to the financing of public services independent of the use they make of those services. Revenue to the risk pool comes from local and national taxation, so public services can have important redistributive functions. In designing any tax and expenditure system, three fundamental decisions must then be made:

- How much should the rich should subsidize the poor? That is, how progressive should the underlying tax system be?
- How much should non-users subsidize service users? For example, what role should user charges play?
- How much should future taxpayers and users subsidize current users? For example, to what extent can the services accumulate financial reserves, run a deficit, or rely on borrowing?

These are key policy decisions that will be guided by public attitudes towards equity and redistribution. They are often poorly articulated, but can equally be crucial influences on the design of funding formulae.

The size of the local government risk pool is in the first instance usually circumscribed by the population it serves. Two basic demand side sources then influence expenditure on services in the risk pool: the propensity of individuals to need a service, and the intensity of that need. In insurance terminology, modelling such need requires estimates first of the number of 'claims' in a given time period, and second of the size of those claims. Some basic mathematics of risk pooling is rehearsed in Appendix A.

The risk pool perspective highlights two crucial elements of demands for public services: the probability of service use, and the intensity of that use. Examples of this insight are readily suggested:

- in health care, an individual's demand for acute treatment is shaped by the incidence of a condition and its severity;
- in education, demand for schooling is determined by the presence of a child in a household, and the educational needs of that child;
- in policing, demand for a criminal investigation is determined by the incidence of a crime and the nature of that crime.

Distinguishing between the probability of service use and the intensity of that use is helpful because it highlights the two broad approaches towards formula funding. In the capitation approach, the payer seeks to fund the locality purely as a risk pool, on the basis of expected activity. In principle, an assessment is made of both the expected incidence and severity of service use (according to some national standard of entitlement), and the jurisdiction is funded accordingly with a block payment. The local government then becomes the public service 'insurer' for the local population.

In contrast, under the case payment approach, the central payer retains responsibility for the insurance risk of the incidence of service use. It must therefore specify national criteria under which a user is entitled to receive a service, and an associated national schedule of fees. A locality (or provider) is then reimbursed according to the fee schedule when providing a service to a user satisfying the national need criteria. Under these circumstances, the main insurance role of the locality is to pool the risks associated with different severity among service users. So, for example, a payer may reimburse schools on the basis of a fixed case payment per pupil. The schools are protected from risk associated with fluctuations in pupil numbers, but continue to be exposed to risk arising from variations in the educational needs of those pupils.

I now consider in turn the two broad approaches to formula funding, capitation and case payments, examining the nature of the mechanism and the incentives it gives rise to.

3.3 Capitation funding: reimbursement according to expected activity

The objective of most of distributional mechanisms for public services is to ensure that equal funds are directed towards individuals in equal circumstances regardless of where they live. Satisfying this principle gives rise to the notion of a capitation payment to the locality for each citizen – in effect, the public insurance premium for the individual. A capitation payment is defined as the amount of public funds to be assigned to a person with certain characteristics for the service in question, for the time period in question. The aggregation of capitation payments for a locality yields the local budget for the service.

The most rudimentary formula for paying the locality according to its expected activity is to reimburse purely in proportion to its population, without regard to variations in the personal characteristics of that population. This approach can be justified when differences in expected service use between citizens in different social circumstances are not substantial, or when the local governments in receipt of funds have only small differences in socio-demographic profile. It may also be justified if there is no further information with which to refine payments. However, simple capitation methods are manifestly crude, and unlikely to satisfy most observers' notions of fair funding when there are substantial differences between the expected service use of different types of citizen.

A modest refinement to the crude capitation payment may be to confine the population 'at risk' to any obvious demographic stratum from which service users will be drawn. For example, school financing is clearly better distributed according to the estimated number of children than the total population. Another example of such simple stratified capitation funding is implicit in the formula for social services for older people in England (Office of the Deputy Prime Minister, 2003), treated in Box 1.1. This formula considers only older people, and in 2003 implied a basic expenditure requirement of £337.77 for each person over 65.

However, capitation methods are usually also adjusted to account for more subtle variations in the expected spending needs associated with certain citizen characteristics. For example, the expected expenditure requirement of a person for personal social services is known to increase with age (Bebbington and Davies, 1983). Therefore the estimates of expected expenditure needs are disaggregated by age. Accordingly, the social services example was refined using an age adjustment that implies a capitation payment of £158.62 for people aged 65–74, £482.97 for people aged 75–84 and £1,252.54 for people aged over 84. Processes such as this, usually referred to as *risk adjustment*, amend the capitation payment attached to an individual according to certain measured characteristics.

When capitation methods are applied to personal public services for which there is no immediately obvious clientele, such as public health or policing, it is usually the case that the client group can be thought of as the entire population in an area. So a starting point will be to allocate funds according to population. Of course, in the same way that individual risk adjustment may be necessary, it may also be the case that certain population characteristics such as unemployment rates or mortality rates are associated with variations in population spending needs, and we show in Chapter 5 how these might be incorporated into a funding formula.

Numerous approaches to risk adjustment can in principle be envisaged, ranging from the rudimentary age adjustment noted above, to extraordinarily ambitious schemes, such as those found in some health care systems (Rice and Smith, 2001a). As new risk adjusters are added, so the capitation payments can be presented in the form of a contingency table. For example, in an early Netherlands health care capitation scheme, five categories of the head of household's

Table 3.1 Adjustments to basic age and sex capitation payments by employment status, the Netherlands health care 1999

	Age group					
	0–14	*15–34*	*35–44*	*45–54*	*55–64*	*65+*
Permanently sick head of household	–	2.60	2.45	1.90	1.42	–
In employment	0.98	0.93	0.83	0.76	0.74	–
Temporarily/partially unable to work	1.04	1.09	1.20	1.18	1.00	–
Unemployed and dependants	1.09	1.06	1.00	0.94	0.88	–
Pensioner	–	–	–	–	–	1.00

Source: Ziekenfondsraad, 1999.

employment status are added to the usual age and sex dimensions. These result in the multiplicative adjustments to the simple age and sex capitation payments shown in Table 3.1. Clearly, the addition of additional dimensions of this sort leads to a rapid explosion in the number of contingency table cells for which capitations are to be estimated.

A particularly comprehensive example of individual capitation payments is a matrix of payments developed for Stockholm health care. This took advantage of a comprehensive register of Swedish citizens that records both personal characteristics and health care utilization in extraordinary detail. In such circumstances, the number of potential distinct capitation payments to be estimated is enormous – for example, with age (8 groups), sex (2), social class (5), employment status (3), housing tenure (2) and marital status (2) the number of payments to be estimated might in principle be $8 \times 2 \times 5 \times 3 \times 2 \times 2 = 2,160$. Under these circumstances, a fundamental challenge is to reduce the potentially massive matrix of capitation payments to manageable proportions, by minimizing the number of risk adjusters used and amalgamating cells of the matrix wherever possible (Andersson *et al.*, 2000). This both reduces complexity of the payment mechanism and smoothes the statistical noise associated with sparsely populated cells. An example of the abridged matrix of capitation payments is summarized in Table 3.2.

Table 3.2 The abridged Stockholm health care capitation matrix (Swedish krona per month), 1994

Age	Medical and surgical		Psychiatric	
	Owner occupier	*Rented*	*Owner occupier*	*Rented*
<1	7,200	0	0	
1–24	1,900	2,100	400	600
25–64 cohabiting				
Higher non-manual	3,100	3,600	400	800
Other non-manual	3,700	4,300	600	900
Manual	4,000	4,400	900	1300
Not employed	5,300	6,400	1,400	2,400
25–64 living alone				
Higher non-manual	3,600	3,900	900	1,600
Other non-manual	3,600	4,200	1,000	2,400
Manual	3,900	4,600	1,400	3,800
Not employed	5,100	5,400	4,900	12,700
65–84				
Cohabiting	13,500	16,500	500	1,000
Living alone	15,400	18,200	1,100	2,100
>84				
Cohabiting	27,600	29,800	300	1,000
Living alone	24,200	29,400	500	1,000

Source: Diderichsen *et al.*, 1997.

Whenever data permit, the contingency table approach is the preferred method for developing capitation payments, as it conforms most closely to insurance methods and keeps to a minimum the empirical difficulties associated with more aggregate data, as discussed in Chapter 5. However, it is often the case that few, if any, individual level data are available that are suitable for developing satisfactory capitation payments. And even when such data do exist they may introduce unacceptable perverse incentives. Many payers have therefore sought out blended methods that are less technically satisfactory, but do take advantage of the much richer data sources available at a more aggregate population level. The capitation payment then comprises a payment based on individual characteristics such as, for example, age and sex, which is then adjusted according to a needs index that is applied at a constant rate to all residents in the locality.

For example, apart from demographic characteristics, it is currently infeasible to use personal risk adjustment characteristics in English health care. Therefore, simple age-related payments form the basis of the payment mechanism. These are then further adjusted according to an index of local area conditions, so that every age-related capitation payment for the population of an area is raised (or lowered) according to the level of the local area index, which has a national average of 1.0. Thus for the area of Bebington and Wirral shown in Table 3.3, the value of the index for acute health care is 0.8956. The age-weighted budget is calculated by multiplying the national capitation payments (a) by the relevant local population (b). This budget (c) is then further adjusted by multiplying by the local needs index 0.8956 to derive the 'needs adjusted' budget. Of course, the crucial analytic question is how to derive the local area needs index. This is considered in detail in Chapter 5.

The reconciliation of the individual and area based capitation methods can be examined by considering a rudimentary algebraic model. Like an insurance premium, an individual capitation payment is a product of two phenomena: the

Table 3.3 Blending individual and area-level data for capitation payments: example of Bebington and Wirral (England), 2004

Age	(a) National Age Weight (£)	(b) Population	(c) = (a) × (b) Age Adjusted Allocation (£)	(d) Needs index = 0.8956
0–4	591.43	5,062	2,993,850	2,681,365
5–14	225.02	12,670	2,850,954	2,553,383
15–44	444.87	34,270	15,245,542	13,654,277
45–64	531.76	27,803	14,784,635	13,241,478
65–74	966.18	11,200	10,821,163	9,691,696
75–84	1,583.87	7,640	12,100,901	10,837,861
85+	2,357.64	2,768	6,526,778	5,845,541
Total		101,414	65,323,823	58,505,602

Source: Department of Health, 2003b.

probability of becoming a service user and the expected expenditure once a user. Suppose x_j^i is a vector of characteristics of person j in area i, and $c(.)$ is the risk adjusted capitation payment associated with characteristics x_j^i. The budget B_i for the devolved organization i is set as:

$$B_i = \sum_{j=1}^{P_i} c(x_j^i)$$

where P_i is the population for which organization i is responsible. The function $c(x)$ is the capitation payment associated with person x, usually set equal to the estimated costs of the service user x. It may of course be zero for some citizens – for example, men rarely use maternity services. If there is no risk adjustment, the tariff is just a constant equal to the single national capitation payment.

The alternative area-based view of the capitation approach first considers the problem as one of developing an estimate $\hat{N}_i$ of the expected number of service users, informed perhaps by a statistical model of the form $\hat{N}_i = n(y_i)$, where y_i is a vector of exogenous influences on user numbers in jurisdiction i, beyond the immediate influence of the budget holder. This approach is exemplified most obviously in the Scottish system of grant-aided expenditure for local govern-ment, which deploys what is known as the 'client group' approach (Scottish Executive, 2001). For each public service, this method develops estimates of the number of individuals requiring the service in each local government area. Regression methods are used to estimate a statistical model of the determinants of the number of service users, and the predictions from this model form the estimate of the expected numbers in each jurisdiction.

If risk adjustment is to be applied to area-based models, one could in prin-ciple envisage using a scaling factor $f(w_i)$ to the estimate of client numbers to yield an allocation $B_i = \hat{N}_i f(w_i) = n(y_i)f(w_i)$ to jurisdiction i, where w_i is a further vector of local area characteristics (that may or may not have elements in common with y_i). The scaling factor increases or depresses the crude estimate of numbers of service users by the expected average *intensity* of their use. The Scottish method does indeed seek to implement this principle, by augmenting the estimate of numbers of service users with an adjustment for the intensity of their spending needs. Funds are allocated to local governments in proportion to these adjusted estimates.

However, a simpler and more common statistical approach is to conflate the estimate of service users and intensity of needs into a single function of the form $B_i = b(z_i)$, where the $b(.)$ is an estimate of the expenditure requirement of organi-zation i given local characteristics z_i, which are a mix of the variables x_i and y_i. The function $b(.)$ is effectively a reduced form estimate of a complex process of demand for the public service. It seeks to predict expenditure requirements without explicitly estimating the numbers or intensity of service users, and this approach is the basis of many practically implemented funding formulae. Com-pared to the 'individual' capitation approach its virtue is that it permits use of a great wealth of area level data z_i that are not available at the individual level. However, the use of area-wide data can create serious statistical difficulties because it is often not clear, from an empirical perspective, whether or not a statistically important influence on client numbers is caused by user needs or local policies or efficiency levels. This issue is discussed further in Section 3.6.

Capitation payments in general create a global budget for the local organization. They are therefore strongly favoured when expenditure control is a prime objective of the payer. On their own, they offer no incentive to stimulate service activity – indeed they usually create an incentive to depress use of services. This may be beneficial (and intended) if it encourages the implementation of cost-effective preventative measures, such as crime reduction. However, it may be harmful if it encourages local organizations to erect barriers to legitimate use of services. Likewise, on its own, capitation funding offers few incentives to efficiency, and may encourage quality skimping in the provision of services. Other instruments such as performance measurement and efficiency audit must therefore often be implemented alongside capitation funding, in order to assure cost-effective delivery of services.

3.4 Case payments: reimbursing according to actual activity

While capitation methods develop estimates of the *expected* number of service users, it is often perfectly feasible to count the *actual* number of users of an organization's services. Payers often resist relying on such local counts as a basis for reimbursement for a number of reasons, such as:

- using the actual number of service users as a basis for reimbursement may encourage the local organization to stimulate demand for services rather than invest in preventative measures or otherwise manage local demand;
- the counts often rely on the local organization's own information sources and so may be vulnerable to fraud and difficult to verify;
- the payer does not know in advance the total number of service users, and so may not be able to control aggregate expenditure satisfactorily.

Notwithstanding these important concerns, there are often circumstances when it is preferable to rely on local counts of the numbers of service users as a basis for reimbursement, in the form of case payments. The crucial difference from capitation methods is that the estimate $\hat{N}_i$ of the *expected* number of service users is replaced with the provider's *reported* number of service users. An example is schooling where, in contrast to the concerns outlined above, the number of pupils is usually outside the control of the locality, can be satisfactorily verified and audited, and is predictable to a high degree of accuracy by the payer (Ross and Levacic, 1999). Under such circumstances it would be perverse of the payer to rely merely on estimates of the expected number of users.

Even when a case payment approach can give rise to difficulties, it may in practice be seen to be the only feasible way of reimbursing providers. For example, the US Medicare payment system for older people's health care relies on a competitive market for service delivery. Most Medicare providers are paid directly by the federal government, using a system of risk adjusted case payments, without any mediation of local organizations to manage demand. This has led to widespread concerns about 'physician induced demand' in US health care (McGuire, 2000). Medicare has sought to experiment with systems of capitation, under which local insurers are paid to manage demand for an enrolled population within a system of risk-adjusted capitation (see Section 5.5). However, to date patients have been reluctant to enrol in large numbers in such schemes, fearing that their traditional unfettered access to health care may be compromised by local demand management (Glazer and McGuire, 2000).

Payers should therefore in general be alert to the dangers of reliance on counts of service users as the basis for reimbursement. For example, further education colleges in England were for a while reimbursed according to numbers of students enrolled on courses, which could be reliably counted. However, without countervailing quality controls, it created an incentive to enrol students in courses without regard to their suitability or probability of success, and led to high student drop-out rates and a clearly inefficient outcome. Subsequent reforms therefore based case payments on the numbers of students completing their courses of study, rather than the numbers enrolling (Learning and Skills Council, 2004).

The usual approach to case payment is to reimburse according to the expected expenditure on a service user, often using some estimate of the national average. This approach may be adequate without risk adjustment when users are reasonably homogenous, such as university students. However, if variations in spending needs exist and a case payment system does not reimburse providers fairly for the costs of more intensive users, providers may seek to 'cream skim' only low cost users. More intensive users may then find it difficult to secure access to services. For example, if reimbursed at a flat rate per student, universities might seek to recruit only students who have a high probability of completing their studies without undue difficulty, and to deter students with higher perceived probabilities of failure or other complications.

The potential for cream skimming has led to the development of risk adjustment schemes that vary payments according to the dependency of users. The most celebrated of such schemes is the system of 'diagnosis-related groups' (DRGs) used in many health systems, under which the case payment varies according to the diagnosis of the patient. DRG payment systems are used in most mature health systems (Langenbrunner *et al.*, 2005). They are demanding to design, and introduce potentially costly data recording and audit requirements to ensure that providers record the diagnosis accurately. However, they are needed in order to reimburse providers fairly and avoid widespread cream skimming. Analogous systems are needed in schooling when the abilities of pupils (and therefore their expenditure needs) show marked variations.

Yet even within a single case payment group there may be considerable variation in patient costs, so there may still be an incentive to cream skim *within* the group. Generally, the local provider always has a clearer picture of the likely costs of a specific user than the central payer. This information asymmetry between payer and provider leads to pressures to define a finer gradation of user types, for example by increasing the number of DRGs in health care. However – even if this is technically feasible – as the gradation becomes finer, so the payment becomes closer to reimbursing providers according to actual costs. The incentive to reduce costs becomes diluted. There is therefore a fine balance to be struck between the coarseness of the case payment categories, the incentives for cost-reduction and the incentives for cream skimming.

Under case payments, local organizations usually have an incentive to reduce unit costs, subject to satisfying the payer's quality requirements. Indeed this was an important objective of early case payment systems, such as the first DRG systems in the US. However, as under capitation, they also have an incentive to stint on quality if the payer places no quality constraints on them.

Local organizations also have an incentive to ensure that they secure the maximum possible case payment for each service user. Where the category of case payment depends on the type of treatment, this may encourage providers to 'gold plate' treatment in order to secure a higher case payment (where the extra case payment outweighs the extra costs of treatment). For example, under many DRG systems, a patient's case payment category may increase if there are 'complications' associated with the treatment, in some cases offering physicians an incentive to over-treat patients in order to secure a higher DRG payment. The phenomenon of 'DRG creep' has been a source of widespread concern.

Even if physician treatment patterns do not change, the DRG system offers incentives to ensure that all possible indicators of case severity are properly recorded, and software packages have been developed to help medical coders maximize DRG revenue, giving rise to the phenomenon known as 'upcoding'. There are also – at least within the US health system – widespread reports of fraud and very large sums are spent on policing the Medicare DRG system (Becker *et al.*, 2005).

Case payment systems are especially prevalent where users have the freedom to choose their provider. They effectively enable the payer to offer the user a 'voucher' for the service in question, which can be spent on approved providers (Steuerle *et al.*, 2000). The voucher will usually be for a fixed payment for a specified service. Therefore, use of vouchers requires a clear assessment of the needs of the user, and the services to which the user is entitled. This might be quite straightforward in (say) education, where pupils are reasonably homogenous. However, it becomes much more problematic in (say) health care, where the professional assessing patient needs may be the same professional delivering the service. A particularly interesting example of user needs assessment is found in English social care, where some local governments are experimenting with offering individualized vouchers to adults requiring long-term care on the basis of a periodic independent 'needs assessment' (Commission for Social Care Inspection, 2004).

A central feature of reimbursing according to activity is that the payer cannot with any certainty forecast the global costs of reimbursement across all jurisdictions. If this is problematic, it can be addressed by 'close-ending' the payment system at the end of the year, so that the payer makes available only a predetermined sum in aggregate. The amount received by a specific organization is proportional to its measure of activity. However, the total amount disbursed equals the payer's budget constraint. For example, in Austria the measure of hospital activity is the number of DRG 'points' (Sommersguter-Reichmann, 2000). The amount received per point is calculated at the year end by dividing the total health system budget by the total number of health system DRG points reported. Effectively, this approach transfers the payer's expenditure risk to the localities. Under such close-ending, the revenue received by any one organization depends to some extent on the activity of all other organizations. As Barrow (1986) shows, this creates a sort of game between localities, and can lead to an incentive for over-provision of services.

3.5 Information needs

Fundamental to any type of formula funding is the information to be used as the basis for reimbursing local organizations. It is very rare to have available independent 'engineering' evidence of what levels of reimbursement each devolved entity should receive. Instead, in order to infer the level of reimbursement needed, payers are highly dependent on historical expenditure patterns among the intended recipients of funds. The reliance on past spending as a basis for current funding can give rise to profound philosophical and practical difficulties for the payer.

These difficulties can be illustrated in their most extreme form when the payer bases reimbursement to each organization solely on the historical spending of that organization – for example, by making the organization's current budget dependent on expenditure last year, plus some allowance for price changes, less some allowance for assumed efficiency improvements. Such budget-setting rules are endemic within many bureaucracies, and were also a central feature of the Soviet planning system, which tended to set production levels and budgets 'from the achieved level' (Nove, 1980). They lead to many adverse consequences, and contain few incentives for efficiency or effectiveness.

As a result, payers have sought out mechanisms that reduce the reliance on an organization's own past expenditure in setting its future budgets, and instead rely on some form of analysis of past expenditure by all or some of the public service organizations that will be in receipt of the payer's funds. This section summarizes the main considerations that arise when relying on such empirical data as the basis for formula funding.

In the first instance, capitation methods require a verifiable count of population, disaggregated where necessary into demographic groups. Although the population count used in a capitation system is often uncontentious, it can give rise to difficulties when it relies on local reporting, as there are obvious incentives for local organizations to maximize the population on which their revenues are based. For example, for many years UK general medical practitioners received a large part of their income on the basis of unreliable estimates of the size of the population registered with the practice. There was widespread acknowledgement that the registered list sizes were inflated to very different extents in different practices, arising from factors such as delay in removing patients from the list when they died or changed provider, transient populations and fraud (Ashworth *et al.*, 2005).

Under case payment methods, the analogous problem is the reliability of the count of service users. This can be straightforward, as in school education, or highly contested, as for example in a count of people in 'need' of sheltered housing accommodation. A prerequisite for satisfactory case payment methods is a clear statement by the payer of the national criteria that entitle a user access to the service. In contrast, capitation methods can allow an element of discretion on entitlement. The costs and reliability of specifying entitlement and counting the numbers of service users will often be an important determinant of whether case payment or capitation methods are preferred.

Although counts of the 'at risk' population or service users can be problematic, it is usually the risk adjustment process that leads to most technical debate, and where the analysis of past expenditure patterns comes into play. Key issues are the choice of personal or area-wide characteristics to include as 'risk adjusters', and the relative weight to attach to each factor. Different technical choices can lead to major changes in budgets, and there is often little methodological guidance for those seeking to design capitation risk adjustment schemes.

The first criterion will always be feasibility, and it is important to note that in many circumstances the range of satisfactory data available for risk adjustment purposes may be highly circumscribed. For example, some obvious risk adjusters in health care would be measures of chronic health status. These can rarely be reliably collected at reasonable cost, although some imaginative schemes have been tested, such as the use of routine prescribing data as a proxy for some chronic health condition (Fishman and Shay, 1999).

Moreover, the proposed risk adjusters must be reliably and consistently recorded across all recipients of funds. There will often be a need for a strong audit function to reassure all localities that payments are fair. Any suggestion that some localities are manipulating information may be seriously corrosive. For this reason, a payer may often feel unable to use some otherwise suitable characteristics as risk adjusters because they cannot be satisfactorily verified. This is an important reason for the use in many capitation schemes of 'area-wide' data, such as that collected from periodic censuses of population. Use of such data may obviate reliance on data provided directly by local governments or providers.

Fraud is an ever-present danger when funding systems are based on data provided by the recipients of funds and has been a persistent concern in the US Medicare scheme (Becker *et al.*, 2005). A fundamental constraint hampering many analytic endeavours is the extent to which the scope for misrepresentation may rule out the use of certain types of risk adjustment. It is potentially the Achilles heel of the innovative general practitioner incentive scheme described in Chapter 7.

Risk adjusters should obviously be manifest drivers of expenditure. But the payer will wish to use only factors that are *legitimate* drivers of expenditure, and will seek to avoid use of illegitimate factors. Loosely speaking, legitimate drivers of expenditure are influences on the costs of delivering the standard level of service that lie entirely outside the control of local organizations, and so can be used as risk adjusters. Examples might be local input prices and some (but not necessarily all) user characteristics. Illegitimate drivers of expenditure are influences on costs function that arise from the organizations' own policy choices, and so should not be used as risk adjusters. There is frequently a tension in the design of formulae between a desire to model expected expenditure accurately, and a desire to avoid perverse incentives. Issues of legitimacy and perverse incentives are described in more detail in the following section.

A persistent theme in the literature is the tension between parsimony in the use of data and the need to model spending needs sensitively. Generally speaking, many payers prefer simple funding mechanisms as they can be more readily understood and therefore promote accountability. However, there will often be an element of rough justice in a simple funding formula, so those local organizations that feel they are adversely affected by the choice of a simple mechanism will press for 'refinement', in the form of an increased number of risk adjusters and added complexity. Balancing simplicity and sensitivity of the funding mechanism is a key role for the payer.

One final issue of great importance relates to the variation in expenditure that is not captured by the chosen capitation model. Even on those rare occasions when the capitation methodology explains a high proportion of individual variation in expenditure, a considerable element of unexplained variation remains. The unexplained variation can be ascribed to two broad sources: omitted explanatory variables and random fluctuation. Clearly, given the paucity of data available, there is an ever-present danger of variable omission, especially as some important but illegitimate determinants of expenditure (such as variations in teacher effectiveness in education) may have to be omitted from the funding model.

However, it is also important to recognize that there is a large element of unpredictable variation in the use of many public services (most notably health care) that will always defy systematic modelling. Thus, although a given capitation sum might be notionally assigned to an individual, there is in general no expectation that the public sector should spend precisely that amount on the individual. For example, in health care, although an average capitation of (say) £550 per annum may be assigned to a male aged 40–44, it would be absurd to expect every such individual to require that level of expenditure per annum. Rather, the capitation offers an *expected* level of expenditure, around which there might exist substantial variation. The issue of expenditure risk is discussed more fully in Chapter 6.

3.6 Legitimate and illegitimate influences on expenditure

The reliance on historical data has led to widespread use of statistical analysis of previous expenditure among all (or a sample of) budget holders to determine future capitation or case payment rates. In particular, regression analysis of past expenditure on a range of service user or broader population characteristics gives rise to a statistical model that explains past spending patterns. Such models offer estimates of *predicted* expenditure of each budget-holder, for a given set of local characteristics, which can be used as a basis for setting a budget for an organization budget that is largely independent of its own past expenditure. Implicit in such methods is the assumption that (loosely speaking) the basis for reimbursement should be the *sample average* of expenditure, subject to certain local characteristics. Thus, an organization's budget is determined largely by the behaviour of its peers, rather than its own behaviour.

The use of statistical analysis is a cornerstone of formula funding, and has without question allowed payers to move away from reliance on historical spending as a basis for reimbursement. Indeed, the existence of an adequate sample on which to develop cost function models is an important benefit of devolved service delivery, highlighted by the decision of the UK Monopolies and Mergers Commission (1996) to reject a merger of two English water companies on the grounds that it would materially reduce (from 10 to 9) the number of units available for the statistical analysis needed to set future pricing regimes.

However, the reliance on statistical analysis as a basis for formula funding brings with it new difficulties:

- first, patterns of current spending may not necessarily reflect the payer's future intentions;
- second, there may be perverse incentives associated with using certain characteristics as a basis for reimbursement, even if in principle they indicate influences on expenditure in line with the payer's intentions;
- third, the methodological difficulties of developing satisfactory statistical models may be profound.

I consider these briefly in turn.

For practical purposes, many payers choose a 'needs factor' as a basis for risk adjustment if it explains actual current expenditure patterns in a statistically significant manner. The use of statistical significance as a basis for choosing risk adjusters is essentially conservative, in the sense that it reflects current (average) behaviour of local organizations. Yet there may be circumstances in which the payer finds current patterns of service delivery unacceptable, and wishes to change patterns of expenditure. It therefore appears perverse to use current spending patterns as a basis for setting budgets.

In particular, it may not be possible to accommodate some aspects of so-called 'unmet' need for services within traditional empirical formula funding methodology. Unmet need arises when particular groups within the population –

such as ethnic minorities or those living in rural areas – are not receiving the services at the same level as the majority of the population, other things equal. Under these circumstances, the use of empirical spending patterns to infer needs is problematic, as the models developed will perpetuate the implied inequity. For example, if – after adjusting for other needs factors – ethnic minorities systematically receive services at a lower level than the rest of the population, an uncritical statistical analysis of expenditure patterns would identify a negative coefficient associated with ethnic minority status. Notwithstanding any statistical significance, it would be wrong to include such factors in a funding formula if the payer wishes to eliminate the existing inequity.

The existence of unmet need or other departures from the payer's intentions implies that empirical data should be used with great caution. Possible solutions may be to restrict the statistical analysis only to organizations that *are* currently delivering services in line with intentions, or to supplement empirically based formulae with payments based on some non-empirical criterion. An example from health care of how this might be done is described in Chapter 4.

More generally, a fundamental statistical difficulty associated with developing adequate statistical models is deciding which local characteristics to take into account when adjusting for differences in expenditure risk between organizations. There usually exist numerous characteristics of local users, populations and organizations that could potentially be used as risk adjusters. However, it is often the case that the payer will not want to compensate for all variations between organizations. To guide the choice of risk adjustment, Rice and Smith (2001b) therefore develop the notion of determinants of public service expenditure that are *legitimate* and those that are *illegitimate* risk adjusters.

Illegitimate drivers of expenditure are influences on costs function that arise from the organizations' own policy or managerial actions, and so should not be used as risk adjusters. The use of this expression does not imply that illegitimate local influences on expenditure are necessarily illegal or even always undesirable. It merely suggests that they should be ignored in any formula used for allocating funds. Examples include variations in professional practices, variations in managerial priorities and variations in efficiency.

The criterion for deciding whether a determinant is legitimate or not should in principle be based on the institutional and ethical framework underlying the public service in question. For example, to what extent should local capital configuration be considered a legitimate influence on costs? And to what extent should poor managerial choices in the past (such as neglect of crime prevention measures, leading to high current crime rates) be accommodated in the risk adjustment process? In principle current management should not usually be held accountable for the actions of their predecessors. Yet payers will usually wish to encourage current management to take into account the consequences of their actions for future performance. These examples mirror debates in the economic productivity literature about whether to focus on long-run or short-run cost functions. They imply fine policy judgements for the payer when developing funding formulae, the resolution of which often depends on context.

Furthermore, the use of some variables as risk adjusters might lead to unacceptable perverse incentives even if they are legitimate drivers of current expenditure. Thus, although the crime rate is considered a legitimate driver of police expenditure, its use as a risk adjuster will often be ruled out because it gives local forces an incentive to increase rather than reduce crime. There is frequently a tension in the design of formulae between a desire to model expected expenditure accurately and a desire to avoid such perverse incentives.

In another setting, the best predictor of an individual's current health care expenditure is her previous history of expenditure and utilization, and such variables are often used in systems of competitive health insurance in order to model individual expenditure accurately (and so reduce the incentive for insurers to cream skim only healthy patients) (Van de Ven and Ellis, 2000). However, policy makers have in general sought to avoid the use of such data in the design of health service formulae, on the grounds that they may offer a perverse incentive for providers to increase provision in order to secure increased capitation rates in the future.

It is often very difficult econometrically to disentangle truly exogenous influences on the demand for services from factors that are correlated with local policy choices or other organizational actions (Duncan and Smith, 1995). In the terminology used earlier, how is it possible to determine whether an observed statistical association with expenditure arises from a legitimate or illegitimate influence on costs? Even where apparently exogenous data are used in constructing a formula, there may be some scope for budget holders to influence allocations.

For example, there has been a long-running debate in English local government about the extent to which concerted action by certain groups of local governments might collectively influence funding formulae in their favour (Bennett, 1982). The formulae are often estimated using regression equations of the form $B_i = b(z_i) + \epsilon_i$, where the units of observation are administrative areas and the usual error term has been added to the budget equation. In practice, choice of the explanatory variables z_i is usually determined by tests of statistical significance. Thus, groups of local authorities with similar social characteristics might be able to bias the regression in their favour by adopting high levels of expenditure, and thereby appearing to have higher service needs than is actually the case. That is, legitimate indicators of social needs z_i might be contaminated by illegitimate indicators of policy preference.

This phenomenon was a strong driver of a search for reform in the early 1980s, when the use of regression analysis was temporarily abandoned in English local government finance. Although the use of regression analysis was subsequently reinstated ten years later, the difficulty of securing estimates of expected demand for services that are independent of local policy choices remained a central concern in more recent reforms (Office of the Deputy Prime Minister, 2002). The statistical problem is one manifestation of what is referred to by sociologists as the 'ecological fallacy': an effect is detected at an aggregate level of analysis that does not exist at the individual level. It implies that choice of z_i may be biased when based on statistical analysis of area-wide data, such as local governments. This is discussed at more length in Chapter 5, and the small area methodology described in Section 5.6 seeks to mitigate this problem by examining relationships between social circumstances and spending *within* administrative areas.

This section has sought to highlight the profound difficulties that can arise when seeking to develop funding formulae on the basis of empirical data. It is almost certainly the case that statistical analysis of existing spending patterns does form the best basis for most funding mechanisms. But it can raise major methodological and philosophical difficulties. In particular, in contrast to traditional statistical analysis, the payer does not always wish to develop an empirical model that maximizes the proportion of variation in expenditure that is explained. Indiscriminately including variables of all types in a model of expenditure may perpetuate inequalities (if unmet need is in existence), may encourage localities to retain poorly organized services, may otherwise introduce perverse incentives, or encourage manipulation of data. Indeed, in the extreme, as more variables are added into the model, so the model's *predicted* expenditure approaches the *actual* expenditure of organizations. The payer's objective of moving away from historical spending patterns is therefore thwarted.

3.7 Modelling supply side costs

Most of the published literature and academic effort relating to funding mechanisms has concentrated on modelling the demand for public services. Yet on the supply side there are often important variations in local cost structures that should be properly modelled and incorporated into the funding mechanism if the objective of securing a standard level of service is to be addressed. To this end, many funding mechanisms incorporate an adjustment for local cost variations.

For example, labour and capital prices vary greatly within England, and 'area cost adjustments' have therefore been designed to reflect such variations (Wilson *et al.*, 2002). In health care, they have resulted in capitation payments that vary from 11 per cent below the national average (in Cornwall) to 29 per cent above the national average (in Westminster). It is important to note that the methodology to derive these adjustments deliberately avoids use of specific public sector input prices. In particular, to use local public service wage rates as a basis for an area cost adjustment would allow localities to increase pay with impunity above efficient rates implied by local labour market conditions. Instead, the English methodology seeks to use economy-wide measures of relative pay from a regular earnings survey, basing the estimates of public service pay on the rates found in comparable parts of the competitive local economy.

There is often considerable scope for adjusting payment mechanisms satisfactorily for input prices. A more intractable difficulty arises for the payer when local geography or other physical constraints affect the cost structure of local services. In particular, geographical remoteness in countries such as Australia and Canada can have a profound influence on the local costs of delivering the standard package of services. Remote areas often cannot feasibly provide the comprehensive package of services enjoyed by their urban counterparts, and even if they seek to do so, they are unable to reap the benefits of scale economies enjoyed by providers serving larger populations. Remote areas may therefore have to deliver services in different ways, perhaps incurring higher transportation costs or otherwise needing to offer more support to service users.

Again, the first point to make in this connection is that it will often be unsatisfactory merely to reimburse passively in line with the higher unit costs reported in rural areas, as this offers those areas no incentive to improve efficiency, and indeed may encourage them to increase expenditure. Rather, the objective should be to seek out independent measures of inescapable higher costs associated with remoteness. It is difficult to see how this can be done without an explicit statement of the standard level of service. For example, if it is really the case that health systems are seeking to offer equal access to care in all localities, this implies a need to provide high quality, comprehensive health care in the most remote communities, with potentially enormous cost implications.

Rather, it is likely that the implicit intention of the payer is to include in the standard level of service a proviso that equal access can be assured only up to a point. Citizens in rural areas cannot realistically expect to enjoy identical services to their urban counterparts. Nevertheless, the payer is likely to expect that some minimum level of services should be available even in the most remote areas. For example most developed nations seek to offer some form of education to all children, irrespective of the difficulty of doing so, although the nature of that education may necessarily be qualitatively different in more remote areas.

An example of how the increased costs associated with rurality could be modelled is a study of the emergency ambulance service in England. The national government has articulated an explicit standard for all services, as follows: 75 per cent of all life-threatening (Category A) calls should be reached within eight minutes of the call being made; and 95 per cent of less serious (Category B) type calls should be reached within 19 minutes. This level of detail has allowed operational researchers explicitly to model the minimum costs of securing the standard, assuming local ambulance services are deployed efficiently (MHA Associates and Operational Research in Health, 1997).

Detailed transportation models were developed for a limited number of localities to identify the least cost location and size of ambulance stations required to satisfy the standard, given the distribution of population, location of hospitals, and road network. Ideally, a model of this type would be developed for each locality, using consistent model-building principles, and would form the basis for financial allocations. However, it was infeasible to develop the transportation model for every ambulance service. Instead, for those localities that were modelled, it was possible to regress the implied efficient costs of delivering the standard against measures of local geographical conditions, such as population sparsity. This regression model was then used as the basis of the cost adjustment in the payment mechanism for all ambulance services.

In practice, such modelling has rarely been used. It is highly complex, and in any case payers rarely articulate the standard level of service to the level of detail needed to develop secure estimates of the inescapable cost variations caused by geography. Instead, the tendency has been for payers to incorporate measures of remoteness (or rurality) in a rather arbitrary and unstructured way (Sheldon and Watts, 1993). Indeed it appears in many cases that additional payments to rural areas are based on political expediency rather than objective evidence. This is not to say that remote areas do not sometimes experience profound cost disadvantages compared to their urban counterparts. However, the scientific basis on which that disadvantage is compensated is often hard to discern. For example, Chapter 8 describes the Special Islands Needs Allowance paid to three Scottish island local governments, and concludes that the amounts involved were almost certainly a political settlement to appease the islands, rather than a principled compensation for higher cost structures.

Such political solutions to the problem of reimbursing remote areas are attractive not only because the technical difficulties of finding a formulaic solution are so daunting. It is also usually the case that the populations involved are small, so that the amounts of money at stake – although large for the remote areas involved – are small relative to the payer's total budget. As a result, the payer can effect large *per capita* increases to remote areas without materially affecting the allocations to other localities. It may therefore be more expedient to 'buy off' the problem of remote areas, rather than to seek out a technically challenging formula funding solution. Note that the political settlement also obviates the need to specify the standard level of service, which may be embarrassing to the payer if it makes explicit a compromise in standards for remote areas.

3.8 Discussion

Chapter 2 discussed the arguments in favour of using some sort of funding formula as a basis for reimbursing local public service organizations. This chapter has highlighted two broad approaches: capitation payments and case payments. In a sense it is artificial to distinguish between the two. A capitation payment is merely a general case payment that reflects the probability of needing a service as well as the expected cost of the service. The case payment reflects only the expected cost of the service once a need has been realized. Yet the chapter has shown that the two approaches may generate quite different sets of incentives and lead to different data requirements.

In its pure form, capitation funding offers strong incentives to local organizations to control demand. Actions to do so might be virtuous (such as introducing appropriate preventative measures) or adverse (such as inhibiting legitimate access to services). If the organizations have freedom to choose their 'insured' populations (as in the case, say, of general medical practices), it also offers an incentive to cream skim members of the population with low expected expenditure needs (relative to their capitation payments). There are few *direct* incentives for improving technical efficiency under capitation, and an obvious incentive to skimp on the quality of services.

Under case payments, the incentives change profoundly. The mechanism encourages increased service use (at least for low cost users for whom the case payment exceeds the expected costs). This also implies an incentive for cream skimming low cost users within case payment groups. Providers are encouraged to reduce unit costs, which they might pursue either virtuously (by increased efficiency) or adversely (by skimping on quality). Also under case payments, there will usually be incentives to 'upcode' the complexity of users, and for more general data fraud and manipulation.

These stark incentives imply that a sole reliance on the funding mechanism for securing the payer's objectives is likely to fail. Rather, formula funding must be designed in conjunction with other instruments that seek to strengthen the beneficial aspects of the approach and mitigate the adverse consequences.

For example, most forms of formula funding offer an incentive to skimp on the quality of services to users. The most powerful instruments available to the payer for securing adequate quality standards are likely to be non-financial, such as independent quality inspection and public reporting of quality. As data sources improve, there is also the prospect of incorporating quality standards explicitly into the funding formula, as discussed in detail in Chapter 7. It is also likely that detailed managerial incentives independent of the funding mechanism are likely to be useful instruments for maximizing the effectiveness of formula funding.

Another approach to addressing the adverse incentives inherent in the pure funding systems is to implement a mix of payment mechanisms. For example, Norway has experimented with reimbursing local governments for health care partly on the basis of capitation (to secure cost control) and partly on the basis of DRG case payments (to encourage reduction of hospital waiting times) (Biørn *et al.*, 2003). In seeking to secure an optimal balance, the national government has experimented with different proportions attached to each element (at the time of writing it is 40 per cent capitation, 60 per cent case payments). In the same way, some sort of matching payment may be needed to reduce cream skimming and quality skimping, and to maintain stability of the local provider market.

The nature, quality, consistency, timeliness and independence of data are key issues in determining the payer's preferred funding regime. Many of the data on which a public service funding regime should be based are in the first instance collected by the local organizations in receipt of funds. There is therefore always a risk that they will be corrupted, and – even if they are not – any suspicion that they are questionable may corrode trust in the payment system. There is, therefore, often a need for a strong independent audit function to assure the quality of the data. Even if the data can be verified, the choice of some as a basis for funding may be precluded because they introduce perverse incentives for local organizations.

For the payer, numerous criteria for selecting risk adjustment characteristics have been indicated. For example, they should:

- be feasible, with low administrative cost;
- be consistently, reliably, verifiably and universally recorded;
- not be vulnerable to manipulation or fraud;
- be legitimate predictors of expected public service expenditure;
- encourage efficient delivery of public services, and be free from perverse incentives;
- respect confidentiality requirements;
- be parsimonious and plausible, thereby promoting transparency and accountability.

In practice, this severely limits the choice of variables, as in most contexts only very restricted information on the characteristics of individuals or areas exists that conforms to such criteria.

In summary the payer is faced with a formidable challenge when designing a formula funding mechanism, in the form *inter alia* of:

- articulating objectives for the public service under consideration;
- identifying appropriate data sources;
- identifying what influences on expenditure can be considered legitimate;
- determining the preferred systems of formula funding, or mix of systems;
- estimating the parameters of the funding formula;
- putting in place appropriate data audit regimes;
- integrating the funding mechanism with other regulatory instruments;
- monitoring and reviewing the operation of the funding formula.

This chapter has sought to offer some guidance on how in general these tasks might be pursued. However, it is likely that the precise nature of any choices will be highly contingent on the nature of the services under consideration, the institutional framework of local public services and the availability of data.

4 Formula funding: a production function perspective

4.1 Introduction

This chapter sets out a more formal theoretical framework for discussing the issues underlying capitation funding or case payments. The fundamental building block is the personal production function (PPF) for a public service, which describes the link between spending on an individual and the associated outcome. The intention is to model the optimal payment for each individual, given a payer's efficiency and equity objectives. In order to simplify the presentation, the chapter focuses throughout on capitation methods. However, with a trivial change of terminology, the discussion is equally applicable to case payments, for example in the form of *per pupil* school payment mechanisms.

The next section introduces the concept of the PPF and Section 4.3 discusses its link with capitation payments and economic efficiency. Using the PPF framework, Section 4.4 examines three fundamental causes of variations in outcome of public services, and Section 4.5 then discusses the implications for risk adjustment if society wishes to apply an equity criterion to capitation payments. The chapter concludes with a discussion of how efficiency and equity concerns might be balanced, and some applications of the principles drawn from the English public services.

4.2 The personal production frontier

The PPF seeks to describe for an individual service user the outcome from the use of services as a function of inputs. In pursuing this analytic device, I necessarily have to make an extraordinary number of simplifying assumptions, but nevertheless believe that it is useful for understanding the issues involved in setting capitation payments. It is illustrated in Figure 4.1. For a particular individual i, the PPF shows the relationship between expected expenditure on a public service and the expected outcome for the user, assuming efficient production and efficient purchase of inputs. The shape of the PPF is not especially important, although one must assume that above some level of expenditure decreasing returns will apply – the curve levels off. Indeed, there is for many services likely to be a maximum level of attainment above which any improvement is impossible.

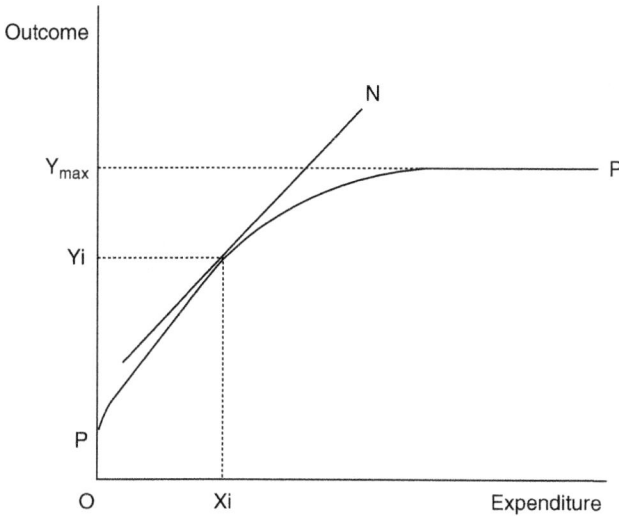

Figure 4.1 An individual's production function for a public service.

Note that inputs have been compressed into a single measure, expected expenditure. I therefore assume that the service provider is purchasing and deploying inputs efficiently, and do not consider the input side of the service in any detail. Equally, a single measure of outcome is used. The analysis could readily be extended to multiple outcomes. Furthermore, there is no special need to dwell on what specific measure of outcome (or indeed output) is under consideration – it could be very simple, merely indicating satisfactory receipt of a service, or it could be very subtle, for example increased lifetime productivity resulting from educational services. For the purposes of this chapter, the precise choice of outcome measure does not materially affect the theoretical argument.

However, the use of a PPF in this stylized fashion does require a number of important assumptions. First, it represents the actions of a single public service provider, other things being equal. In practice a citizen may make use of a number of providers. For example, a child's educational outcomes might be enhanced by private tuition supplementary to her public education. For the purposes of this chapter such effects can be considered just one of numerous potential exogenous influences on the shape of the PPF shown in Figure 4.1. More generally, the precise nature of an individual's PPF is likely to be highly dependent on personal characteristics, complementary public services, environmental factors, and numerous other personal and societal influences on outcome. The implications of the associated heterogeneity in PPFs are considered in Section 4.4.

I also sidestep the issue of what time period the analysis refers to. For long-term services, such as health care, personal social services and education, we might think of expenditure as being expected lifetime expenditure on the relevant service, discounted to birth. In practice, most capitation schemes use a very limited period, such as a year. Once again, this is not a major theoretical difficulty: if necessary, we can merely think of 'age' as one of the personal characteristics that affects outcome over the year. I must also assume a constant service technology over the period under consideration. Rapid change in technologies might complicate practical problems of setting capitation payments, but this is not germane to the theoretical discussion.

More generally, the analysis is restricted to the deterministic case, and uncertainty in outcomes arising from technologies, individual characteristics or external circumstances is not considered. In practice, the effectiveness of a public service is likely – to a greater or lesser extent – to fall some way short of the ideal indicated by the PPF. *Random* inefficiencies of this sort do not materially affect the theoretical argument. *Systematically* larger inefficiencies suffered by particular groups relative to others are however discussed in some detail in Section 4.4 below.

4.3 Selecting the level of capitation payment

Given the shape of an individual's PPF, how much expenditure should the public service devote to that individual? In systems that are not budget-constrained, we might in principle expect to observe expenditure up to the point where marginal benefit is zero (the PPF becomes horizontal). However, within the realistic case of a budget-constrained public service we must assume that some other criterion applies.

In selecting a payment for an individual, the payer is implicitly signalling a preferred level of outcome. Therefore, with knowledge of the PPF of all individuals, the policy maker should be able to optimize a social welfare function that balances the aggregate expenditure on the service with the benefits expressed in terms of the aggregate magnitude of outcomes and its distribution between individuals. In the simple case of identical individuals this might entail balancing the aggregate benefits of the service against its aggregate costs, leading to the choice of expenditure X_i (with associated outcome Y_i) in the case in Figure 4.1. The slope of the line NN indicates the chosen marginal social value of the relevant public service, determined by the aggregate budget set for the service.

In general, personal production functions vary greatly between individuals. For example, for a given level of expenditure, some school pupils will secure poorer educational attainment than others. More generally, PPFs for a particular public service might vary for the following reasons:

- variations in an individual's inherent characteristics;
- variations in lifestyle;
- variations in state of physical or mental wellbeing caused by external factors, such as the environment or occupation;

- variations in wealth, for example leading to different capacities to supplement the public service with other resources;
- variations in the ability to secure access to the public services, for example through geographical, language or cultural barriers;
- variations in access to substitute or complementary services;
- variations in information regarding the availability and optimal use of the public service.

Each of these sources of variation can affect the shape of the PPF, often in a major fashion. For example, the lifestyle and wealth of individuals are known to have a major impact on their responsiveness to health care interventions. Indeed, it may be the case that some desired levels of outcome cannot be secured for some especially disadvantaged individuals, whatever the level of expenditure.

This heterogeneity among individuals has major implications for payment policy. Even if the payer has no equity concerns, and is prepared merely to add up individual outcomes, risk adjustment becomes necessary if aggregate outcomes are to be maximized. In this case, the marginal social benefit from an extra unit of expenditure should be equal for all individuals, so the decision rule becomes one of applying the same sloped line NN to all individuals, whatever the shape of their PPF. Figure 4.2 illustrates for two individuals with different PPFs. The application of a uniform cut-off entails selecting expenditure X_1 for individual 1 and X_2 for individual 2, leading to unequal outcomes Y_1 and Y_2. Assuming no externalities, this can be thought of as the pure efficiency solution. A fundamental efficiency argument for implementing risk adjusted capitation

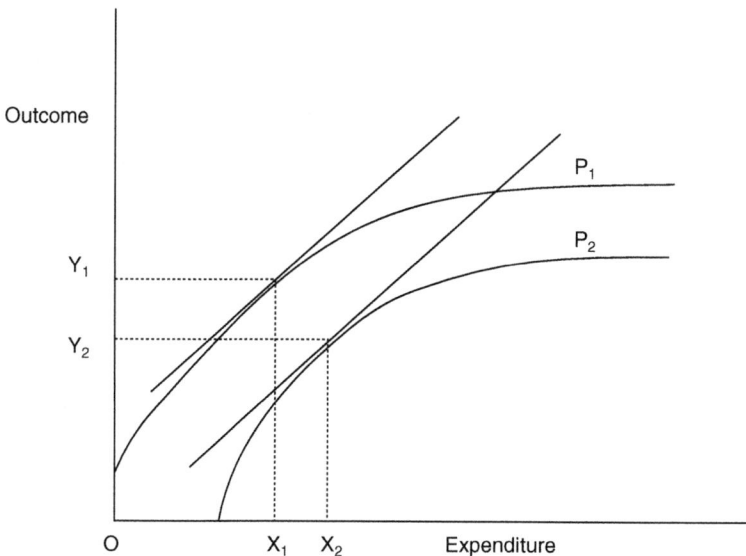

Figure 4.2 Efficient payment rates for two individuals.

funding is that it facilitates the most productive use of fixed resources by maximizing aggregate outcome. Any variation from this allocation leads to a net reduction in the sum of individual outcomes.

This pure efficiency model underlies much of the literature on economic evaluation of public service interventions (Davies *et al.*, 1999). It is moreover important to note that – *if and* only *if* we define an individual's 'need' in terms of marginal capacity to benefit from the public service – the pure efficiency model is consistent with the widely used equity principle that those in equal need should have equal access to services. I return to this and other notions of need in Section 4.5.

4.4 Why do variations in outcome arise?

In practice, large variations arise in the outcomes secured for individuals by public services. These can arise from three sources: variations in managerial efficiency, variations in inputs and variations in individual PPFs. They are often the subject of considerable policy concern, yet the three sources of variation have very different policy implications. We consider them in turn.

4.4.1 Managerial inefficiency

Suppose first that all individuals have the same PPF and that the same cut-off criterion is applied to all individuals. That is, given the budget constraint, the efficient level of expenditure X_i is being directed at all individuals i. However, services for some classes of individuals are managerially (or technically) inefficient, in the sense that the levels of outcome secured lie below the optimum level implied by the PPF. That is, services for two equally needy individuals differ due to variations in technical efficiency. This situation is represented in Figure 4.3 by the point L for the disadvantaged individual, giving rise to outcome Y_L, as opposed to Y_H for the individual receiving better quality services.

Services to disadvantaged population groups may be less technically efficient than other services for a number of reasons: expenditure may not be allocated optimally across an individual's lifetime, staff may be less motivated to secure good outcomes or may communicate poorly with disadvantaged individuals, recruitment of staff may be more difficult or capital configurations less appropriate in areas where the affected groups live, and so on. In this case, it is important to identify the true production possibilities, and to distinguish between improvements in outcome that can be secured by improved use of existing public services, and those that require additional resources.

Addressing inequalities arising from technical inefficiency requires no change to capitation payments, because existing allocation of expenditure is *allocatively* efficient – it is the use of resources that is *managerially* inefficient. In this case, policy attention should focus not on changing capitation methods, but on instruments to secure better use of resources in services for disadvantaged

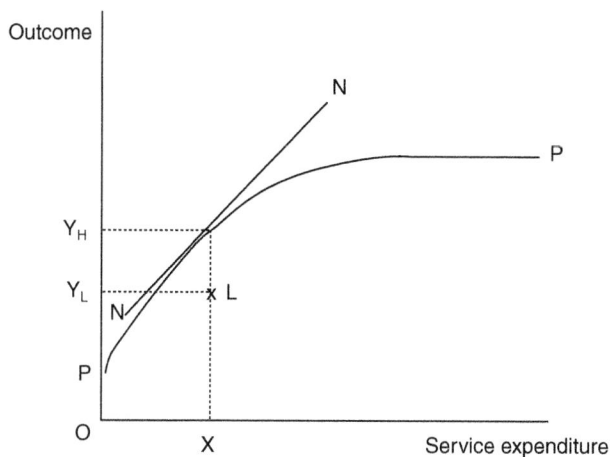

Figure 4.3 Inequalities in outcome arising from variations in managerial efficiency for two individuals.

populations. Initiatives such as the publication of performance data and systems of audit and inspection may help secure progress towards this objective.

4.4.2 Allocative efficiency

Suppose now that all individuals continue to have the same PPF and all are being served technically efficiently (that is, on rather than below the production function). However, a stricter cut-off criterion is applied to some classes of individuals than to others, implying the existence of allocative inefficiency. Although needs are identical, expenditure on the public service is less for some groups than others. This may be due to market or informational failures on the demand or supply side. Figure 4.4 illustrates the principle for two individuals, with the stricter treatment criterion applied to the disadvantaged individual L resulting in lower expenditure X_L and poorer outcome Y_L than for the other individual H.

If a stricter cut-off criterion is currently being applied to some individuals than to others, a fundamental equity principle underlying many public services is being breached – that of equal access for those in equal need. Systematic variations in expenditure of this sort were discussed in Section 3.5, under the rubric of unmet need. Aside from any equity concern, the presence of this sort of unmet need also implies that outcome maximization is not being secured, because the underserved have a greater capacity to benefit from expenditure than the rest of the population.

A redirection of resources towards the disadvantaged groups is therefore required, with an implication that capitation payments for disadvantaged

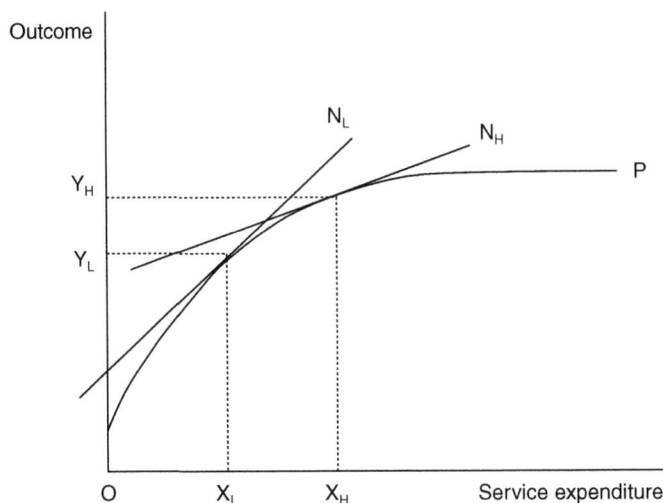

Figure 4.4 Inequalities in outcome arising from variations in access for two individuals.

populations should rise relative to the remainder of the population. In terms of Figure 4.4, the requirement is to quantify the shifts in expenditure $X_L X_H$ required to ensure that all citizens receive the same level of service. It is important to note that use of capitation payments based on historical empirical data (X_L and X_H) will perpetuate the implied disparity. Therefore more creative methods of setting capitation payments will have to be employed. For example, Sutton and Lock (2000) and Blundell and Windmeijer (2000) show how an empirically-based capitation formula could be based only on the subsample of institutions that are thought to be closest to delivering services in line with the payer's equity policies. Alternatively, empirically derived payments might be augmented with a 'premium' for the disadvantaged groups, perhaps based on a policy judgement rather than empirical evidence.

However, although capitation payments based on empirical data may need to be adjusted, addressing unequal outcomes caused by allocative inefficiency does not require definition of a new criterion for setting capitation payments. The main policy requirement is to formulate strategies to eliminate the allocative inefficiency in the provision of the services; that is, to design interventions that reduce systematic inequalities in service utilization. The nature of these will of course be highly dependent on the reason why inequalities arise. Problems on the demand side might be caused by informational, cultural, financial or geographical barriers to access. Examples of supply side factors that may inhibit use by disadvantaged groups include the design or location of services, failure to address language or cultural barriers, and the attitudes of staff.

4.4.3 Individual heterogeneity

The third source of unequal outcomes arises because of the heterogeneity in individuals' PPFs. Figure 4.2 illustrated that – even if there is no technical or allocative inefficiency in the deployment of resources – individual outcomes will in general vary, because of the variations in individuals' personal and environmental circumstances. If these outcome variations are considered unacceptable, the policy implication is that the public services need to skew resources towards the disadvantaged groups, to compensate for the poor outcomes that would arise under a pure efficiency set of capitation payments. That is, a fundamental change to capitation policy is required. This is considered in more detail in the following section.

4.5 Equity and risk adjustment

Chapter 2 discussed the possible equity criteria that a payer might wish to pursue, and noted that they fall into two broad categories – horizontal equity (equal treatment of equals) and vertical equity (greater priority for those with greater needs). Horizontal equity is concerned mainly with seeking to equalize inputs, while vertical equity is concerned mainly with outcomes. The principle underlying both notions is that social welfare depends on both the level and distribution of the benefits secured by public services.

4.5.1 Horizontal equity

The horizontal equity criterion implies a desire to secure equal outcomes for those in equal circumstances (however defined). It does not explicitly consider whether different groups receive their 'fair share' of resources. Rather, the key policy decision is to determine which personal characteristics are 'legitimate' and which 'illegitimate' causes of variations in service utilization (see Section 3.5). These define what is meant by 'equal circumstances'. The legitimate causes should then be incorporated into the capitation formula, the illegitimate should not. Thus horizontal equity is concerned mainly with the first two reasons for variations discussed in Section 4.4: technical and allocative inefficiency.

For example, researchers in Stockholm found that 'immigrant' status had a negative impact on expected health service expenditure, other things equal (Diderichsen *et al.*, 1997). The payer judged that this reflected 'unmet' need rather than a healthier population, so did not include the variable in the health care capitation formula. In contrast, many health care capitation formulae use 'age' as a part of the capitation formula, suggesting that most policy makers believe that age is a legitimate reason for variations in expenditure. Most capitation schemes adjust for age according to empirically derived variations in expenditure between age groups. They therefore do not question whether or not that existing distribution of resources between age groups is in line with policy intentions.

Many public services employ a horizontal equity criterion that implies that capitation payment levels should be equal for people in equal 'need'. However, few capitation methods consider explicitly what is meant by the concept of need, and the associated choice of legitimate causes of variation in utilization (Culyer, 1995). As discussed in Chapter 2, a pure equity principle would in principle seek to ensure that a representative individual should enjoy the same level of utility regardless of where she lives or which institution she uses. Making operational such a principle is infeasible, and the equity principle usually adopted (explicitly or implicitly) is that the formula should seek to offer comparable public sector organizations the opportunity to deliver some standard level of service.

As discussed in Chapter 3, the standard level of service can be defined in terms of inputs, processes or outcomes. These give rise to increasing levels of methodological complexity, and must be translated into an expenditure consequence in order to compute the associated capitation payment. Examples would be a fixed expenditure per pupil (inputs), the amount required to ensure that all older people satisfying some entitlement criterion receive some specified level of domiciliary care (processes), or the amount required to ensure that avoidable mortality below the age of 75 is prevented (outcome). The chosen definition of the standard defines what equity criterion is being employed and what is meant by 'need'.

If the emphasis is on equalizing inputs (for example in the form of equalizing expenditure), then the requirement is to ensure that the funding formula reflects only legitimate sources of expenditure variation. If empirical utilization data are used to derive the formula, this results in a statistical estimate of expected expenditure on an individual, given the individual characteristics that are considered legitimate sources of expenditure variation. Although it is even-handed, the horizontal equity approach is intrinsically conservative because it does not question whether or not current expenditure patterns between different groups are in line with social objectives.

4.5.2 Vertical equity

In contrast, a vertical equity criterion signals a concern with variations in outcomes, and the precise measure of outcome deployed is the key policy decision (Mooney *et al.*, 1991). Once it is specified, it becomes (in principle) possible to determine the amount of inputs required to 'meet' that need for each individual, and therefore the associated capitation or case payment. Public services are frequently set targets such as maximizing the number of pupils securing five or more public exam passes at age 16, an important performance measure in English schools. Case payments associated with a pupil might therefore in principle reflect the effort required to secure this benchmark, given the pupil's characteristics. However I am not aware of any school funding schemes that are informed by such explicit performance criteria. Moreover, service standards are in practice much more complex than this single dimensional example. Risk adjustment methods should nevertheless in principle reflect the performance measures used to assess public sector organizations.

As noted in Section 4.2, if individual need is defined as the 'capacity to benefit', then allocating resources according to need will be both efficient and equitable. For example, if 'need' in health care is defined as the expected health gains from treatment, and society's objective is to maximize aggregate health gains, then allocating resources according to this concept of need implies the application of the pure efficiency criterion. However, any other criterion of need implies a departure from the pure efficiency solution to formula funding.

A 'pure equity' solution to risk adjustment based on vertical equity principles can be illustrated in Figure 4.5. Under the efficient funding solution, persons 1 and 2 secured different outcomes (say, examination results). If the intention is now to secure equal outcomes (Y_e with an unchanged budget), then capitation payments must be skewed towards the disadvantaged person 2, resulting in revised payments Z_1 and Z_2. Notice that there will in general be a loss of efficiency (in terms of aggregate outcome) in comparison with the pure efficiency solution. That is, $(Y_1 + Y_2) > 2Y_e$.

In practice, most funding mechanisms seek to secure a balance between pure equity and pure efficiency. This trade-off can be examined using the production function approach (Culyer and Wagstaff, 1993). I continue to assume a fixed expenditure constraint. Figure 4.6 then replicates (in a transposed state) the production functions for the two people shown in Figure 4.2. The top left corner of the diagram represents person 1 while the bottom right corner represents person 2. The straight line in the bottom left quadrant represents the fixed expenditure constraint $E_1 + E_2$. All expenditure choices must conform to this constraint. They are then reflected, via the production functions, into the top right quadrant, which yields the production possibility frontier.

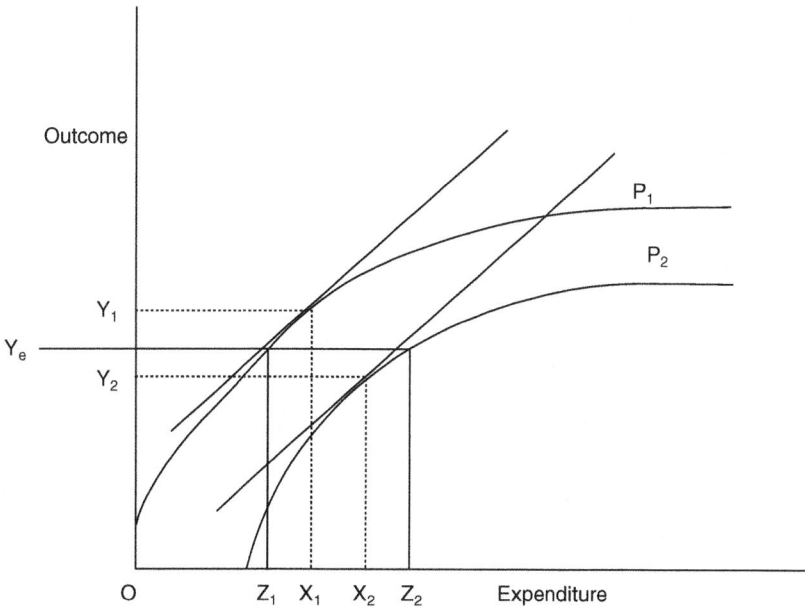

Figure 4.5 Payments to secure equal outcomes for two individuals.

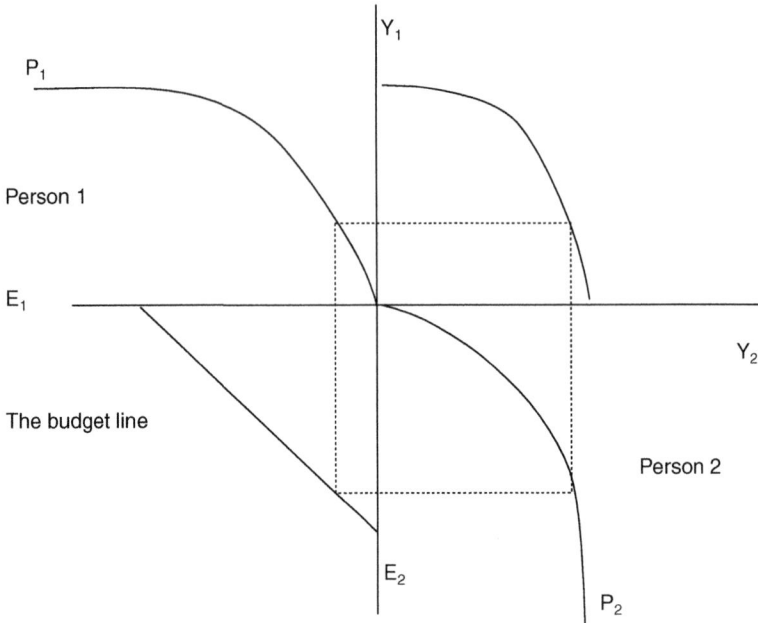

Figure 4.6 Derivation of the production possibility frontier with two individuals.

The frontier indicates the locus of feasible outcome distributions between the two individuals, given the budget constraint, and is reproduced as Figure 4.7. If individual outcomes are presumed to be simply additive, then the pure efficiency solution that maximizes aggregate outcome would be the point W*. Equal outcomes, on the other hand, would be secured at the point Q*. Depending on the relative value placed on efficiency and equity, as expressed in the payer's welfare function, a position somewhere between W* and Q* will in general be adopted.

4.6 Examples from England

Capitation methods in English health care seek to reflect just such a balance of efficiency and equity objectives. The policy objective is to allocate resources to geographical areas in order 'to contribute to a reduction in avoidable mortality'. Underlying this policy is the belief that existing services are resulting in an unacceptable outcome (disparities in health), and that resources have therefore to be skewed further towards individuals with low life expectancy. Using the production function model outlined above, Hauck *et al.* (2002) examine the implications of adopting this criterion. By seeking to target disadvantaged groups more intensively, it implies a desire to change existing patterns of service delivery, and to change capitation payments accordingly.

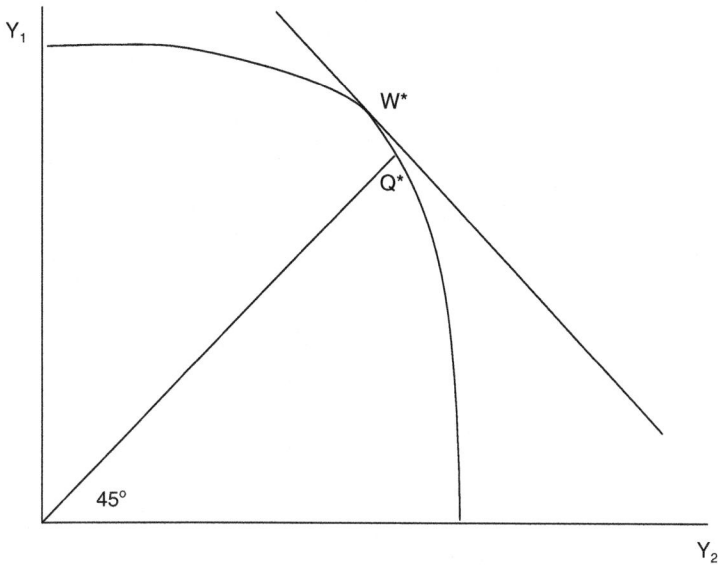

Figure 4.7 The trade-off between equity and efficiency implied by the production possibility frontier.

In principle, implementing appropriate funding mechanisms to address the health inequalities adjustment requires the resolution of the following issues:

- Identification of effective health care interventions designed to reduce the health inequality.
- Identification of disadvantaged groups at which the intervention should be directed.
- Identification of the areas where such groups live.
- Designing a formula to direct appropriate funding to all localities.
- Ensuring that the resources are spent appropriately on the disadvantaged groups and the necessary interventions.

Such detailed modelling is usually infeasible, and in its first year of operation, the English system used a health inequalities adjustment that was based simply on the magnitude of an area's 'avoidable mortality'. This was defined as the number of years of life lost in the area under the age of 75 over a three-year period, where diagnosis of death was in certain broad categories deemed to be 'avoidable'. That is, additional funding was directed to areas in proportion to a crude measure of the magnitude of the unacceptable outcomes. In the first year these amounts represented a very small (1 per cent) proportion of the budget, but this was subsequently increased.

The concern with equalizing outcomes has parallels with initiatives in further and higher education in the UK to broaden access to students from disadvantaged backgrounds. The policy objective is to reduce inequalities in educational outcomes. The policy response has been to introduce augmented case payments for students from areas that currently make low use of further and higher education (Higher Education Funding Council for England, 2002).

Note that introducing such vertical equity payments does not guarantee that the associated funding will be spent as intended on the disadvantaged groups. Indeed, it is more likely that localities in receipt of additional funding will merely continue to deliver services in line with previous practice, albeit at a higher level of funding than hitherto. Additional rules or incentives, such as ring-fenced funding for the disadvantage groups, may be needed in the short term. However, in the longer term, as all localities begin to spend in line with the payer's intentions, the need for a vertical equity adjustment disappears, and the capitation formula can instead be based on a conventional analysis of empirical patterns of spending.

4.7 Discussion

There are powerful efficiency and equity arguments for allocating public service resources formulaically. The efficiency arguments are well understood, and reflect a desire to ensure that public expenditure is employed most effectively. The equity arguments underlying formula funding have been less well developed, and in practice careful specification of equity criteria is usually avoided. Instead, most payment mechanisms are based on some observed relationship between current spending and individual characteristics, suggesting an implicit desire to pursue an equity criterion of equal treatment of equals.

As Chapter 5 explains, this is a pragmatic approach that secures widespread acceptance, but is not generally intellectually coherent (Smith *et al.*, 2001). Empirical methods model existing average responses of service providers to the demands of users, including any equity criteria they may currently be applying. There is however no explicit consideration of whether current service delivery is in line with the payer's equity objectives, and in practice the observed relationship is likely to reflect a jumble of preferences, constraints and informational weaknesses. The use of such pragmatic methods suggests that the implicit criterion underlying the design of most payment systems should be reworded as follows: the payments seek to offer comparable public sector organizations the opportunity to deliver some average type of service, assuming average responses to social and economic circumstances, and an average level of efficiency.

One should also note the implications of information shortcomings for modelling efficiency and equity concerns. The policy of risk adjustment recognizes the heterogeneity among individuals, and seeks to adjust payments accordingly. The 'pure efficiency' solution would be to select capitations such that the marginal benefits from public service expenditure are equal for all individuals. This might alone result in quite large variations in payment rates between individuals, even before any further equity considerations are applied.

In practice, because of data limitations, the payment mechanism may be unable to discriminate between individuals. For example, notwithstanding evident heterogeneity among service users, no risk adjustment may be possible, and the chosen capitation payment is therefore equal for all. The increase in welfare secured by moving from simple capitation to risk-adjusted capitation can be thought of as the value of risk adjustment information. The pure efficiency solution presumes perfect information, a situation that cannot apply in practice. Furthermore, assuming 'perfect' risk adjustment would lead to higher payment rates associated with more disadvantaged groups, information imperfections are likely to discriminate against those groups.

The chapter has shown how a payer can move towards a vertical equity criterion, if the current distribution of outcomes is considered unacceptable. By definition, conventional use of empirical data for the purposes of risk adjustment is likely to be problematic under these circumstances, and more imaginative approaches to setting payments will be required. Furthermore, in order to move away from existing patterns of service delivery, additional instruments will usually be needed to ensure that services are delivered in line with a policy to reduce unequal outcomes. These might, for example, take the form of introducing services aimed at only disadvantaged groups, or offering financial incentives on either the demand or supply side.

5   Empirical methods

5.1 Introduction

The purpose of this chapter is to discuss the methodological and practical issues that arise when developing empirically based capitation formulae for public services. It concentrates on capitation payments, although many of the arguments are also relevant to case payment methods. The chapter starts with a summary of some of the important modelling issues that arise when seeking to develop a capitation funding formula using statistical methods, and Section 5.4 then develops a general theoretical model of the supply of and demand for public services.

Chapter 3 advocated the use of contingency table methods. Section 5.5 therefore shows how individual level data can be used to derive a set of capitation payments in line with this approach, using an example from US Medicare. Generally, however, the sort of individual level data needed to construct contingency tables are often absent. Because of the limitations of data sources, it is often possible to relate service utilization to only very basic individual characteristics, such as age and sex. Many payers have therefore augmented these rudimentary individual data with information about the characteristics of the areas in which individuals live, as an important additional basis for capitation payments. This entails developing a simple contingency table of capitation payments based, for example, on age and sex, which is then further adjusted according to some index reflecting the social and economic circumstances of local areas. Section 5.6 describes such 'blended' methods, using examples from English public services.

5.2 Empirical considerations

Most capitation formulae seek to reflect some observed relationship between legitimate needs factors and actual expenditure. For example, it may be considered that the unemployment rate is a primary indicator of the spending needed by police forces to deliver a standard level of service. A statistical analysis of the historical link between *per capita* spending and the unemployment rate might therefore be used as the basis for deciding how much grant-in-aid should be allocated to each police force on the basis of contemporary unemployment

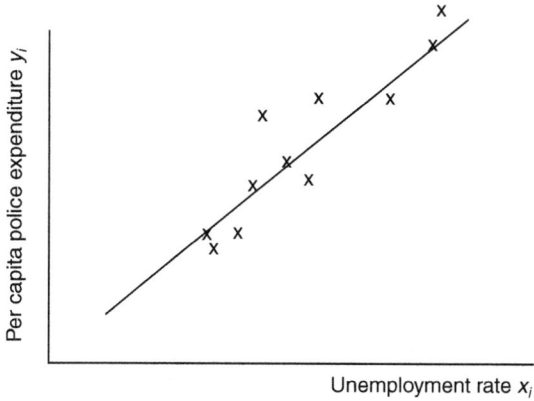

Figure 5.1 Empirical link between unemployment rate and *per capita* police expenditure.

rates (as shown in Figure 5.1). The use of such methods implies that – on average – police forces are currently delivering the 'standard'. The statistical methods then estimate the expenditure needs for a police force of securing that implicit standard, given its prevailing unemployment rate.

It is however frequently the case that many putative indicators of spending 'need' exist, some of which are legitimate, some illegitimate (as defined in Section 3.6). An indiscriminate multivariate statistical analysis of observed spending patterns will reflect a jumble of influences on expenditure, only some of which conform to the definition of 'legitimate'. The statistical challenge is to explain expenditure variation caused by legitimate needs factors, and to ignore variation caused by irrelevant factors such as variations in local efficiency levels, accounting methods or policy choices.

In much empirical work on formula funding, the principal yardstick for deciding whether a plausible 'needs factor' should be used as a basis for a risk adjustment is whether it explains actual spending patterns in a statistically significant manner. That is, the actual spending behaviour of public service organizations is used to infer appropriate needs factors. As discussed in Chapter 3, this has two implications. First, it may not be possible to accommodate some aspects of so-called 'unmet' need within the capitation methodology; and second it may be necessary to adjust for illegitimate 'supply' influences on expenditure.

Unmet need can be considered under two headings: general and specific. *General* unmet need arises when the services provided by a local agency are considered inadequate to meet expected standards for the population at large, perhaps because of inadequate funding. In these circumstances, the usual assumption is that the organization under scrutiny will nevertheless allocate spending to citizens in proportion to legitimate need, albeit at a lower than socially optimal level, so that its spending pattern offers useful information on the *relative* needs of recipients of services. *Specific* unmet need arises when particular groups within the population – such as ethnic minorities or those living in rural areas – are not receiving the services intended by the payer. Under these circumstances, the use of empirical spending patterns to infer needs is problematic, as the models developed will perpetuate the implied inequity. In effect, there is an illegitimate influence on observed demand for services.

In the same way, illegitimate supply side influences on expenditure can be partitioned into two broad categories: *agency-wide* factors, which can reasonably be expected to apply to all citizens for whom a local agency is responsible; and *specific* factors, which apply to different extents to different citizens within a locality. Agency-wide factors might include levels of funding, levels of efficiency, and more general policies of the local organization. Specific illegitimate supply factors might arise from geographical considerations, such as proximity to a hospital, which leads to variations in hospital utilization rates within the agency. Such phenomena may arise because of supply side effects (such as supplier induced demand) or demand side effects (such as transportation costs).

Use of empirical data may therefore be problematic because (a) the existence of specific unmet need may lead to depressed coefficients for the disadvantaged population group in the estimated statistical model and (b) unless handled carefully, the existence of supply effects may lead to coefficients that reflect illegitimate supply side influences on spending as well as legitimate demand factors. In such circumstances, the development of models that maximize the statistical explanation of existing spending patterns is not necessarily a desirable objective in itself. Rather, the intention should be to explain that part of variation that is attributable to legitimate needs factors.

Of course, as noted in Chapter 3, the analyst should also avoid use of needs factors that are vulnerable to manipulation by the recipient agencies, or that create perverse incentives, and to constrain the analysis to factors that are universally available and reliably measured. These considerations often impose severe constraints on the nature and scope of any empirical analysis.

5.3 Adjusting for supply side influences

The following sections discuss how researchers have sought to develop empirical capitation formulae in the light of such complications. The methods do not consider the problem of specific unmet need, as by its nature this problem implies the need to depart from strict empirical methods (see Chapter 4). Instead the emphasis is on adjusting for supply side influences on utilization. This section summarizes the methodological issues associated with modelling illegitimate supply influences on observed public service utilization.

There may exist agency-wide illegitimate influences on expenditure that the payer does not wish to see reflected in the funding formula. For example, there may be systematic variations between local governments in spending levels, service priorities, efficiency or data recording methods. A fundamental insight is then that a statistical analysis of public service spending on individuals may identify a relationship between spending and some population characteristic that is a reflection of agency-wide supply factors, and that does not necessarily reflect individual needs. Conversely, an analysis of aggregate agency level spending data might fail to detect a relationship with a legitimate needs factor that does exist at the individual level. In short, any statistical analysis at individual or agency level is at risk of modelling a jumble of needs and supply factors, rather than the desired modelling only of legitimate expenditure influences.

This problem is associated with a phenomenon known as the ecological fallacy (Steel and Holt, 1996), and can be illustrated with reference to a diagram (Figure 5.2). In this example there are three local agencies. The numbers in the diagram refer to individuals within each agency. It is assumed that some measure of legitimate needs exists. The expenditure responses of each agency to variations in individual needs are roughly similar, as shown by the slopes of the regression lines for each agency. However, agency LG1 devotes a higher level of resources to the services than LG2, which in turn devotes more than LG3. The *average* needs and costs of each agency are indicated by the black circles. If these aggregate measures are used in a regression, the thick regression line SS will result. This line bears little relation to actual responses to needs within local agencies, and is in this case mainly determined by variations in expenditure policy between the local agencies. Notice also that an uncritical regression based on just individual observations (the numbers in the diagram) will in general give a misleading indication of the relationship between needs and expenditure, as the individual level data are contaminated by systematic area-wide effects.

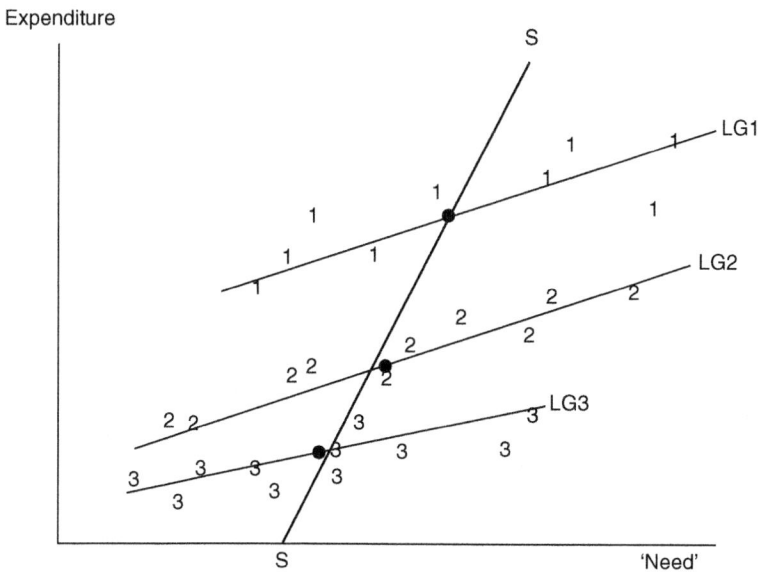

Figure 5.2 The ecological problem illustrated.

Thus, unless properly addressed, the ecological problem might contaminate statistical analysis of individual level data, small area data, or agency-wide data on service expenditure. However, distortions are likely to be most serious when examining aggregate, agency-wide data. This analytic insight implies that – wherever possible – use of aggregate agency-wide data should be avoided as a basis for developing funding formulae. However, even where more disaggregate individual or small area data are used, it is essential that the hierarchy of agency and individual influences on expenditure should be properly modelled.

However, methodologies used to develop spending needs assessments in the English local government sector have often used aggregate local government level data, and so are vulnerable to the problems summarized above. The use of aggregate local government expenditure data in a regression analysis may be capturing a jumble of historical spending variations between local governments as well as genuine responses to needs. If we are searching for some 'standard' agency response to needs, we should be seeking to identify the individual slopes of the sort LG1, LG2 LG3 in Figure 5.2. The payer then has to select a particular slope as the 'standard'. A natural choice would be to favour the national average of individual authority slopes, but there is no reason why the national average response should be used as the basis for allocating funds. One could for example envisage using some estimate of 'best practice', as suggested by the Scottish Executive Health Department (1999). However the average is for practical purposes a relatively uncontentious choice.

Although use of agency-wide data is unacceptable, for many public services data sources on individuals are absent or certainly less comprehensive than required to adopt a contingency table approach. As a result, some payers have introduced an intermediate solution of augmenting individual level data with data from the small areas in which those individuals live. The use of data relating to the characteristics of small areas rather than individuals – often necessitated by confidentiality requirements and the high cost of tracking services received by individuals – can be justified on the grounds that area characteristics might be a rough approximation to individual characteristics (Tranmer and Steel, 1998). This approach is widely used, for example, in the insurance industry, which for many risks uses post code of residence as well as individual characteristics to determine premiums.

It is of course possible to argue that – once one departs from an individual level of analysis – there is no necessary reason why the use of small areas should yield more satisfactory models than the use of larger areas. However, there are very strong grounds to believe that organizational pressures create numerous illegitimate influences on expenditure at the level of the administrative area that are independent of need, and that some element of disaggregation below that level can offer distinct analytic advantages.

5.4 Modelling the determinants of expenditure

This section introduces a simple model of expenditure on individual citizens, assuming that social factors pertaining to the individual and (possibly) to the broader community give rise to the need for a particular service. In seeking to meet the citizen's needs, a local agency incurs costs. For a citizen with given needs characteristics, reported unit costs may vary between agencies because of policy variations, data recording differences and area cost variations (brought about by differences in costs of labour, capital and other relevant factors). Assuming there are no specific illegitimate supply factors, this gives rise to the following theoretical model:

$$EXP_{ijk} = f(n_{ijk}, s_{jk}, a_k) \tag{5.1}$$

Expected expenditure EXP_{ijk} on citizen i living in small area j within administrative area k depends on the personal circumstances of the citizen n_{ijk}, the broader characteristics of the small area s_{jk} and agency factors a_k. This is the model that analysis of individual level data seeks to estimate. Where individual data n_{ijk} are absent, or limited in scope, an important policy question for the payer will then be the extent to which small area factors s_{jk} can reasonably be used within the funding formula. Agency-wide factors a_k will usually be considered illegitimate spending influences.

Suppose the absence of adequate individual level data leads us to consider use of the many socio-economic data relating to small areas. For example, in England many potentially useful data, the purposes of capitation funding (most notably population estimates and socio-economic data), have historically been prepared only at the level of local authority electoral wards, which have average populations of about 7,000. Therefore for many practical applications small areas such as the electoral ward may be the smallest unit available for analysis. Under these circumstances, it becomes necessary to model *average* individual characteristics within a small area as a proxy for individual data. This small area methodology is therefore a compromise between seeking to minimize the ecological problem and gaining access to a suitably rich dataset.

The model to be used must then be amended as follows:

$$EXP_{jk} = f(\bar{n}_{jk}, s_{jk}, a_k) \tag{5.2}$$

The dependent variable is now expenditure *per capita* in small area j within local agency k. We now assume that expenditure depends both on *average* individual characteristics $\bar{n}_{jk}$ within small area j as well as the broader characteristics of the small area s_{jk}. In general, of course, only in very particular circumstances, such as a linear function $f(.)$, will the expenditure requirements of a representative ('average') individual citizen in an area $f(\bar{n}_{jk}, s_{jk}, a_k)$ equal the average spending requirements of all citizens in an area $\sum_{i=1}^{N} f(n_{ijk}, s_{jk}, a_k)/N$. Although not used in this study, there exist methods to adjust for within-area heterogeneity, and future research might examine whether such adjustments materially affect results (Steel and Holt, 1996).

In practice, one does not know which small area needs variables $\bar{n}_{jk}$ and s_{jk} should be used in the model, although – on the basis of research evidence and practical knowledge – it is possible to propose a range of potential candidates. The statistical challenge is to select relevant variables for inclusion in the model as legitimate needs factors. For the purposes of inferring capitation payments, the agency effect a_k is considered to be an illegitimate (supply) influence on costs, and is therefore not of direct analytic interest. Rather, the chosen methodology must extract the agency effect in order that the small area needs effects of direct interest can be correctly identified and modelled.

The partitioning of observed variation in expenditure into within and between groups such as local governments and other agencies can be achieved using various statistical methods. Regression-based approaches include multilevel (or hierarchical) modelling (Goldstein, 1995), using iterative generalized least squares as a particular example of the general class of the so-called random effects models, and fixed effects models using the least squares dummy variable estimator or the within groups estimator. In determining which model specification to favour, the analyst should be guided by economic theory, prior knowledge of the characteristics of the data and good statistical modelling practice.

For example, if correlation between regressors and group effects exists, the random effects multilevel approach may lead to inconsistent estimation. Yet it is often the case that needs and social circumstances are correlated with agency supply effects. The fixed effects model has the virtue of allowing correlation between the regressors and the group effects, and may therefore be preferred as being more robust, even though it may appear costly in terms of degrees of freedom lost (Greene, 2000). Hausman (1978) proposes a test for in random effects models that may offer some guidance on model choice.

If *specific* (local) supply factors apply, then – instead of operating at a discrete agency level – supply effects may also be operating differentially at a small area level. It is then necessary to amend the analytic model to include the possibility that there exist both legitimate and illegitimate factors at work at the small area level. That is, Equation (5.2) becomes:

$$EXP_{jk} = f(\bar{n}_{jk}, s_{jk}, p_{jk}, a_k) \tag{5.3}$$

where the p_{jk} are the local supply effects. This model calls for a refinement in statistical methods, as it becomes necessary to disentangle legitimate (needs) effects from illegitimate (supply) effects at the small area level. Given the frequent data limitations, such as a single year cross-section of observations, modelling becomes complicated because local supply p_{jk} might itself in turn be a function of local needs – that is, p_{jk} might be endogenous. Under these circumstances, there will be a need to test whether estimation methods such as those provided by instrumental variables, two-stage least squares or control functions may be required (Greene, 2000).

A further methodological consideration is the functional form of the relationship depicted in Equation (5.3). In its simplest form this might be modelled using a linear relationship between explanatory factors and expenditure. In such a model the constant term assumes an important role, as it corresponds to a fixed average capitation rate for all citizens (conditional on the needs and supply variables). The relative size of this term determines the level of funds that will be distributed on a purely *per capita* as opposed to a needs basis. Alternatively the model may be specified to be multiplicative (or linear in logarithms). The estimated coefficients then represent elasticities. Where the capitation formula is to be used to distribute an exogenously fixed sum of money, this form of specification has the effect of rendering redundant the constant term in the estimation. It is in effect an arbitrary scaling factor that has no impact on the relative estimates of needs, and the allocation is made purely on the basis of the chosen needs factors. An additional refinement that may be important in some applications is to incorporate explanatory variables that capture the interaction between individual needs factors.

5.5 Individual data methods

This section discusses an empirical approach to capitation when individual level data are available. Once the risk adjustment factors have been identified – in whatever fashion – weights must be attached to them that reflect their relative influence on the need to spend. If the contingency table approach is used, in principle this entails quantifying the entry to be placed in each cell of the table. However, as discussed in Chapter 3, this can quickly lead to an infeasible proliferation of contingency table cells and the associated payments to be estimated. A cruder but more practical approach is therefore to treat the factors independently, and merely to quantify the marginal contribution to the capitation payment of each needs factor. That is, an individual's risk factors are simply added up to create a capitation payment, and no interactions between risk factors are considered. This section gives an example of this marginal approach adopted in US health care.

Medicare is the statutory federal insurance scheme for elderly people (aged 65 and over), disabled people, and those with end stage renal failure. It is administered by the federal Centers for Medicare and Medicaid Services (CMS). Most Medicare beneficiaries are covered under a traditional case payment arrangement, under which CMS reimburses providers directly according to a fixed schedule of fees, based on diagnosis related groups. However, under a scheme now known as *Medicare Advantage*, Medicare members have been encouraged to enrol in Healthcare Maintenance Organizations (HMOs), which agree to cover enrolees for most health service needs in return for a fixed annual capitation payment. About 15 per cent of Medicare enrolees currently take this option in preference to the traditional fee-for-service insurance.

Until 1999, risk adjustment of Medicare capitation payments took into account the enrolee's age, sex, county of residence, welfare status and whether or not they live in a nursing home (Health Care Financing Administration, 1998). The essence of the adjustment was as follows. For each care group (elderly or disabled people) a matrix of relative needs was constructed from a large database of individual Medicare beneficiaries' claims. The matrix for hospital care for elderly people is shown in Table 5.1, with the average Medicare beneficiary given a weight of 1.0. The Medicaid category indicates qualification for Medicaid support, the health care scheme for low income citizens. The appropriate weight was applied to 95 per cent of the adjusted average per capita cost (AAPCC) for fee-for-service Medicare beneficiaries for the county of residence. The AAPCCs were considered to be excessively volatile and widely dispersed. They were therefore damped and 'blended' with the national average.

The weights reported in Table 5.1 were derived empirically from expenditure patterns on traditional fee-for-service Medicare beneficiaries, not the AAPCC beneficiaries. There was some concern that – because healthier patients tend to be attracted to the capitation option – the rates used may be excessively generous for the insurers, even with the 5 per cent discount to the local AAPCC. However, empirical data on expenditure for capitated patients were not available.

The AAPCC methodology explained only about 1 per cent of the variation in expenditure on individual Medicare enrolees, and was clearly inadequate in failing to adjust for the sickness level of the beneficiary. It therefore gave plans a considerable incentive to cream skim healthier patients. The federal Balanced Budget Act of 1997 therefore introduced a much more aggressive risk adjustment mechanism, and from 2000 a scheme known as *Medicare + Choice* was introduced that included previous inpatient experience as a risk adjuster, in an attempt to model the beneficiary's health status (Health Care Financing Administration, 1999).

The basis of the revised capitation payments was a risk factor table that incorporated: age, sex, whether or not the beneficiary qualifies for Medicaid support, and (for elderly people) whether or not the patient was previously a Medicare younger disabled beneficiary. In addition, an adjustment was made for what was known as the Principal Inpatient Diagnostic Cost Group (PIP-DCG) of the

Table 5.1 Medicare 1999 demographic capitation weights

Sex	Age	Nursing home	Non-nursing home		
			Medicaid	Non-Medicaid	Working
Male	65–69	1.75	1.15	0.65	0.40
	70–74	2.25	1.50	0.85	0.45
	75–79	2.25	1.95	1.05	0.70
	80–84	2.25	2.35	1.20	0.80
	85+	2.25	2.60	1.35	0.90
Female	65–69	1.45	0.80	0.55	0.35
	70–74	1.80	1.05	0.70	0.45
	75–79	2.10	1.45	0.85	0.55
	80–84	2.10	1.70	1.05	0.70
	85+	2.10	2.10	1.20	0.80

patient (Iezzoni *et al.*, 1998). This indicated the most severe category of inpatient diagnosis experienced by the citizen over a previous one-year period. Each citizen was allocated to one of 16 PIP-DCG categories of increasing severity, and capitations adjusted accordingly. Table 5.2 contains illustrative data, which are based on empirical analysis of expenditure on a 5 per cent sample of Medicare fee-for-service enrolees in 1996.

The national average factor was 1.0. An individual's factor was built up additively. The base was determined by age and sex. To this was added a disability or Medicaid factor if appropriate. Then, if the beneficiary underwent hospital inpatient treatment in the base year, a further factor was added based on the highest PIP-DCG score of all qualifying inpatient spells. Thus a male aged 78 who qualifies for Medicaid and had an inpatient spell with PIP-DCG score 11 would have a total factor of $0.907 + 0.461 + 1.271 = 2.639$. That is, the HMO would receive 2.639 times the average capitation for accepting that beneficiary. This risk adjustment scheme was also phased in slowly alongside its predecessor.

The PIP-DCG model was a clear improvement on the AAPCC method, in that it acknowledged some aspects of an enrolee's sickness level. It offered a dramatic improvement in predictive power, explaining about 6.2 per cent of the

Table 5.2 Medicare + Choice 2000 risk adjustment capitation weights

	Age	Base	Previous disability	Medicaid	PIP-DCG score	Factor
Male	0–34	0.367	–	0.125	0	–
	35–44	0.380	–	0.283	5	0.375
	45–54	0.487	–	0.370	6	0.458
	55–59	0.615	–	0.397	7	0.697
	60–64	0.760	–	0.418	8	0.822
	65–69	0.541	0.415	0.440	9	0.915
	70–74	0.705	0.398	0.457	10	1.170
	75–79	0.907	0.334	0.461	11	1.271
	80–84	1.077	0.287	0.445	12	1.662
	85–89	1.258	0.237	0.404	14	2.000
	90–94	1.376	0.189	0.331	16	2.438
	95+	1.357	0.141	0.242	18	2.656
					20	3.392
Female	0–34	0.362	–	0.192	23	3.823
	35–44	0.403	–	0.312	26	4.375
	45–54	0.526	–	0.367	29	5.189
	55–59	0.643	–	0.397		
	60–64	0.891	–	0.412		
	65–69	0.453	0.605	0.433		
	70–74	0.588	0.576	0.440		
	75–79	0.747	0.519	0.454		
	80–84	0.918	0.415	0.423		
	85–89	1.096	0.313	0.327		
	90–94	1.162	0.232	0.231		
	95+	1.128	0.152	0.168		

costs of traditional Medicare beneficiaries (Ash *et al.*, 2000). However, its reliance on inpatient diagnosis was highly selective, and introduced potentially serious adverse incentives, by encouraging inpatient care in preference to potentially more cost-effective care in other settings. It was always seen as a transitional instrument, and CMS continued to seek out more suitable risk adjustment mechanisms.

The outcome was a scheme known as the CMS hierarchical condition categories (HCC) model. The essence of the HCC approach is unchanged from the preceding PIP-DCG model. Capitation payments are adjusted for the severity of a beneficiary's sickness level, as indicated by previous health care diagnosis. However, the new diagnosis cost groups are based on both ambulatory and inpatient diagnoses, and are very much more refined than the PIP categories. This exposition summarizes the comprehensive description given by Pope *et al.* (2004).

In essence, the HCC researchers developed a hierarchy of diagnoses, so that for *related* diagnoses a patient was assigned to only the most serious category (so avoiding double counting). On the basis of previous research, the researchers first collapsed over 15,000 health care intervention codes into 804 diagnostic groups. These were then further aggregated into 70 HCCs that reflected clinically meaningful categories of diagnosis. The predictive power of the model diminishes as the number of HCCs is reduced, so a careful balance had to be struck between a manageable number of HCCs and good predictive power. Although related diagnoses within a HCC are counted only once towards the capitation payment, if a patient has more than one *unrelated* diagnosis, then both can contribute to the payment calculation.

The initial HCC model was estimated using ordinary least squares regression of preceding year (1999) diagnoses on individual costs of Medicare fee-for-service patients in 2000. The explanatory variables were 24 age/sex categories, four Medicaid status variable, a disability marker and the 70 HCC categories. Restrictions were imposed to ensure there were no perverse signs on coefficients. Statistical tests were undertaken to determine whether certain diagnoses interacted to create expenditure needs in excess of the simple sum of the associated adjustments. In the event, only six interaction terms (such as the simultaneous presence of congestive heart failure and chronic obstructive pulmonary disease) were found to be necessary. Measured on a consistent basis, the use of the HCC model increased model R^2 from 6.2 per cent under PIP to 11.2 per cent.

Space precludes presentation of the payments matrix. To illustrate, the payment calculation for a female aged 72 with Medicaid entitlement, with diagnoses of acute myocardial infarction (AMI) and chest pain is as follows. The basic payment for a female aged 70–74 is $2,061. To this is added the $616 sum for a female Medicaid beneficiary, and the $1,885 for a diagnosis of AMI in the preceding year. The chest pain diagnosis makes no contribution to the payment, as it is included hierarchically in the AMI HCC. The total capitation payment is therefore $4,562. This is further adjusted for average Medicare *per capita* expenditure levels in the county of residence.

The development of the HCC model sought to apply a number of criteria to guide model building (Pope *et al.*, 2004). These included the requirements that diagnostic categories should:

- be clinically meaningful;
- predict medical expenditure;
- be based on adequate sample sizes;
- be based on hierarchies that – within a disease process – record only the most serious diagnosis;
- encourage specific (rather than vague) clinical coding;
- not reward proliferation of diagnostic coding;
- not penalize the recording of additional diagnoses;
- be internally consistent;
- be exhaustive;
- exclude discretionary diagnoses.

Clearly these criteria are often in conflict, and not always attainable. Moreover, other criteria (such as model parsimony and data collection costs) were also important considerations in the development of HCCs. CMS, the payer, therefore had to come to a judgement on how to balance the criteria.

The major omission from the methodology is any explicit treatment of supply side factors in the modelling. The imperative was to develop a model of individual spending needs that minimized cream skimming and reduced the risk of market failure. In such circumstances, the payer must often act passively, accepting local utilization levels and prices even if they do not appear to be competitive. To fail to do so might run the risk of destabilizing the local insurance market. As a result, CMS feels constrained to accept local provider practices in adjusting national capitation rates for expected local area expenditure. This gives rise to accepting very large *ceteris paribus* county level variations in Medicare expenditure that cannot be explained by input price variations.

Also, for all its strengths, the HCC approach highlights certain limitations of individual level capitation methodology. It relies on health system diagnostic coding, and therefore has onerous data requirements. It is noteworthy that a central reason for an initial lack of enthusiasm of insurers for the *Medicare + Choice* initiative was the heavy reporting requirements it placed on participating insurers, and one of the central features of the HCC system was a requirement for parsimony in data provision. It nevertheless still places extremely heavy demands on information flows.

Furthermore, it relies on diagnoses reported by doctors and other clinicians, who have a clear incentive to report diagnoses with high expenditure weightings, to upcode, and to misrepresent. Data audit is therefore a high priority with a potentially very large cost. Moreover, notwithstanding the inclusion of diagnoses in settings outside the hospital, the use of diagnoses codes may still offer incentives for over-treatment or sub-optimal treatment. To some extent this incentive may be abated by the potential for beneficiaries to change insurer periodically. However, the reliance on service encounter data may be an unattractive feature for many health systems. Finally, although the HCC capitation payments reflect the expected *current* costs in the light of *previous* health care experience, there is nevertheless the risk that – as the categorization becomes finer – so the payment system comes closer to retrospective reimbursement of previous health care utilization. The paradox of the more refined risk adjustment method is that, in becoming more accurate, it may steadily reduce the incentive for providers to economize on service provision.

Nevertheless, accurate prediction of expected health care costs is a central requirement of any competitive health insurance system. In this context, the HCC system is a stupendous technical achievement. It succeeds in collapsing the enormous number of potential medical diagnoses, in a variety of settings, into a manageable number of diagnostic categories, and represents the apotheosis of individual level capitation payment methods at this time.

5.6 Small area data methods

For many public services, the use of individual level data either is infeasible or would lead to unacceptable perverse incentives. In this section I therefore demonstrate how small area data can be used as a feasible approach to setting capitation payments in the absence of adequate individual level data. The examples pay particular attention to seeking to take account of supply side effects. First the multilevel agency effect is modelled to inform the allocation of grant for Children's Personal Social Services (PSS) to English local governments (Section 5.6.1). Then Section 5.6.2 presents a method for allocating hospital funds to health authorities in the English National Health Service (NHS) that seeks to accommodate local (small area) supply effects.

5.6.1 Children's Personal Social Services

In England there is a long history of the government payer seeking to estimate the spending needs of local authorities, as a basis for distributing grants in aid. The general principle since 1981 has been to develop spending needs assessments for individual services that are subsequently aggregated into a measure of total spending needs for each local authority. These service needs assessments are intended to provide an estimate of how much an authority should spend if it were to deliver some common level of services, given the demographic, social, economic, meteorological and geographical characteristics of the area. For example, in 1995 the Government defined the needs assessment to be 'the amount which the Government considers appropriate for each authority to calculate as its budget requirement ... consistent with the amount the Government considers it would be appropriate for all authorities to incur' (Department of the Environment, 1995). This unhelpful definition explicitly omits mention of standard levels of service. However, the notion of some 'common' level of service is implicit in the methodologies adopted for constructing spending needs assessments.

A variety of distributional methods have been adopted, but most rely on a statistical regression of some measure of local authority expenditure on certain socio-economic characteristics at the local authority level thought to be associated with the need to spend (Department of the Environment, 1995). Local authorities are not constrained to spending their budget in line with the individual service needs assessments calculated by the government. In general, they are free to set their own service budgets, subject to fulfilling their statutory obligations and restraining total expenditure within any central government spending limits.

Spending needs assessments in England have been the subject of wide-ranging criticism from the Audit Commission (1993), the House of Commons Select Committee on the Environment (1994) and academics (Hale and Travers, 1993; Flowerdew *et al.*, 1994; Goldstein, 1994; Duncan and Smith, 1995; Hall *et al.*, 1996; Thomas and Warren, 1997). Many of these criticisms reflect tension between the conflicting objectives of technical accuracy and operational simplicity, a theme that emerged as a central issue in a review of local government finance (Revenue Grant Distribution Review Group, 2000).

Children's Personal Social Services are charged with caring for vulnerable children, through the provision of supervision, foster care and residential care. In 1995 they accounted for £1.755 billion, or 4.4 per cent of local government expenditure. In common with most other needs assessments, the funding formula for Children's PSS was until 1999 based on a statistical regression analysis at the local authority level (Department of the Environment, 1995). Two regression equations estimated at a local authority level were used. The first used numbers of children 'at risk' in a local authority as the dependent variable and a selection of needs indicators as the explanatory variables. This model yielded a prediction of the expected numbers of children at risk in each local authority. A second regression analysis then sought to explain variations in unit costs (costs per child) as a function of a different set of needs variables. The final stage in the calculation of the needs assessment was the application of an area cost adjustment, intended to account for variations in the costs of inputs required to provide a common level of service independently of personal social service unit costs. In 1995/96 it implied that, compared with authorities outside the southeast of England, costs were 24.70 per cent higher in inner London and 12.56 per cent higher in outer London.

These methods were theoretically and practically inadequate for a number of reasons, many of which have been rehearsed earlier in this chapter. In particular, local authority spending is a function of many factors as well as needs, such as local preferences and income, competition from other services, central government spending limits, central government grant, the local tax base, local policies, local levels of efficiency and local accounting methods. Under these circumstances, the use of local authorities as the unit of analysis is vulnerable to the ecological fallacy. The study described by Carr-Hill *et al.* (1999) sought to address some of these problems. The study was pioneering, in the sense that it applied multilevel statistical methods for the first time to British local government finance, although the methods had previously been successfully applied in the National Health Service (see Section 5.6.2).

The dependent variable used in the study was the expenditure on children's personal social services in each small area within a sample of 25 of the 107 English local authorities responsible for social services. Construction of the dependent variable involved obtaining a list of all Children's PSS users on the project survey date, and estimating the annual costs of those users. It resulted in 74,493 valid children in the sample actively known in some way to the social services department on the date of the survey.

The chosen unit of analysis was small areas, in the form of electoral wards, with populations of about 10,000 (all ages). The dependent variable chosen for use in the study was then the costs of Children's PSS per head of total population aged 0–19, deflated by the appropriate 1995/96 Area Cost Adjustment. The distribution of the resulting dependent variable among the 1,036 small areas used in the study is shown in Figure 5.3. Mean estimated cost of PSS per head was £140.8 with a standard deviation of £122.1. The average number of clients in each small area was 72, or 3.0 per cent of all children aged 0–19.

The study sought to explain variations in the small area costs of Children's

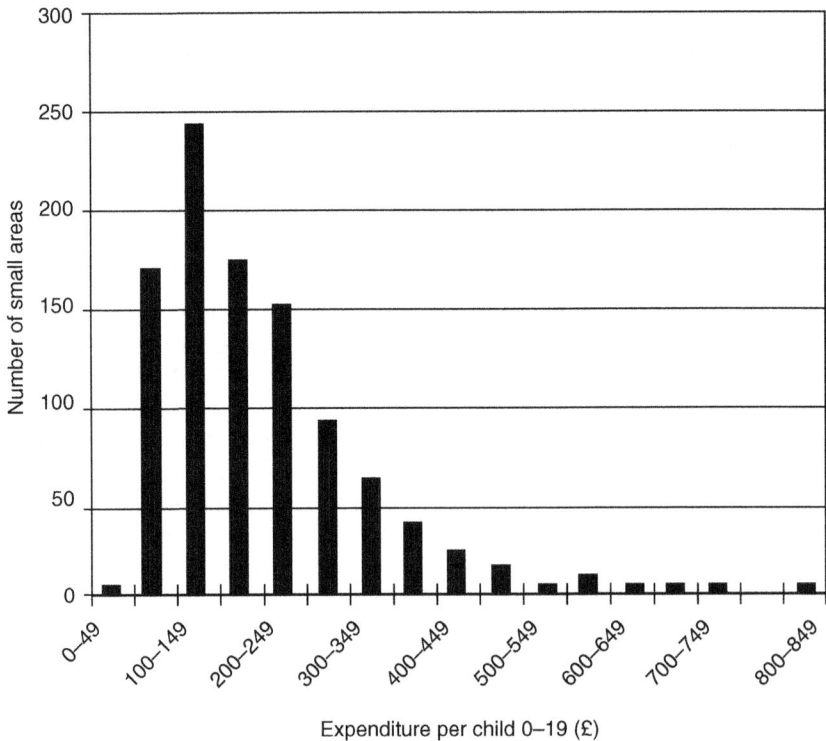

Figure 5.3 Distribution of costs per child aged 0–19.

PSS in terms of socio-economic conditions within those small areas. Many of the potential explanatory variables were derived from the 1991 Census of Population, but important other sources were available, relating to issues such as mortality, low birth weight, welfare payments and population sparsity. Numerous variants and combinations of variables were created.

The statistical model used in the study can be summarized as follows. Costs of children's PSS in small area j within local authority k depend on a vector of small area social circumstances n_{jk}.

$$EXP_{jk} = \alpha + \beta n_{jk} + \nu_k + \epsilon_{jk}$$

The model contains two error terms, ν_k and ϵ_{jk}. The latter represents the small area residual, the former the local authority residual, which applies to all small areas within authority k. The vector n_{jk} comprises the PSS needs indicators, which were to be identified in the course of the modelling procedure. All illegitimate factors were therefore assumed to operate at a local authority level (rather than the specific small area level). The model was estimated using iterative generalized least squares multilevel methods proposed by Goldstein (1995).

The principal modelling problem was to select a suitable explanatory model from the innumerable potential candidates. This entails selecting appropriate needs variables (components of n_{jk}). In this respect, the development of the models must be based partly on the basis of known relationships between social circumstances and PSS use, and partly on statistical criteria. We required a strategy for selecting among variables for four reasons:

- given the high intercorrelations between variables, it would be possible to develop a wide range of models containing different variables but with roughly similar statistical properties;
- although similar in statistical properties, competing models may have markedly different resource consequences for a small number of localities;
- a formula with too many variables would be unwieldy and unacceptable to policy makers, who have persistently (if not always successfully) sought 'simplicity' wherever possible;
- it is important for policy purposes that the variables are widely accepted as being reasonable indicators of PSS needs.

In summary, we were searching for a model that was not only statistically satisfactory, but that was also plausible and parsimonious.

The general approach adopted in the light of these criteria was as follows:

- preference was given to indicators based on the circumstances of children rather than those of the more general population;
- indicators based on large proportions of the population were preferred to those based on relatively rare events, although the latter may have been necessary to refine the model;

- we gave priority to those variables that are most germane to the phenomena and processes that might be generating the different rates of use of Children's PSS, and sought to avoid variables that are rather distant proxies.

A first step was to check whether there were important demographic determinants of PSS costs. These may have arisen if a child's age or sex turned out to be major influences on expected costs. If this turned out to be the case, a first stage in the analysis would have been to have developed rudimentary capitation payments based on relative expected costs by age group and sex (effectively standardizing for age and sex) before checking whether the socio-economic data offered additional explanatory power. In the event, analysis of the individual data detected no material variations due to demographic factors, so this stage proved unnecessary, and there was no need to apply variable capitation payments for different age or sex groups.

We therefore moved directly to estimation of multilevel models of PSS costs, with the small area as the smallest unit of observation. The full methods used in arriving at our favoured models were documented in a publicly available 'audit trail'. Throughout, each observation was weighted by the total number of children in the small area. Although we undertook some experiments with a non-linear functional form, the results were less well specified and we therefore chose to concentrate on a linear regression model, as such models are simple to implement and in the event performed well. Careful checks were made to ensure that the statistical model was well specified, and only well-specified models were considered acceptable, as measured by the Ramsey's reset test for specification (Ramsey, 1969).

The modelling process described above resulted in the derivation of a model containing the following variables:

LPAR   proportion of dependent children aged 0–18 in lone parent families;
IS   dependants of welfare claimants as a proportion of all children;
FLAT   proportion of dependent children living in flats;
LLSI   proportion of children 0–17 with limiting long-standing illness;
DENS   persons per hectare.

The model based on these variables reflects the commonly accepted risk factors associated with Children's PSS: family breakdown; poverty; housing need; and long-standing childhood illness. The inclusion of density (DENS) in the model offers evidence that, other things being equal, urban areas give rise to more utilization than rural areas. There was considerable debate among the study's advisors as to whether this was a legitimate influence on expenditure (reflecting otherwise unmeasured influences on need arising in urban areas) or illegitimate (perhaps reflecting unmet need in rural areas). In the event, the former viewpoint prevailed, and the variable DENS was retained in the model.

The model is presented in Table 5.3. It is statistically well specified, as tested by the reset test ($t = 1.92$). The residuals from this model were examined in some detail. Visual inspection confirmed that they appear to exhibit no manifest

Table 5.3 Preferred model of Children's Personal Social Services expenditure

Variable	Coefficient	Standard error
Constant	−7.393	13.49
FLAT	126.4	28.39
LLSI	1,016	441.0
IS	184.4	36.38
LPAR	364.8	77.56
DENS	0.3192	0.1273
Variance authority level	2,498	759
Variance small area level	4,721	211
Reset test	1.92	

Source: Carr-Hill *et al.*, 1999.

outliers or skewness. Numerous variants of this model were tested and an extensive sensitivity analysis was undertaken.

The model based on these five variables accounted for 45 per cent of the variation in small area costs. As expected, the variation between local authorities is substantial. Even after controlling for the five explanatory variables, which themselves vary widely between authorities, over one third of the remaining unexplained variances are at the local authority level.

The model described in Table 5.3 represents responses to needs factors within local authority areas. Assuming the multilevel analysis had satisfactorily extracted the local authority supply effect, the model could therefore be directly used as an indication of how a 'typical' local authority might respond to needs within its jurisdiction. We felt that the model passed each of the criteria of statistical adequacy, plausibility and parsimony, and therefore recommended that it would form the basis for a more satisfactory expenditure needs assessment than that used at the time. The predictions from the model indicated wide variations in needs among local authorities, ranging from 270 per cent of the national average per capita (aged 0–19) in Islington, to 40 per cent of the national average in Rutland, more than a six-fold difference.

An important outstanding issue remained to be resolved. Our methodology implicitly presumed that any local authority effect on expenditure was illegitimate from the point of view of estimating 'standard' spending needs. However, one local authority effect is clearly an important legitimate reason for variations in expenditure – namely, the considerable variation in the costs of goods and services found within England. It is therefore necessary to adjust funding formulae to accommodate cost variations. For many public services it is possible to use general indices of variations in labour and capital costs to model this phenomenon. However, for personal social services there is in addition clear *prima facie* evidence of large cost variations specific to the service, most notably in the allowances paid for foster care (National Foster Care Association, 1998). The payer therefore had to undertake additional work outside the scope of this study in order to estimate an appropriate cost variation index.

The revised needs formula was implemented in 1999/2000. Financial allocations are calculated by multiplying the model expenditure predictions by the relevant population of children and area cost adjustment in each area, and rescaling the consequent allocations so that they sum to the total national finance available. The needs element of the new formula resulted in major shifts of assessments, most notably an average 20 per cent reduction in needs assessments in inner London, an 11 per cent reduction in outer London, and a 7 per cent gain in other areas (Carr-Hill *et al.*, 1999).

5.6.2 Hospital and Community Health Services

The national government has the annual task of seeking to distribute English NHS resources to geographical areas. In the early years of the NHS, this distribution was based on incremental changes to historical spending patterns, and was widely perceived to be grotesquely inequitable (in favour of the southeast of the country). The celebrated report of the Resource Allocation Working Party (RAWP), described in Chapter 1, sought to address this inequity. It recommended that expenditure targets for health authorities should be based on population size, adjusted for age and sex, and further weighted by local standardized mortality rates for specific groups of conditions, assumed to be proxies for morbidity. The RAWP approach gave rise to the notion of 'weighted capitation' that is still in force in the NHS today. The RAWP targets were first implemented in 1976 for distributing funds to the 12 health regions, where most of the regions used analogous systems to distribute revenues to their constituent health authorities.

RAWP remained in force until 1990, by which time most regions were spending very close to their expenditure targets. However, increasing pressure developed in the 1980s to place NHS resource allocation on a more empirically sound basis. In particular, the assumption that there was a one-to-one relationship between condition-specific mortality rates and the associated NHS expenditure needed to be tested. Consequently, the national government set up a Review of RAWP, which introduced the notion of a small area study of NHS utilization, designed to minimize the problem of the ecological fallacy (Royston *et al.*, 1992). The intention was to identify social factors associated with NHS hospital utilization, as measured by inpatient episodes. An additional innovation was an attempt to introduce a measure of the local supply of hospital beds as a possible explanatory variable, as there was a widespread belief that a small area's proximity to inpatient beds might affect its utilization.

The Review of RAWP recommended a major simplification of resource allocation methods. It retained an age adjustment, but substituted for the condition-specific standardized mortality rates (SMRs) a combination of just two variables: the SMR for all causes of death for ages under 75, and an index of social deprivation. In the event, the government of the day rejected the use of the deprivation index, and in 1990 implemented an amended version of the recommendations that comprised the square root of the under-75 SMR only.

The Review attracted widespread criticism, related to execution, interpretation and implementation, and the amendment implemented by the government had little scientific justification (Sheldon and Carr-Hill, 1992). Considerable pressure therefore developed for a further review that would have available more extensive datasets, take advantage of the 1991 Census of Population, and employ more appropriate statistical methodology. A team from the University of York undertook that study, which is described in brief below (Carr-Hill *et al.*, 1994; Smith *et al.*, 1994).

In line with the principles set out above, two types of determinant of demand were considered to be important in driving utilization: the health care needs of the population, and the supply of health care facilities. The study tested a wide range of potential indicators of health care need, including indirect social determinants of demand for health care as well as direct measures of health status. In contrast to the PSS study, where the local supply effect was found to be negligible, it was necessary to consider variations in supply not only at the health authority level, but also *within* a health authority, on the grounds that access to specific local facilities (such as hospitals) may have an important local influence on utilization.

The units of analysis were 4,985 small areas covering the whole of England, with average populations of about 10,000. For each small area, potential explanatory data were assembled relating to socio-economic conditions, the supply of health services, and the utilization made of inpatient services. Socio-economic variables comprised detailed demographic data, health status variables derived from statutory returns, and broader social and economic variables derived from the 1991 Census of Population. Health status variables included a variety of age-specific standardized mortality ratios, standardized limiting long-standing illness ratios (derived from the Census), and low birth weight data. A total of 42 socio-economic variables thought to be possible influences on demand for health care were abstracted from the Census.

Four supply variables were created, reflecting the local availability of health services to the small area's population. They sought to measure the accessibility of NHS inpatient facilities, the accessibility of general practitioner (GP) services, the accessibility of private inpatient facilities, and the provision of residential and nursing homes. The problem of deriving accessibility measures is that it is necessary simultaneously to reconcile the supply of facilities, their proximity to the small area of interest and the impact of competing populations. This was achieved using the methods of spatial interaction modelling (Wilson, 1974). For example, if the measure of facility size is taken to be the number of hospital beds (say), the associated access measure is directly analogous to the familiar 'inpatient beds per head' ratio, but takes account of distance and competition from other small areas (see Appendix B for details).

The dependent variable was calculated from the 1990/91 and 1991/92 Hospital Episode Statistics (HES), a database of all hospital inpatient episodes (including day cases). A cost was attached to each episode, and a small area's utilization thereby measured in terms of costs. This facilitated the construction

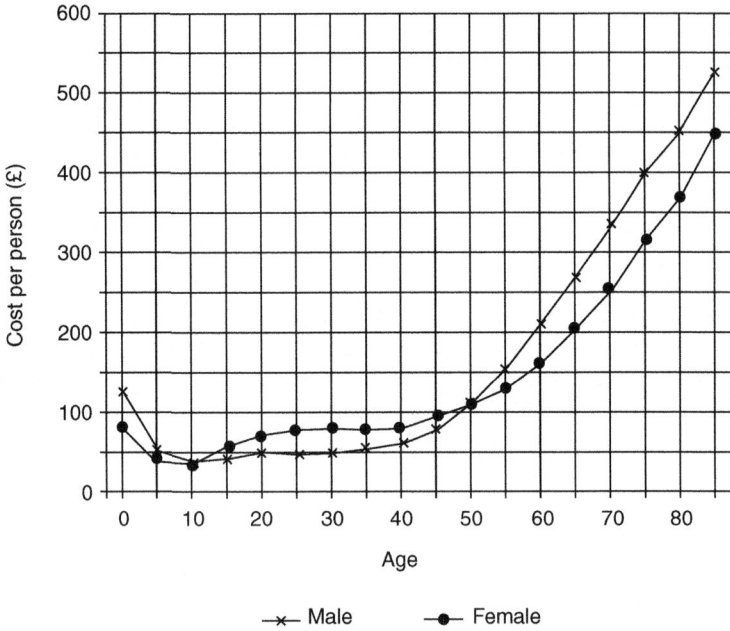

Figure 5.4 Age-related capitations for hospital and community service (£), 1991/92.

of an 'age-cost' curve, defined as the national average costs per head of population within 36 age/sex bands. These age-cost curves formed the basis for the first element of NHS capitations, and are summarized in Figure 5.4.

A particular problem caused by the introduction of small area supply factors is that the supply variations might themselves reflect variations in local needs. That is, there may exist simultaneity in the determination of supply. In essence, using the notation of Section 5.4, although there exists a small area relationship of the form:

$$EXP_{jk} = f(n_{jk}, p_{jk}) \tag{5.4}$$

where EXP_{jk} is expenditure, n_{jk} a vector of health care needs factors and p_{jk} a vector of supply factors in small area j (we ignore agency-wide effects at this stage), there may simultaneously exist a relationship of the form:

$$p_{jk} = g(n_{jk}, EXP_{jk}, z_{jk}) \tag{5.5}$$

where z_{jk} indicates social factors associated with supply rather than health care needs. This set of equations implies a need for careful modelling. In particular, if Equation (5.4) is estimated, it is necessary to test whether the variables p_{jk} need to be treated as endogenous. This analysis also indicates that indiscriminate

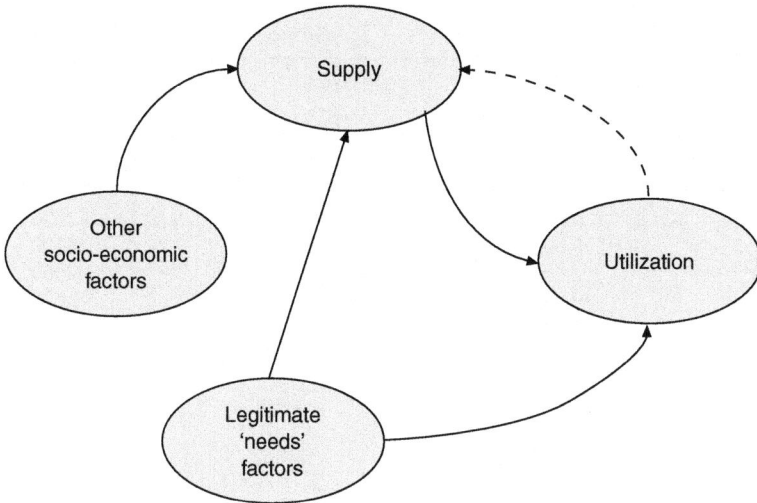

Figure 5.5 Representation of the econometric model of determinants of utilization.

regressions of utilization on social factors (effectively the reduced form for EXP_{jk} fund by eliminating p_{jk} from Equations (5.4) and (5.5)) may lead to the inclusion of illegitimate factors z_{jk} as well as the legitimate needs factors n_{jk}. The essence of the model is represented diagrammatically in Figure 5.5.

A small area's utilization, standardized for age and sex, was therefore modelled as a function of supply and needs, using two stage least squares regression methods, with the supply variables treated as endogenous. Two separate models were estimated for acute and psychiatric specialty groups. Throughout, the models were found to be better specified when natural logarithms were taken of all variables. The instruments used in the modelling were the entire set of socio-economic variables.

In the first instance, in addition to the supply variables, a large number of potential determinants of health care needs were included in the model. The initial selection of needs variables was on the basis of high statistical significance and *a priori* judgement about the importance of the variable. Thus, for example, in the acute sector a model comprising four supply variables and 25 needs variables was specified as the 'unrestricted' model. This model was then progressively restricted by omitting needs variables on the basis of lack of statistical significance. This process was continued until deletion of another variable would have resulted in a statistically significant alteration to the model. Possible health authority effects were modelled using authority dummy variables (not shown). Although methodical, the precise nature of this model selection process is of course open to challenge, and care was taken to prepare an audit trail which was open to scrutiny. The preferred model in the acute sector is shown in Table 5.4.

Table 5.4 Model of NHS acute sector utilization based on supply and needs

Variable	Coefficient	Standard error	T value
ACCNHS	0.0234	0.0497	0.4720
ACCGPS	0.3769	0.0809	4.6580
HOMES*	0.1290	0.0671	1.9230
ACCPRI	0.1214	0.0362	3.3530
DENSITY	−0.0370	0.0051	−7.2920
MANUAL	0.0733	0.0138	5.2970
OLDALONE	0.0915	0.0240	3.8100
S_CARER	0.0577	0.0178	3.2360
UNEMP	0.0475	0.0134	3.5520
HSIR074	0.1090	0.0291	3.7430
SMR074	0.1179	0.0210	5.6040

Source: Carr-Hill *et al.*, 1994.

Key to variables:

ACCNHS	Access to NHS acute beds
ACCGPS	Access to GPS
HOMES*	Proportion of population aged 75+ not in nursing or residential homes
ACCPRI	Access to private hospital beds
DENSITY	Persons divided by hectares
MANUAL	Proportion in households with head in manual social classes
OLDALONE	Proportion of pensionable age living alone
S_CARER	Proportion of dependants in single carer households
UNEMP	Proportion of economically active unemployed
SIR074	Standardized limiting long-standing illness ratio for ages 0–74
SMR074	SMR for ages 0–74

Numerous variants were tested, and the model was subjected to extensive sensitivity analysis.

According to the conventional Sargan test for misspecification errors in simultaneous equation models, the model is well specified ($\chi^2(33) = 69.7$) (Godfrey, 1988). The supply variables were confirmed as endogenous, justifying the use of the two stage least squares procedure. Of the supply variables, NHS hospital beds (ACCNHS) and nursing homes (HOMES*) were found to have little influence on utilization. However, the local supply of GPs (ACCGPS) and private beds (ACCPRI) were both positively strongly associated with higher NHS utilization.

The model described in Table 5.4 was not suitable as it stood as the basis for a funding formula because it contains indicators of supply. The final stage of the study was therefore to run a regression of utilization on the needs indicators alone, as selected by the two stage least squares methods, omitting the supply variables. This equation is in effect a truncated reduced form of utilization, and captures not only the direct impact of the selected needs variables on utilization, but also the indirect effect, to the extent that supply reflects legitimate needs. The rationale behind this methodology is based on Equations (5.4) and (5.5). Needs influence utilization directly and indirectly via supply. The truncated

Table 5.5 Acute sector multilevel model (standard errors in parentheses)

Variable	ML model
Constant	−1.651 (0.1168)
SMR for ages 0–74	0.1619 (0.0131)
Standardized limiting long-standing illness ages 0–74	0.2528 (0.0183)
Proportion of pensionable age living alone	0.0765 (0.0130)
Proportion of dependants in single carer households	0.0436 (0.0121)
Proportion of economically active unemployed	0.0287 (0.0092)

Source: Carr-Hill *et al.*, 1994.

regression models these legitimate determinants of supply. However, it does not incorporate the illegitimate socio-economic characteristics that are correlated with supply but not with health care needs. This final regression was estimated using multilevel modelling techniques in order to extract any potential effect at the health authority level.

The multilevel regression on the needs variables yielded a model containing five variables, as shown in Table 5.5, with MANUAL and DENSITY dropped through lack of statistical significance. This model formed the basis of the recommended index of health care needs in the acute sector. An analogous model was developed for the psychiatric sector.

Note the models described above indicate relative utilization after adjusting for age and sex. Therefore, although the emphasis here has been on explaining the small area element of the modelling, the methods in effect used a blend of individual level and small area level data. As a result, in developing expenditure allocations, a set of age-weighted capitation payments was first applied to the local population (differences attributed to sex were considered negligible). The predictions from the model in Table 5.5 were then applied to the age-weighted population. Because of their logarithmic specification, the indices had the effect of raising or lowering the capitations for each age group in an area by a fixed percentage. In the acute sector, the magnitude of this adjustment among health authorities ranged from plus 30 per cent in Central Manchester to minus 18 per cent in mid-Surrey, suggesting a much shallower needs gradient than that found in Children's PSS. The variation in the psychiatric sector was however larger, ranging from plus 108 per cent (Central Manchester) to minus 37 per cent (Huntingdon), implying a three-fold variation in *per capita* needs between the two areas. The net variation in *per capita* grant in the 183 health authorities arising from the risk adjustment process is shown in Figure 5.6.

A cost adjustment (known as the market forces factor) was then applied to the resulting allocations, and the allocations rescaled to sum to the total national finance available. Peacock and Smith (1995) give full details of how the expenditure allocations were calculated. The York formulae have since been superseded, but the basic approach towards calculating formulae for the bulk of NHS funding has remained unchanged (Sutton *et al.*, 2002).

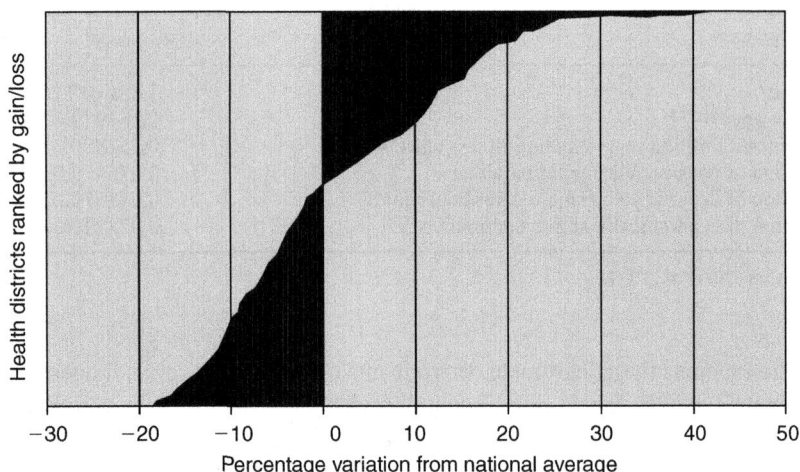

Figure 5.6 Percentage gain (loss) from equalization grant, 183 English health districts.

The models described above were developed deliberately in ignorance of the consequences for financial allocations, so that technical advisors would not be influenced by the political implications of the redistribution. However, it turned out that the use of the formulae would lead to a distinct shift of resources from richer to poorer areas, against the electoral interests of the then Conservative national government. Thus, although the study findings were accepted by the government as the basis for distributing 76 per cent of NHS hospital and community revenues in 1995/96, the remaining 24 per cent was contentiously distributed on the basis of age weighted population alone – that is, with no additional needs index – thereby seriously diluting the redistributive effect of the formulae. This decision underlines the pre-eminence of political considerations in the implementation of funding formulae, and is discussed further in Chapter 8.

5.7 Discussion

Capitation funding is based on expected individual consumption of public services, and it is therefore natural to seek to focus on individual level data in developing capitation payments. Use of such data:

- yields a capitation payment attached to every citizen that is portable between providers or insurers;
- can reduce 'cream skimming' of citizens or service users expected to make less intensive use of services;
- is heavily reliant on accurate individual utilization data collected by providers;

- may introduce a perverse incentive for providers to encourage more service utilization (in order to gain higher capitation ratings in future).

Because of data difficulties and perverse incentives, many payers have resorted to the small area methodology. This approach:

- economizes on the need to collect personal level data, and makes it feasible to use a large amount of readily available population level data;
- can lead to very simple funding formulae;
- circumvents confidentiality difficulties;
- can gives rise to serious analytic difficulties when estimating a risk adjustment formula;
- can be inaccurate for small populations.

In short, use of area-wide data is often a pragmatic and cost-effective way of developing funding formulae in the absence of satisfactory individual data. However, more widespread availability of individual level data should be an objective to which payers aspire, as it would facilitate the development of contingency tables of the sort advocated in Chapter 3. To that end, the potential for opening up new data resources is increasing as public service IT systems expand in scope and relevance. The Medicare Advantage example offers an indication of the potential in this domain, and in UK health care the emergence of an electronic health record for all citizens in the foreseeable may offer immense opportunities. Chapter 9 returns to this issue.

6 Budgetary risk and formula funding

6.1 Introduction

The word 'risk' in English has a number of different connotations, giving rise to a potential for ambiguity. In capitation terminology, 'risk adjustment' means adjusting financial allocations for the expected expenditure on a particular user. However, in this chapter I consider budgetary risk in the sense of the unpredicted variation in outturn expenditure from expected levels.

Such risk is an intrinsic feature of expenditure on public services. If expenditure requirements could be predicted with certainty, then the problem of setting budgets becomes trivial, and the task for the devolved entity becomes that of merely carrying out agreed policies. However, if significant risk does exist, it can induce both intended and unintended behaviour on the part of local organizations. Without some element of risk for the budget holder, a budgetary regime becomes little more than reimbursement of expenditure, destroying the intended incentive for financial discipline. In contrast, excessive risk can lead to unintended adverse responses from risk averse budget holders, as they seek to avoid risk or shift it on to other agencies or service users. Finding a satisfactory distribution of risk between payers, purchasers, providers and users is therefore often a central preoccupation of the designer of formula funding systems.

Chapter 3 introduced the notion of local government as a risk pool. This chapter explores in more detail the distribution of risk in public services under formula funding. It first examines the components of budgetary risk. It then describes possible behavioural responses of local organizations to such risk. Finally, it summarizes some potential strategies on the part of the payer to share risk with the budget holders.

6.2 What is budgetary risk?

Budgetary risk can be defined as the propensity for outturn expenditure to vary from forecast expenditure. It can be interpreted and formalized in a number of ways, but is often measured by statistical measures of dispersion, such as the variance of outturn expenditure. If demand for public services is independent of the budgetary regime, the aggregate of budgetary risk in the system as a whole cannot be altered.

But how it is shared between various parties can be profoundly altered by the chosen organizational structure and payment mechanisms. Moreover, in practice demand for services is likely to be highly influenced by the funding mechanism, implying that both the level and distribution of risk is amenable to policy choices.

Risk can therefore be important under any system of formula funding. In capitation systems, risk is concentrated on the budget holder because a fixed budget is allocated to manage uncertain demand and unit costs. Under case payment, some of the demand risk is transferred to the payer. However, a local organization still bears the case intensity risk. Also, under case payments, a local provider might suffer budgetary risk if it faces risky demands but its cost structure includes a high degree of fixed costs. In that case, an uncertain revenue stream may not cover the fixed costs to which the provider is committed.

Funding mechanisms usually seek to reflect the *expected* expenditure on an individual with certain measured characteristics if some standard set of policies is applied. As noted in Chapter 3, there is of course no expectation that the recipient of funds will spend that amount on each relevant individual. For many services, such as health care, there is enormous variance in expenditure around this mean. Rather, the sum of the budget holder's formula funding payments creates an insurance risk pool, and its role is to ensure that the expenditure made from the risk pool is in line with some agreed set of policies.

Newhouse *et al.* (1989) present a model of individual annual expenditure on a public service that can be paraphrased as follows:

$$\text{Expenditure} = \boldsymbol{b}.X_i + u_i + e_{it}$$

where $\boldsymbol{b}$ is the universal (national average) response to known risk factors, X_i is the vector of risk factors used in the payment system that are exhibited by individual i, u_i is a time-invariant component of variance associated with individual i that is independent of the chosen risk factors, and e_{it} is a person-specific time-varying component of variance. The component $\boldsymbol{b}.X_i$ can be thought of as the part of the total variance in expenditure that is predicted by the payment formula. Component u_i represents the additional part of variance that could in principle be predicted if it were possible to incorporate all potential risk factors of an individual into a formula. The component e_{it} is the random part, which is independent of any patient risk factors, known or unknown. This model implicitly subsumes variations due to different provider practices into the random element e_{it}. In health care, Newhouse *et al.* (1989) estimated that this random component is likely to account for at least 85.5 per cent of the variance in expenditure on any one individual.

This insight can be adapted therefore to partition variability in public service expenditure into four components:

1 an element that is due to individual characteristics – such as age – that are captured by the chosen risk adjustment process in whatever formula is used to allocate funds;

2   an element that is due to service user characteristics that are not captured by the formula, such as – for example in health care – the presence of diabetes;

3   an element that is due to the practices of local providers – for example, the level of local efficiency;

4   an element that is totally random, caused by the unpredictable incidence and severity of service need, such as a car accident in health care.

Payers will seek out a formula that captures as much of (1) as possible, and minimizes (2), thereby promoting fairness and reducing the scope for local organizations to indulge in cream skimming and other adverse behaviour. Element (3) reflects illegitimate influences on expenditure, and so should be ignored in a formula, while (4) is inherently unknowable. The chosen formula will predict expenditure according to (1). All remaining expenditure will be perceived by the local organization to be expenditure 'risk'.

6.3 The causes of budgetary risk

Under capitation systems there are two broad determinants of the budgetary risk for a budget holder: the number of users, and the magnitude of the expenditure on each of those users. The relative importance of these two elements can vary considerably between services. For example, a further education college might experience considerable uncertainty about the number of students who will enrol in the forthcoming year, but can forecast with relative ease the expenditure per student. In contrast, a prison might be able to forecast with some confidence the number of users, but experience extreme variability in the costs of each individual prisoner. These concepts, which derive from the insurance literature, are treated more formally in Technical Appendix A.

A fundamental choice in any system of formula funding is who should bear each of these sources of risk: the payer, the budget holder, or some other party, such as the user. In the relatively rare situation when the payer reimburses the budget holder for all service expenditure, all budgetary risk remains with the payer. The budget holder has no direct incentive to restrain expenditure and one would expect to see services provided technically inefficiently, and in excess of socially desired levels. In contrast, where the payer sets a fixed budget independent of number of users, all budgetary risk is transferred to the budget holder. Here the budget holder's incentive is equally clear: to restrain both the numbers and expenditure of users. Without additional incentives, one would expect to see both the volume and quality of public services below the social optimum. It is because of the stark incentives inherent in these two extreme models of risk apportionment that an intermediate arrangement of mixed funding is frequently adopted.

Under formula funding, the level of budgetary risk borne by a budget holder depends on a number of factors, such as:

•   the intrinsic variance in demand for the service, a function of both the expected number of users and their individual expenditure needs;

- unexpected variations in input prices and other supply side factors;
- the size of the devolved entity (number of users or potential users);
- the time period over which financial risk can be spread;
- the degree of policy autonomy enjoyed by the devolved entity;
- the risk sharing instruments put in place;
- the nature and quality of the funding formula;
- the consequences to the budget holder of breaching budgetary levels.

Many of these sources of risk are generic to all budgetary regimes. However, the choice of funding mechanism can profoundly affect their importance for the payer, budget holders and service users. The remainder of this section concentrates on the issues most relevant to formula funding.

6.3.1 Intrinsic variance in demand

The variance in the incidence and expenditure of potential users is not in itself a major difficulty providing that the risk adjustment used to estimate payments does a good job in predicting expenditure. However, except for highly homogeneous user groups such as university students, it rarely does so, as the information requirements of good risk adjustment are usually too demanding. Instead, budget holders will be exposed to shocks in expenditure that are not modelled by the funding formula. For example, if the local football team enjoys an unanticipated sequence of victories, a police force might have an unexpectedly large number of football matches to police. A particularly extreme shock may be a catastrophic event – such as a major fire, a prison riot, or a complex murder investigation – that by definition cannot be captured by a formula. In the extreme, such incidents might be the subject of exceptional retrospective funding from the payer, outside the scope of the formula funding regime.

6.3.2 Supply side budgetary pressures

Supply side sources of risk, such as the detailed characteristics of physical or human resources, can often be important, particularly for small institutions. The treatment of capital endowments can be particularly challenging for formula design. In the long run, capital should be treated like any other input, making a case for allocating capital funds within the usual formula funding mechanism. However, in the short to medium term, public service providers are severely constrained in the extent to which they can alter capital stock or configurations, so there is a case for allocating capital resources in the light of capital endowments. This tension is illustrated by a report by the Audit Commission (2003) on school funding that noted that '[too many] of the capital resources are distributed according to the number of pupils, rather than more critical factors, such as the age and condition of school buildings. As a result, not enough of the most urgent need is being adequately resourced to immediately fund improvements.'

Because of these difficulties, capital resources are removed from many funding formulae and responsibility for capital retained by the payer. Of course this can itself lead to difficulties. Organizations with more efficient capital stock enjoy an operational advantage over others, and the payer now has a complex task of deciding how to allocate capital resources in the absence of an explicit formula.

While recognizing the constraints of current endowments, any funding formula must also seek to avoid offering current management the opportunity to 'game' the system, by running down capital stock to secure favourable allocations in future. In housing, the inheritance of capital stock is largely the legacy of previous management, and beyond the control of current management. There is therefore a case for treating the capital endowment as exogenous, and using it as a basis for a funding formula in conjunction with housing demand data. However, such treatment offers little incentive to purchase and maintain capital efficiently. Efforts to design satisfactory funding formulae for housing capital have found it difficult to balance the conflicting pressures of immediate needs and longer-term efficiency (Glennerster *et al.*, 2000; Audit Commission, 2005b).

Similar considerations might apply to human resources. For example, because of the vagaries of personnel turnover, some schools might have higher unit salary costs than others. Here one possible solution is to measure performance against budgets assuming schools pay an *average* salary for each grade, rather than budgets based on actual salaries paid. However, while allowing for possibly inescapable salary risk, this mechanism in turn gives budget holders no incentive to restrain salary costs within each grade, and so may lead to a tendency for some salary growth.

6.3.3 *'Size' of budget holder*

In general, the magnitude of budgetary risk will increase as the organizational units to which funding is being devolved become smaller (Bachmann and Bevan, 1996; Bojke *et al.*, 2001). There is therefore often a trade-off between the managerial benefits brought about by devolution to a local level and the increased financial risk such devolution introduces (Baxter *et al.*, 2000). For example, if a schools funding formula implies that spending per pupil not explained by the formula has a variance of σ^2, then the per pupil standard error for a budget devolved to a school covering n pupils will be $\sigma/\sqrt{n}$. While this error is usually small for large n (say a secondary school), it may become very important for smaller units of organization.

Martin *et al.* (1998) examine the risk inherent in the formula for English health care described in Section 5.6.2. The chosen statistical model explained about 55 per cent of the variation in small area expenditure on acute health services. The unexplained element represents the expenditure risk to local health authorities. Martin *et al.* (1998) then examine implications for different sizes of health care purchasers. Figure 6.1 summarizes the findings by indicating the 95 per cent confidence limits for actual expenditure relative to the York formula as the population covered by the purchaser increases. The probability of a material

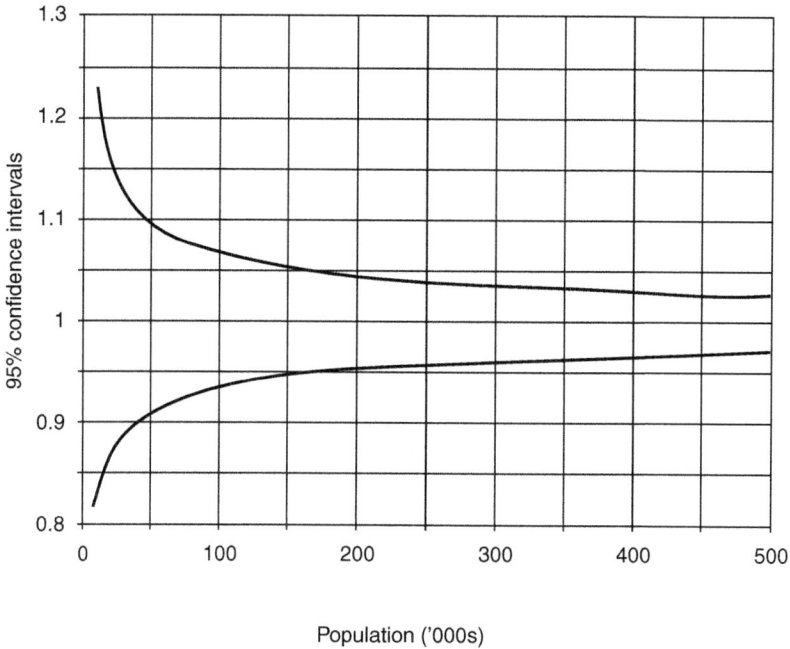

Population ('000s)

Figure 6.1 Ninety-five per cent confidence intervals for outturn expenditure, budget = 1.0 (source: Martin *et al.*, 1998).

divergence from the formula for a health authority covering a population of 500,000 is negligible. However, if the population is as low as 10,000, there is a one in three chance of a divergence in expenditure of more than 10 per cent from the formula. They conclude that a formula that is entirely satisfactory for paying large health authorities may be unsuitable for paying small general practices.

A further example from the UK is the discretionary Social Fund, a social security programme that offers emergency one-off loans to low income households (Huby, 1995). Local benefits offices receive fixed annual Social Fund budgets within which they are expected to meet local demand for discretionary (that is, non-statutory) loans to low income households. This approach secures expenditure control and delegates individual decisions to local offices, thereby obviating the need for detailed guidance on the eligibility of claimants. The formula for funding local offices seeks to ensure that 'applicants with broadly similar personal circumstances [receive] the same level of available budgeting loan debt wherever they live' (Secretary of State for Social Security, 2000). In principle the formula seeks to model the local level of demand for loans and the ability of the local office to recover loan repayments. In practice, the programme has proved 'vulnerable to changes in the anticipated level and pattern of demand', and exceptional payments have been made to certain offices to reflect unanticipated surges in demand. Thus the social security benefits office area may be too small to act as a satisfactory basis for devolved Social Fund budgets.

One solution to handling local risk might be to devolve mechanically to a regional level, thereby securing national expenditure control, but then to allow considerable flexibility to the regions as to how their allocations are spent locally. The English Housing Corporation adopts this approach. A Housing Needs Index is used to allocate capital allocations to regions, but the regions use a 'fully strategic' (that is, non-formulaic) approach to allocating to local government areas (Housing Corporation, 2001). As well as reducing local risk, this approach seeks to target resources at a small number of well-planned initiatives, rather than spread finances purely on a fair shares basis. There is therefore an implication that some equity may be sacrificed in the interests of efficiency.

One associated consideration under this heading is that – if a devolved agency holds a pooled budget for a range of services – it can absorb expenditure risk more readily than if it must secure financial balance on each of its services in a single budgetary period. For example, English local government comprises 24 separate services, and separate formulae are used to set grant levels for each (Office of the Deputy Prime Minister, 2003). However, the budget constraint for the local government is the aggregate of the sub-programme calculations, and there is no obligation to conform to each of the implied sub-programme budgets. Such arrangements permit the budget holder to spread risk between services. In loose terms, negative expenditure shocks in one service may to some extent be offset by positive shocks in other services.

This indicates that – through cost sharing with other services – multipurpose organizations may often have a greater capacity to bear budgetary risk than single purpose equivalents. This form of risk sharing may of course be less effective if there is a high degree of positive correlation between risks in individual services (perhaps because demand for many services depends on underlying economic conditions). The ability of pooled budgets to absorb risk on individual services is then not so pronounced.

6.3.4 Budgetary time horizon

The time period over which budgets are set is an important determinant of budgetary risk. Government payers typically use a one-year budgetary cycle, and seek to secure adherence to budgets over that period. Where uncertainty in spending needs is high, a strictly enforced annual budget can lead to seriously adverse consequences, as discussed below. Therefore some governments are implementing longer time horizons. For example, the UK now expects many public service organizations to secure budgetary balance over a three-year period.

The most common mechanism for managing this source of budgetary risk is to allow public service organizations to accumulate or run down financial balances. Balances allow organizations to smooth shocks in expenditure across time periods, and models of financial management can be used to determine optimal levels of financial reserves, given expenditure uncertainties. Note that, in general, as the size of budget holders reduces, so the relative need for prudent levels of financial balances increases, as the organizations become more vulnerable to unexpected expenditure shocks. Thus one of the costs implicit in a highly devolved organizational structure may be the high aggregate level of balances held by budget holders. Furthermore, rather than acting as a risk management tool, the use of balances could be used as a means of transferring the costs of providing services from current taxpayers to future taxpayers, an outcome that may not be intended.

6.3.5 Policy autonomy

If a public service is subject to an unexpected spending shock, it has two broad choices under a hard budget constraint. It can either continue to deliver the standard level of service, in which case it will overspend its budget, or it can reduce the standard of service it offers to something below the assumed standard. If the first alternative is ruled out, variable levels of service will arise, not because of policy choices on the part of providers, but because of the limitations of the funding formula, and the random shocks to expenditure that it fails to capture. Thus the level of policy autonomy enjoyed by the budget holder is an important determinant of the risk it bears. With full autonomy it may be able to absorb imperfections in the funding formula by varying service levels. However, if the payer leaves little room for discretion in the services to be provided, or the performance standards it expects, then the financial risk increases correspondingly.

Inescapable expenditure commitments might be imposed on a public service from numerous sources other than central decree, such as capital repayments, payments in settlement of negligence claims, and an inheritance of users or services that must be maintained (a particular feature of long-term social care). The greater the extent of these 'ring-fenced' commitments, the greater the risk attached to the residual service.

6.3.6 Cost sharing

Many cost sharing arrangements can be put in place between the payer and the budget holder as a means of sharing financial risk (Newhouse, 1996). In particular, under case payments the risk relating to numbers of users is retained by the payer. For example, school budgets are often dependent on the number of pupils, implying that the budget holder avoids some of the risk associated with variations in pupil numbers. Hospital case payments based on the diagnosis-related group (DRG) of patients are a more complex example of the same principle.

Other approaches to cost sharing include cost matching (under which the payer pays a proportion of all incremental expenditure beyond some threshold), stop loss arrangements (under which the payer takes responsibility for expenditure in excess of some fixed amount on a particular user) and 'carve outs' (under which financial responsibility for particular users or services reverts to the payer). Each of these arrangements introduces a different set of incentives for the budget holder (Van de Ven and Ellis, 2000). Some examples are given in Section 6.4. Formula funding can assist in making some of these cost sharing arrangements operational. For example, the case payment could serve as the baseline above which matching payments are triggered. And carve outs might be modelled by returning an agreed portion of the full capitation payment to the payer.

The budget holder might also have important cost sharing arrangements with the service user (in the form of user charges) or the local voter (in the form of local taxes). Some budget holders may be able to share costs with other agencies, such as other public services or charities, or be in receipt of voluntary donations or capital gifts from local benefactors. The possibility of local cost sharing can pose a particular challenge for funding formula methodology. It may become necessary to incorporate into the formula variations in the capacity of local public services to raise local income. For example, English social services for elderly people (Box 1.1) raise substantial income in the form of user charges from users able to pay, but there are large variations between jurisdictions in personal income levels. The associated formula set therefore has a 'low income' adjustment designed to reflect variations in the ability of local governments to recover costs through user charges.

6.3.7 *The quality of the funding formula*

This analysis reinforces the critical importance of the nature and the quality of the funding formula for the budgetary risk experienced by the budget holder. A lack of proper risk adjustment imposes greater risk on the budget holder, and may induce some of the adverse responses discussed later in this chapter. However, note also that the payer may use the funding mechanism to put in place explicit incentives. So for example a payer may deliberately decide not to use counts of existing service users in a funding formula in order to promote reductions in the level of service utilization.

In particular the population to be used as the basis for capitation payments is an important choice. In general, as the population gets increasingly specific, so the risk is transferred from the budget holder to the payer. For example, consider public provision of an adolescent psychiatric service. A hierarchy of population bases can be considered:

a   the entire geographic population for which the provider is responsible;
b   the population in the relevant age groups;
c   the number of service users registered with the service provider;
d   the number of service users disaggregated by diagnosis.

Under (a) the provider bears the risk even of the relative size of the adolescent age group in its population. Under (b), the payer assumes that probably modest element of budgetary risk, while under (c) it assumes the risk associated with the relative propensity of local adolescents to become users. Under (d), refinement of the reimbursement scheme transfers further risk to the payer.

In general, each refinement of the capitation formula reduces the level of risk borne by the budget holder. To the extent that this reduces the adverse responses noted below, there are beneficial. However, refinement of the formula can itself introduce adverse incentives, particularly when some elements of the formula are under the control of the budget holder. For example, I have described in Chapter 3 how successive refinements of DRG payments in health care might lead to an incentive to 'DRG creep', as providers assign patients to more complex diagnostic categories in order to attract higher case payments. Likewise, an individual's previous service utilization is sometimes used as a basis for risk-adjusting capitation payments in health care. While this reduces the financial risk faced by budget holders, it may also introduce a perverse incentive to increase services for patients above optimal levels, in order to attract higher capitation payments in the future.

6.3.8 Sanctions and budgetary risk

The responses of managers to risk will be strongly determined by the sanctions they incur for overspending. A budgetary system may appear nominally to transfer a great deal of risk to the budget holder – for example, being based on a rudimentary *per capita* formula, yielding a fixed budget that must be balanced within the year, without any potential for cost sharing. However, if managers or their organization suffer few consequences for a breach of the budget, the high levels of risk they bear may not materially affect their actions. In particular, if budget holders in financial difficulties can expect to be periodically rescued financially by the payer, then there is little incentive to conform to budgets, and the formulaic approach to budget setting becomes little more than an annual ritual.

The incentives associated with formulaic budgets may be quite subtle. For example, a formula used to allocate funding to English housing associations sought to give recipients the opportunity to set 'fair rents', given their housing stock characteristics and assuming some standard level of efficiency in repair and maintenance (Glennerster *et al.*, 2000). However, the consequences for the associations of levying rents in excess of the assumed level were initially very modest, as many tenants were in receipt of welfare benefits that automatically paid any level of rent, funded by the national government. Many associations therefore felt they could increase rents with impunity. A harder constraint was subsequently introduced that made associations with high rent increases ineligible for future capital grants. This policy radically altered incentives, and effectively set an upper limit on rent increases in most associations.

6.4 Budget holders' responses to risk

Some degree of budgetary risk in public services is essential, as it encourages local organizations to operate prudently and efficiently. However, depending on the payer's chosen financial mechanism, budgetary risk may also induce unintended and adverse behavioural responses among public service organizations. This is likely to be especially important when the organizations are small, such as local schools or general practices, and are risk averse. This section discusses the stratagems that such organizations might adopt if they perceive there to be high degrees of budgetary risk.

Recall the four sources of variation in expenditure on a particular public service user discussed in Section 6.2:

a   variation that is predicted by the relevant funding formula;
b   other variations that were predictable (given the user's personal characteristics) but that was not captured by the current formula;
c   variation that is due to the practices of the service provider;
d   variation that is random (that is, entirely unpredictable).

The budget holder is compensated only for (a). The budget holder may in principle be able to observe (b), and therefore have an informational advantage over the payer. For example, a school may have detailed information about the truancy record of potential pupils that is not available to the payer. The budget holder may also be able to control some of the actions leading to (c), perhaps through improving the level of efficiency of the organization or by changing its policy on the level of services delivered to users. By definition, (d) is outside the control of payer or budget holder.

Thus the scope for budget holders to manage their budgetary risk through their own actions may be quite considerable. Some of the actions are intended and desirable consequences of budgetary risk, such as adopting cost-effective approaches to service delivery. However, other actions are unintended and potentially undesirable. We examine three examples:

- 'spending to the budget' in order to retain a strong budgetary base for future years;
- discouraging users with high contribution to the budget holder's expenditure risk;
- seeking out risk avoidance mechanisms

6.4.1 Spending to the budget

Notwithstanding the intentions of formula funding, current budget holder actions often affect future budgets. For example, many formulae use previous expenditure as one component of the budget calculation. Under these circumstances, budget holders have an incentive to maintain higher levels of expenditure than intended by policy in order to protect future budgets. So for example if a budget-holding general practice perceives during the course of the year that it is going to underspend its current budget, it may feel it needs to increase the quality of services offered to patients or otherwise 'pad' its spending over the remainder of the year in order to justify its current budget and protect future years' budgets. Similarly, if an underspend cannot be retained by the budget holder (perhaps because the payer uses it to balance overspends elsewhere) there is little incentive to leave any of a budget unspent.

Conversely, if strong sanctions are imposed for overspending, a school (say) that perceives during the year that it is going to overspend may implement dramatic cuts in service levels in order to avoid exceeding the budget. The prevalence and importance of such responses is likely to increase as both the magnitude of risk and the severity of the sanctions increases. Of course, such behaviour – familiar to students of bureaucracies and the Soviet Union – merely emphasizes the need to put in place good funding formulae systems that are independent of the organization's previous expenditure or activity.

In UK public services, variations in service provision have become known as 'postcode rationing', and are a central policy concern. In order to address perceived service standard variations, the payer might seek to secure rigid service standards for an increasing proportion of the service. This might secure the desired equity in the 'mandated' proportion of the service. However, the expenditure risk for the residual 'unmandated' services becomes ever larger as its proportion of spending gets smaller. This can lead to gross inequalities in service standards in unmandated services if budgets must be adhered to. Thus, although the pursuit of equity objectives is usually an important motivation for formula funding, the risk inherent in public service provision given can paradoxically give rise to profound *inequity* between localities when a strictly enforced fixed budget is implemented alongside strict standards for some services (Smith, 1999).

A similar but distinct form of postcode rationing *within* a provider occurs if a budget holder has a hard budget constraint and its perceived budgetary position changes during the course of the year, because of stochastic shocks to demand. Then it might alter service standard over the course of the year as the apparent budgetary position alters, and a user might therefore receive a different level of service depending on the time of year he or she seeks access (Glazer and Shmueli, 1995; Pollack and Zeckhauser, 1996). Such 'dynamic' inequities will also usually contradict the payer's equity intentions.

A number of policies to counter such tendencies can be envisaged. Most fundamentally, the use of current expenditure to inform future budgets should be minimized. However, use of some element of historical expenditure to inform future budgets is often considered inevitable, in order to avoid large swings in budgets. Alternatively, budget holders might be allowed to carry over deficits to future years, through the use of balances. Again, there is a danger that this may serve merely to transfer the inequity from current users to future users, who will bear the costs of satisfying current equity objectives. Finally, as the discussion of quality skimping in Chapter 3 underlined, performance reporting and inspection can be used to reduce variations in service levels.

6.4.2 Cream skimming

A persistent theme throughout the book has been the incentive for the budget holder to cream skim only those service users whose marginal costs are expected to be lower than the associated capitation or case payment. This incentive applies particularly to service providers, and will be most marked when the variance of expenditure is high, and budget holders therefore have a strong incentive to seek out private information about potential users in order to secure better estimates of expected costs. As the units of devolution become smaller, so risk increases and the potential for asymmetry of information between the payer and provider increases. Small units of organization, such as schools, are likely to have access to extensive private and informal information about potential users that larger organizations do not possess. So the potential for cream skimming increases accordingly.

The payer's obvious policy response to this problem is to make the risk adjustment scheme more refined, so that payments can more accurately reflect all known client characteristics. In principle, risk adjustment of payment mechanisms should be designed so that – assuming a standard level of service is to be provided – all potential users are equally attractive to providers. However, this can – in the extreme – lead to a system closer to complete reimbursement of expenditure, and considerable heterogeneity even within risk adjustment groups will often remain.

Risk aversion implies that the perceived *variability* in the user's expenditure requirements to achieve specified performance criteria may also be a consideration. In the English higher education sector, a 'postcode premium' is attached to the case payment for students living in areas with high deprivation scores (Department for Education and Skills, 2002). It is quite plausible to interpret this premium as an attempt to compensate for the perceived risk in terms of outcome uncertainty (for example, adverse impact on the university's drop-out rate), rather than a reflection of expected additional costs.

This example emphasizes that the performance criteria to be reported publicly may also serve to induce risk aversion in a provider. More generally, the postcode rationing debate suggests that localities can rarely vary quality standards with impunity. Moreover, the specific choice performance measure on which local organizations are judged may be important. For example, if the performance of a university is measured by extreme outcomes (such as the prevalence of drop-outs) rather than (say) average grade attainment, then the provider is encouraged to concentrate on one tail of the ability distribution rather than the entire range of circumstances. I return to the link between performance measurement and funding mechanisms in the final chapter.

6.4.3 Risk avoidance

Devolved purchasers of public services (such as local governments) may seek to transfer risk to other parties through a variety of mechanisms. One of the most common is to negotiate a 'block' contract with a service provider, under which the provider is required to satisfy all demand that arises for a fixed budget. Clearly to be effective the contract must also specify service standards in the form of performance criteria. This arrangement transfers all the local government's risk to the provider. There may be circumstances when this is desirable (for example, when a large provider, such as a hospital, can pool the risk borne by a number of small purchasers). However, the entire transfer of risk to the provider may thwart some of the original payer's intentions, such as making the local government more active in controlling demand for the service.

While a block contract transfers all the devolved purchaser's budgetary risk to the provider, less extreme transfers can be effected through use of cost sharing arrangements in the contractual arrangements between purchaser and provider. More generally, a purchaser might seek to moderate financial risk by pooling its budget with other agencies in the interests of risk management. Such pooling might be especially effective in the case of services that are potential substitutes, such as school education and children's social services. Also, small budget holders (either purchasers or providers) might pool their budgets in order to reduce their levels of budgetary risk. For example, some general practice fund holders in UK general practice formed various types of purchasing alliances that reduced budgetary risk, reduced transaction costs and increased purchasing power (Smith, 1999). While often beneficial, these arrangements may dilute some of the direct accountability of the devolved budget holder to the payer.

A radically alternative approach is for the local entity to transfer some risk to the service user by requiring a copayment of some sort. This might take the form of

- an excess or deductible, which in effect creates a fixed fee for securing access to the service;
- a matching payment, under which the user shares a fixed proportion of the costs incurred by the provider;
- a residual payment, under which the user pays all costs in excess of some pre-determined upper limit.

The topic of user charges for public services is large and complex, and beyond the scope of this book, and the main objective of many systems of charging is to moderate demand rather than to manage financial risk.

However, some types of user charge do have important risk reduction objectives. For example, many systems of vouchers for public services offer only a fixed financial contribution towards the provision of a service (Steuerle *et al.*, 2000). If the user chooses a provider that charges in excess of the voucher sum, they must meet the difference out of their own pocket. A specific example observed widely in health care is the user of 'reference prices' for drugs (examples include Sweden, Germany, Spain and Italy) (Kanavos and Reinhardt, 2003). Under this regime, pharmaceuticals with similar properties are grouped into discrete 'clusters'. Patients are reimbursed at a fixed rate for all drugs within a cluster, and if they choose a more expensive drug they must pay the difference between the drug price and the reference price out of their own pocket. The intention is to encourage use of cheaper generic replacements of branded drugs. However, the system also has the effect of reducing expenditure risk for local governments or providers.

Risk averse providers might also hold financial balances in excess of socially optimal levels, or even taking out insurance against overspending with third parties, leading to an unproductive outflow of funds from the public services (Smith, 1997). While these responses are not necessarily associated with formula funding *per se* (they would exist whatever the budget-setting method), it may be the case that setting budgets for very small units is seen to be feasible only if a funding formula is in place. To that extent, formula funding is a prerequisite for the devolution that gives rise to risk averse responses.

Policy responses to these actions might include the payer acting as an insurer (so that the reinsurance 'premiums' remain within the service). This is effectively a form of retrospective cost sharing. Similarly, the payer could act as the banker for financial reserves. In this way it can both reduce the aggregate need for reserves and also use its market power to secure favourable rates of interest.

6.5 Policy instruments for risk management

This chapter has indicated that the nature and importance of risk in systems of formula funding is highly dependent on context. However, it suggests that there are many circumstances in which the distribution of risk may be an important determinant of the effectiveness of the system, and that any payer may need to consider its formula funding decisions alongside its policies for institutional design and risk management. The chapter has raised numerous possible issues associated with risk management policy. This concluding section summarizes the policy instruments discussed in the chapter that may need to be implemented alongside a funding formula when financial risk gives rise to adverse behavioural responses among devolved entities.

Pooling budget holders. Budgets become less susceptible to random *per capita* variations as the population to which they refer increases. This suggests the need to consider carefully the size of the organizations to which budgets are being devolved under formula funding. There are numerous conflicting objectives to be considered when determining the optimal size of devolved entities, such as promoting accountability, securing scale economies and minimizing transaction costs. However, risk management may be an important consideration when deciding whether to devolve expenditure mechanically to entities as small as schools, or to rely on local planning systems for such budget setting.

Where risk is important, consideration might be given to creating a joint budget for voluntary associations of local organizations that wish to collaborate. However, accountability may be diluted in such partnerships, leading to weaker budgetary control (Audit Commission, 2005c). This highlights an important tension that exists between the goal of managing financial risk (which would favour large organizational units) and the goal of maximizing accountability (which often favours small organizational units).

Pooling years. Random fluctuations become less important as the time period associated with a budget increases. Organizational budgets may be more meaningful if they refer to a period longer than the conventional one-year planning horizon, or if organizations are able to retain reserves. Again, this will have to be balanced against the potentially adverse consequences of excessive use of balances, noted earlier in the chapter.

Excluding predictably expensive service users. A small number of service users with very high needs may account for a large proportion of the unpredictable variation in a local organization's expenditure. An example in schools might be pupils with severe learning difficulties. Where the characteristic is readily verified, there may be an argument for incorporating the characteristic as a risk adjuster into the capitation formula or transferring budgetary responsibility directly to the original payer. For example, in Israeli health care, reimbursement for people with certain serious chronic diseases, such as Gaucher's disease, thalasemia major, haemophilia, dialysis and AIDS, have been modelled separately to the capitation system, and mental illness services reimbursed separately by the national government (Shmueli *et al.*, 1998).

Excluding certain services. In the same way, certain rare but expensive services may have important implications for budgetary control where they occur. Again, in health care, patients with severe mental illness may lead to high and uncertain treatment costs. Consideration might be given to transferring the whole or part of the costs of such services to the payer. More generally, when there exists a hierarchy of public service organizations responsible for delivery (for example, schools within local governments within states within nations), careful consideration should be given to how to share the intrinsic risk optimally between the tiers (Van Barneveld *et al.*, 1998).

Cost sharing. The payer might retain a certain amount of the aggregate expenditure for the period for the purposes of cost sharing. For example, in case payment systems this might take the form of meeting all or some of the costs incurred on a particular service user once they exceed some threshold. Alternatively, cost sharing might take the form of meeting all or some of any total budgetary overspend during the time period in question. Of course such cost sharing arrangements may create their own adverse incentives, but they do have the effect of moderating local risk.

Careful analysis of variations from budgets. The above discussion indicates that – before any action can be taken – it is imperative that the payer examines with some care the causes of variations from local budgets. Such variations may arise from a number of sources, the policy implications of which are very different. Defects in the funding formula are a policy issue for the payer. Variations in delivery methods might be addressed by increased use of benchmarking and practice guidelines. Variations in contract prices may be inescapable, or may reflect weaknesses in local managerial bargaining skills. Variations in service standards might be captured by suitable performance reporting. Random variations in demand may be by their nature largely resistant to policy intervention. Investigation of the causes of budget violations may increase the payer's management costs, but it is difficult to see how a budgeting system can be made to function without running alongside other managerial instruments.

In summary, there exist a multitude of risk management instruments that should be considered by the payer seeking to implement formula funding. The precise choice will be heavily dependent on context. Furthermore, risk management cannot be considered in isolation from other objectives – indeed it will often be the case that risk management initiatives may directly compromise certain other of the payer's objectives. However, it is unlikely that many systems of formula funding can be introduced without the need for careful scrutiny of its implications for the level and distribution of risk. This chapter has indicated the challenges confronting the payer when seeking to integrate funding mechanisms with considerations of risk management instruments and broader organizational design.

7 Paying for quality
The case of UK general practitioners

7.1 Introduction

The quality of public services is a fundamental concern when designing funding formulae. In particular, as Chapter 3 highlighted, the incentives implicit in most systems of formula funding run the risk of compromising the quality of services, defined as their effectiveness in securing desired standards of service. To some extent poor quality can be addressed by implementing appropriate service inspection and public reporting regimes alongside funding mechanisms. However, these can often be costly or ineffective in enforcing quality standards, and there is a growing conviction that carefully designed explicit incentives have a central role to play in securing desired levels of effectiveness in public services, particularly as the scope and timeliness of data on quality improves. This chapter examines incentives for quality specifically in the context of health care, where there has arisen widespread concern with poor quality (Institute of Medicine, 2001). However, the principles identified are likely to be of relevance to any public service for which usable quality metrics are available.

To date there have been remarkably few experiments with incentives designed explicitly to improve health care quality. Instead, research effort has concentrated mainly on the *implicit* implications of payment mechanisms for quality. However, payers have recently begun to recognize the potential for securing quality improvements by directly rewarding measured quality. The chapter first briefly reviews existing evidence on incentives in health care, and then reviews the relevant elements of the principal/agent model, which acts as a good framework for designing quality incentives. The chapter then discusses the development of quality incentives in UK primary care, particularly a contract for general practitioners introduced in April 2004 that marks one of the most ambitious attempts to incentivize health care quality to date. We discuss the opportunities and risks associated with the contract, and conclude with some more general observations on the design of quality incentives.

7.2 Incentives in health care

All providers of health care – in whatever institutional setting – operate within the context of a complex mix of contractual arrangements with patients, payers, insurers, governments and other relevant parties. However, even where there is a formal, explicit service contract (say between local government and provider), it is rare that it can even remotely anticipate all possible turns of events, and therefore the contract will to a greater or lesser extent be incomplete. One could argue that the development of the health care professions was a response to this incompleteness. In the words of Kenneth Arrow, 'when the market fails to achieve an optimal state, society will, to some extent at least, recognise the gap, and non-market social institutions will arise attempting to bridge it' (Arrow, 1963). The medical professions are the most celebrated of these non-market institutions in health care. One of their most important functions is to transmit to their members an ethic that seeks to transcend immediate contractual incentives.

Any formal contract embodies funding rules that define a set of explicit incentives. The most rudimentary of these is that a financial payment is conditional on delivering (or promising to deliver) some good or service. The vast majority of explicit incentives in health care are of this type. For physicians, three broad types of financial incentive have been predominant: fee for service, under which the provider is offered payments in proportion to the services offered; capitation, under which the provider is offered payments in proportion to the number of patients cared for (but not the services they receive); and salary, under which payment is unrelated to any explicit measure of activity or coverage.

Whatever the payment mechanism, physicians have almost always operated under some sort of incentive to deliver good quality in health care. In antiquity, Chinese villages are said to have paid their doctors only when healthy. In contemporary health systems, reputation for poor quality care can pose an obvious threat to a physician's livelihood. Systems of accreditation offer a rudimentary incentive for physicians to conform to some very basic quality standards. And more generally a requirement to conform to professional standards can offer a powerful incentive to offer high quality care.

There is a large research literature in US health care on the impact on quality of payment mechanisms (Miller and Luft, 1994). This literature has sought preeminently to evaluate the theoretical prediction that capitation will deliver cost-containment more effectively than fee-for-service or salary. A strand of this literature has also examined the theoretical prediction that (broadly speaking) fee-for-service will produce levels of treatment (and perhaps quality) in excess of socially desirable levels, while capitation and salary may lead to under-treatment and various forms of 'quality skimping' (Hillman *et al.*, 1989; Miller and Luft, 1994; Kralewski *et al.*, 2000).

One normally thinks of incentives in terms of financial payments, either to an individual or organization. However, it is worth bearing in mind that a number of other rewards, either implicit or explicit, may be incorporated into an incentive scheme, such as professional advancement, an 'easy time', increased professional autonomy and freedom from inspection, prestige and reputation, and simply intrinsic satisfaction in a job well done.

The impact on quality is a central design concern for health care incentives. Some have argued that, particularly in the US market-based system, there is a business case for quality, in the sense that providers might naturally wish to provide high quality care without direct incentives to do so, in order to minimize costs and increase market share. However, this effect appears to be weak, and there is a growing belief that providers therefore need explicit incentives to promote clinical quality (Casalino *et al.*, 2003; Leatherman *et al.*, 2003). This requirement is likely to be even stronger in a non-market system. Yet, in contrast to the work on implicit incentives, there is to date little research evidence on explicit quality incentives in health care, although a literature is starting to emerge (Dudley *et al.*, 1998; Bazzoli, 2004).

There are a number of reasons for the slow progress. First, and most obviously, measuring quality is still in its infancy. Second, even where measurement is feasible, quality incentives are still relatively rare and where they have been tried they are not a large component of overall remuneration. To have discernible results, an incentive scheme may require the commitment of considerable financial resources, with uncertain implications for outcomes. Third, few of the schemes that have been tried have been properly evaluated. The scope for using randomized experimentation is limited, given practical and ethical considerations, evaluation of voluntary schemes is intrinsically difficult because participants are self-selected, while evaluation of compulsory schemes is difficult because there are no controls. Furthermore, evaluation should embrace unintended side-effects, such as neglect of unmeasured quality or longer-term outcomes, by definition a complex task.

7.3 The principal-agent paradigm

The principal-agent approach, introduced in Chapter 2, provides a robust and now widely studied set of models for generating testable predictions about how individuals will respond to incentives, and consequently how incentive schemes can be designed (Prendergast, 1999). Agency theory has proved a rich source of insights into contractual relationships within health care and the consequent behaviour of professionals and the health care system as a whole (McGuire, 2000). In its most rudimentary form the principal-agent model examines the relationship between a single principal (the patient) and a single agent (the physician).

However, the models have been extended in various ways to make them more relevant to real life settings. Some of the most important, from a health care perspective, are: rewarding more than one dimension of performance; incentives in the form of 'tournaments' (in which performance relative to peers, rather than absolute performance is rewarded); the extension to multiple principals; and the use of non-pecuniary rewards. In addition, the use of incentives for situations in which outcomes depend on collaboration between independent agents is likely to be important for many aspects of health care, particularly for patients with chronic conditions. The principal-agent models that look at 'multi-tasking' seem particularly relevant to health care quality incentives. The strength of incentives attached to what can be measured may need to be moderated in order that they do not squeeze out the inevitably large aspects of health care that are not measured (Dewatripont *et al.*, 1997).

Three fundamental components of the economist's agency model are:

- the nature of information availability to the two parties;
- the objectives of principal and agent, and the extent to which they are aligned;
- the nature and strength of the incentive instrument.

There is great variability among different health care settings in the nature and importance of these considerations. However, Conrad and Christansen (2004) offer a general model of how quality incentives can readily be integrated into this conventional view of physician agency.

In most agency models, it is usually assumed that the agent's objectives are fixed. However, there is considerable evidence that clinicians' objectives are to some extent malleable. In particular, the health care professional may yield benefits simply from delivering a high quality of health care to the patient. Given a favourable organizational culture, therefore, it is possible that clinicians' objectives could be even more closely aligned with the principal's, thereby reducing agency costs. Conversely, autonomy is important to professionals. Shifts towards explicit incentive mechanisms for monitoring and rewarding performance may signal a lack of trust, and therefore adversely affect the intrinsic motivations clinicians bring to the job (Frey, 1997).

If agents' objectives are malleable, there is therefore a case for seeking out methods of nurturing favourable attitudes, and ensuring that any incentive regime does not undermine them. In this respect, there may be important institutional arrangements (for example the role of professional self-regulation in safeguarding quality) that have developed over many years in response to the informational and non-market nature of health care. Any incentive regime must be designed with such arrangements in mind (Francois, 2000; Le Grand, 2002).

Finally, it is important to note that the design of incentive mechanisms is a complex undertaking. There are important decisions to be taken on issues such as:

- which measures of performance to use as a basis for rewards;
- how targets are to be set;
- over what time period is the scheme to operate;
- how performance measures along several dimensions are to be combined;
- how much reward is dependent on attainment;
- what is the link between improved performance and reward;
- what risk sharing arrangements are used?

In developing an incentive scheme, especially in a new setting, there may be a need for considerable experimentation in a least some of these considerations. More generally, almost all incentive schemes involve substantial managerial costs in the form of writing and monitoring the associated contracts.

7.4 UK General practitioners

General practitioners are a distinctive and important feature of UK health care. Most of them are independent contractors with the National Health Service (NHS), and enjoy considerable autonomy of action. Every NHS patient must be registered with a GP, and GPs act as gatekeepers to NHS secondary care. Except in the case of emergencies, no patient can gain immediate access to specialist NHS care without a referral from a GP.

General practitioners have traditionally been offered a wide range of direct financial incentives, embodied in what became known as the 'Red Book' (the General Medical Services Statement of Fees and Allowances). This national contract offered a mix of remuneration methods, including fee for service (accounting for about 15 per cent of GP income), capitation (40 per cent), salary (30 per cent), and capital and IT (15 per cent). The fee-for-service element includes incentive payments for reaching coverage targets for services such as vaccination and cervical screening.

The traditional GP contract therefore sought to encourage important public health interventions, in the form of vaccinations, immunizations and screening, up to the point where the relevant payment threshold is reached. The capitation payments were crude, and risk adjustment (for age, rural patients and patients living in disadvantaged areas) was rudimentary. Although refusal of enrolment is formally disallowed, the capitation system could in principle have discouraged GPs from seeking out high-risk patients (Glennerster *et al.*, 1994). There has been, more generally, some concern at the low quality of primary care provision in disadvantaged areas.

In recent years about 30 per cent of GPs have opted out of the traditional contract to work under alternative locally negotiated arrangements known as Personal Medical Services (PMS) contracts, which are based mainly on salary but can vary according to local circumstances. There have also been additional primary care incentive payments for practices, outside the traditional GP contract, for example for prescribing and access.

General practitioners are therefore used to working within an incentivized environment (Scott, 2001). One of the most important schemes in which they played a central role was the GP fundholding experiment, under which general practices that volunteered to participate were given annual budgets with which they were expected to purchase most routine (non-emergency) secondary care and pharmaceuticals for their patients. The fundholding scheme ran from 1991 to 1998, and by the end of the period over 50 per cent of NHS patients were cared for by a fundholding general practice (Audit Commission, 1996). A comprehensive analysis of the fundholding scheme suggests that fundholders reduced inpatient procedures by about 5 per cent relative to non-fundholders, and also secured lower waiting times for their patients (Dusheiko *et al.*, 2005).

More recently, a primary care quality improvement scheme was tested in East Kent over a three-year period. The majority of local GPs enrolled in a programme that required them to meet challenging chronic disease management targets across 13 conditions. In return for enrolment, the GPs were offered £3,000 per GP per annum. If they failed to meet the targets for all 13 conditions the financial incentive had to be repaid. An evaluation of this scheme concluded that it had led to major changes in the management of chronic diseases in the East Kent area (Spooner *et al.*, 2001). It also suggested that the success of the project had been partly due to its multi-faceted approach; it included quality standards, audit with feedback, leadership, education and financial incentives. Aligning the management priorities with doctors' and nurses' own professional values, and preserving the autonomy of professionals were also seen as important.

7.5 The 2004 GP contract

The East Kent scheme influenced a major change to primary care incentives embodied in an entirely new GP contract, introduced in April 2004 (Department of Health, 2003a). The new contract incorporated a number of elements, including a simplification of remuneration rules, a fairer capitation scheme and a major injection of expenditure into primary care (approximately £1.9 billion annually, an increase of 33 per cent over three years). A central element of the new contract was a system of quality incentives known as the Quality and Outcomes Framework (QOF). In the first year, about £1.3 billion was distributed on the basis of quality measures, accounting for around 18 per cent of GP income. This is expected to increase markedly in future years. The scheme has been developed in close negotiation with physicians, and was approved by 79.4 per cent in a ballot of GPs, with a response rate of 70 per cent.

In its initial form, the QOF incentive scheme used 146 indicators of quality across seven areas of practice, as summarized in Table 7.1. In each area of practice a certain number of quality 'points' are available for attainment of certain levels of quality. A maximum of 1,050 points are available. The most heavily weighted area of practice is the clinical, for which 550 points are available. Other areas include indicators for practice organization (184 points) and patient experience (100 points). The clinical indicators are in turn distributed across ten domains of care, as shown in Table 7.2, which indicates that the three most heavily weighted domains are coronary heart disease (121 points), hypertension (105) and diabetes (99).

An example of the points scheme for hypertension is shown in Table 7.3. Five indicators are used, covering structure (clinical records), process (diagnosis and initial management) and outcome. For most indicators there is a lower limit (at which points can start to be earned), and an upper limit at which all available points are secured. The number of points available for each indicator is shown in

Table 7.1 The GP contract: numbers of performance indicators and points at risk

Area of practice	PIs	Points
Clinical	76	550
Organizational	56	184
Additional services	10	36
Patient experience	4	100
Holistic care (balanced clinical care)	–	100
Quality payments (balanced quality)	–	30
Access bonus	–	50
Maximum	146	1,050

Table 7.2 The GP contract: the clinical indicators

Domain	PIs	Points
CHD including LVD etc.	15	121
Stroke or transient ischaemic attack	10	31
Cancer	2	12
Hypothyroidism	2	8
Diabetes	18	99
Hypertension	5	105
Mental health	5	41
Asthma	7	72
COPD	8	45
Epilepsy	4	16
Clinical maximum	76	550

the right hand column. So, for example, for indicator BP2, points start to accumulate once the notes of 25 per cent of patients with hypertension record smoking status at least once. A maximum of ten points is secured when the smoking status of 90 per cent of such patients is recorded.

7.6 Assessment

The 2004 GP contract is one of the most ambitious attempts yet to incorporate quality incentives into paying for health care. It embodies a number of important strengths, in line with the prescriptions of the principal/agent model. Most importantly, it seeks to reward 'what matters', in the form of the structure, processes and outcome of health care. The scheme has been developed in close collaboration with physicians who have sought to apply evidence-based principles to the selection of performance indicators. In particular, efforts have been made to ensure that the indicators are consistent with national clinical guidelines that are now promulgated in the form of 'National Service Frameworks' for clinical areas such as diabetes and coronary heart disease (Department of Health, 2003a).

Table 7.3 The GP contract: the hypertension indicators, scale and points at risk

	Min	Max	Points
Clinical records BP 1. The practice can produce a register of patients with established hypertension			9
Diagnosis and initial management BP 2. The percentage of patients with hypertension whose notes record smoking status at least once	25	90	10
BP 3. The percentage of patients with hypertension who smoke, whose notes contain a record that smoking cessation advice has been offered at least once	25	90	10
Ongoing management BP 4. The percentage of patients with hypertension in which there is a record of the blood pressure in the past nine months	25	90	20
BP 5. The percentage of patients with hypertension in whom the last blood pressure (in the last nine months) is 150/90 or less	25	70	56

The structure of the scheme offers some important advances. The use of a 'balanced scorecard' seeks to reflect the relative importance of different primary care activities in terms of its impact on health. By basing remuneration on an aggregate score, GPs remain free to decide on their own priorities, and to seek out improvements where they have comparative advantage. Many of the distortions associated with more piecemeal schemes may therefore be avoided. The scheme rewards practices (rather than individual physicians), so is likely to encourage teamwork and peer review. Furthermore, in contrast to many previous incentive schemes, the contract offers tangible financial rewards that are a significant component of GP remuneration. Finally, there is a commitment to review and update the incentive scheme, an essential undertaking given the uncertainty about exactly how it will work, and the constant emergence of new clinical evidence.

Notwithstanding these apparent strengths, it is also important to note some potential risks associated with the GP contract. First, primary care clinical practice is enormously heterogeneous and – notwithstanding the deployment of 146 indicators – there remain large areas of activity that are not covered at all by the incentive scheme, or are treated inadequately. There is therefore a risk that some of the important primary care activity not covered by the scheme will be downgraded or even abandoned. More generally, it is quite possible that the scheme will distort practice in unintended ways. Some of the targets will be too easy, others too tough, and the balance between different areas of activity, reflected in the distribution of points, may be inappropriate.

For example, clinical practice associated with mental health is allotted a mere

41 points, a figure that seems at odds with the importance of mental health problems in primary care activity. The contract documentation notes that 'it was not possible to develop indicators that could be rewarded in this type of framework for many of the most important aspects of mental health care. Mental health care is however an example of a number of conditions where some markers of good clinical care have been included in the organizational indicators.' It will be very important to evaluate the impact of the scheme on patients in this and other less well represented clinical domains.

More generally, an urgent role for evaluation is to check whether the scheme adversely affects some of the 'softer' attributes of primary care that are generally acknowledged to affect quality, such as continuity of care, or discourages collaborative actions with other public services (such as education and social services) that may have important long-term public health benefits, but are not directly rewarded.

As with all incentive schemes, there is a danger that the new contract will discourage clinical practice in challenging localities. Formally, GPs are supposed to show no discrimination in which patients they accept onto their lists, and are not allowed to cream skim healthy or compliant patients. However, in practice there exist means whereby GPs can discourage enrolment of patients that may adversely affect performance measures. Perhaps even more importantly, the scheme may not do enough to encourage GPs to set up practice in disadvantaged areas. The initial implementation sought to adjust performance measures for local environmental difficulties by weighting payments in the clinical domain according to measures of local disease prevalence. An important evaluation task is to determine whether these adjustments are operating effectively and fairly.

As with all funding formulae, there is an ever-present danger of gaming and misrepresentation. Some of the performance measures appear to be particularly vulnerable to gaming. For example, in the patient experience domain, 30 points are allocated in part according to whether the average length of consultation with patients exceeds eight minutes. The potential for misrepresentation is large, given that the scheme relies mostly on self-reported data. This is a critical area that needs very careful attention at an early stage. Even if fraud is rare, a perception among GPs that there is widespread inaccuracy in reporting may fatally undermine the scheme. There is therefore a need for a cost-effective audit regime, combined with encouragement of a professional culture that will not tolerate misdemeanours.

The scheme requires constant monitoring and reviewing. The key tasks are to identify unintended (and unwanted) consequences, and to incorporate new clinical evidence as it emerges. The design of the scheme is a major achievement in itself, but careful updating must be a central priority. In doing so, a balance will have to be struck between maintaining continuity (so that GPs can plan future initiatives with some certainty) and responding to new evidence (so avoiding ossification).

This discussion implies that the policing, monitoring and reviewing of the incentive scheme may impose a substantial managerial burden. Traditionally,

UK health care has reported very low managerial costs, and there is a reluctance among the public and politicians to recognize that management activity may make an important contribution to clinical quality. Yet there is a clear need for investment in information technology, consultation and managerial processes if the full benefits of the QOF scheme are to be secured.

Finally, perhaps the most uncertain element of any incentive scheme is the extent to which it might undermine the professional ethic and moral of physicians. As noted above, the emergence of the medical profession arose in part from a need to guide the actions of physicians in circumstances where there is no direct remuneration. Will such a heavy reliance on explicit use of incentives lead to a diminution of the willingness to respond in the best interests of patients when not directly rewarded (Frey, 1997)?

In the light of these comments, the evaluation of the scheme is a high priority, although at the time of writing results are not available. Evaluation will be methodologically challenging as there is little in the way of a quantitative baseline against which progress can be monitored. For many of the clinical areas covered by the scheme, implementation represents the first attempt to collect data systematically across the whole NHS. Furthermore, there has been no possibility of any piloting or randomization, so any evaluation will have to rely on observational data, and all the associated perils. Yet there are also clearly major opportunities to evaluate natural experiments, for example when the weight on a particular indicator is changed.

Evaluation should also, in principle, test for unintended side-effects of the scheme, the nature of which – almost by definition – cannot be predicted with any confidence, and for which there may be little quantitative evidence. It should also address issues of data reliability and managerial effort that have in the past proved resistant to reliable evaluation. Notwithstanding these methodological challenges, the scope and the power of the contract mean that it offers an unprecedented laboratory for evidence on the use of quality incentives in public service funding mechanisms.

7.7 Discussion

The design of incentives intended explicitly to improve service quality is a complex undertaking. Some of the priorities for future policy development include:

- carefully embedding such incentive schemes within the broader design of the public service system;
- scrutinizing economic theory and the existing evidence base from other sectors to identify pointers for improving the design of incentives, such as:
  - determining the most appropriate measures on which to base incentives;
  - identifying the optimal size, power and degree of difficulty of incentives;
  - achieving appropriate risk sharing, taking account of the degree of uncertainty and noise in the measurement of performance;

  - studying the motivations of physicians, including career concerns and professional motivations, and building these features into the incentives;
  - examining how team or group incentives can best be deployed;
- developing better measures of quality and better risk adjustment methodology;
- engaging with the relevant professions to ensure that incentives will challenge but at the same time resonate with the professionals charged with delivering services;
- enhancing the research evidence base to embrace careful evaluation of specific schemes (such as the GP contract) and the analysis of other natural experiments.

Specifically, the success (or otherwise) of the GP contract is likely to be highly conditional on the nature of other important influences on health care quality, such as:

Guidelines: is good clinical practice disseminated rapidly and effectively to front line professionals?
Information: is the information base adequate to measure quality for the purposes of informing professional actions and acting as the basis for rewards?
Culture: is the professional and managerial culture aligned with the quality objectives of the health system?
Managerial capacity: is there capacity in place to set appropriate targets and avoid gaming, misrepresentation and other perverse outcomes?
Clinical capacity: is the professional capacity in place to act on information and secure quality improvements?
Institutional arrangements: what is the institutional context within which health care is delivered, including consideration of issues such as market structure, organizational ownership and the regulatory regime.
Cross-agency working: are other instruments in place to ensure that the health system works as intended with other agencies, such as social care and housing?
Research: are there mechanisms in place to ensure that incentives systems are properly evaluated and lessons can be quickly transmitted?

In many of these respects the climate of the NHS appears favourable (Smith, 2002). The issues that give cause for greatest concern are the reliability of performance data and the managerial and research capacity for monitoring and refining the GP scheme.

The GP contract is an extraordinarily ambitious quality improvement initiative. Although it embodies a number of risks, many of its design features accord well with the principles of incentive design as set out in the principal/agent literature. Provided the contract is developed and evaluated with care, and necessary adjustments made as experience is accumulated, it offers the prospect of enormous gains in the quality of primary health care in the UK, and offers the potential for informing policy in many other types of public services.

8 The political economy of formula funding

8.1 Introduction

The essence of formula funding is that it seeks systematically to resolve competing claims for limited resources. It may appear that, by delegating the rules for setting budgets to the technical domain, formula funding circumvents the political problem. However, Glennerster *et al.* (2000) suggest a three-layered motivation for the development of funding formulae: a long-term principled or moral predisposition towards fairness; a medium-term concern with political expediency, for example seeking to minimize political conflict; and a short-term preoccupation with feasibility and practical concerns. They conclude that 'devising, implementing, and justifying formulae is an intensely political process' (Glennerster *et al.*, 2000: 50).

Funding formulae are put in place by governments and other payers to secure policy objectives. It is therefore imperative that the designer of a funding mechanism understands the payer's underlying objectives, and ensures consistency with any formulae recommended. If the formulae fail in this rudimentary respect they are unlikely to last long, however technically refined they might be. Policy judgements having important implications for system design are needed at all stages in the development of funding formula.

Hitherto, this book has implicitly assumed an enlightened payer wishing to design a payment mechanism that furthers the society's objectives in respect of its public services. However, enlightenment may not be the only principle informing the payer's motivations, and a more self-interested payer may wish to use a funding formula to further its own interests. Moreover, there are numerous actors associated with the funding of public services beyond the immediate payer who may seek to influence the deployment of funding formulae, including politicians, bureaucrats, local governments, providers, interest groups and the general public. Depending on the institutional arrangements in place, such actors may play an important role in influencing, constraining or enabling the design and implementation of funding formulae. Indeed, the payer may use the formula funding mechanism to reconcile these various interests. In short, there is a potentially rich political economy underlying the design of public service funding mechanisms.

This book is concerned mainly with the technical aspects of developing funding formulae. However, in the light of their fundamentally political nature, this chapter offers some comments on the political environment within which such formulae are developed. The next section discusses the various forms the payer's objectives – both overt and covert – might take. Section 8.3 then explains the flexibility a payer has when designing any funding mechanism to secure those objectives. Finally, the chapter examines the role of formula funding as a cost-effective way of resolving the bargaining process between the payer and other interest groups. It is important to emphasize that this is not a comprehensive treatment of the topic. For more extended discussions of the political economy of formula funding from a UK perspective, see the valuable treatments by Glennerster *et al.* (2000) and McLean (2005).

8.2 The payer's objectives

The formulaic approach to funding has become popular not just because it leads to more efficient and equitable outcomes than other methods (although – for all its limitations – it usually does), but because it serves the payer's more general objectives. Of course, those objectives often include equity and efficiency criteria. But they may also include important political considerations such as: allowing the criteria for funding to be set out explicitly; treating the budget-setting process systematically; avoiding the need for case by case scrutiny of budgets; binding politicians, bureaucrats and other parties to a set of distributional rules; and more generally economizing on political effort. Glennerster *et al.* (2000) also suggest that – in a unitary state such as the UK – national governments need to demonstrate that they are treating localities even-handedly in order to retain the allegiance of their elected representatives and to demonstrate that they are a national party.

McLean (2005) discusses at length the political context of formula funding in the UK. He cites a government minister, whose concern was manifestly not with the technical content of the payment mechanism. Instead, the principal interest is on the 'exemplifications' – the impact of alternative technical choices on the finances of individual English local governments (McLean, 2005: 127). The distributional consequences of formulae often have profound political ramifications, and it would be a very brave (or foolhardy) minister that made decisions on formulae purely on the basis of technical advice.

The interest in exemplifications arises because, whatever the strength of the science underlying a formula, the payer almost always enjoys considerable flexibility in the mode of implementation. Ward and John (1999) and John and Ward (2001) find that under a Conservative government the English local government grant system appeared systematically to favour marginal constituencies, and so-called 'flagship' Conservative authorities (but not Conservative local governments in general). They argue that the formulae mechanisms are sufficiently opaque to make such manipulation feasible. Gibson (1998) examines the case of inner London education services, and concludes that 'there was pure (that is, unadulterated) political manipulation of the Education [funding formula] by the Conservative government in 1990' in order to favour inner London authorities.

In the extreme, the payer can supplement any formula with non-formulaic elements, or additional formulae that target specific classes of budget holders. Of course this may not always be in the payer's interests, as it suggests special treatment for the beneficiaries. However, the political consequences of an explicit extra-formula payment may outweigh any negative consequences. For example, for many years the three island local governments in Scotland received additional grants in the form of a 'special islands needs allowance' (SINA). The rationale for SINA payments was never explicitly articulated. The amounts involved were not based on any scientific evidence or formula, and appeared to be well in excess of any sum justified by additional needs or costs associated with island status. SINA was therefore probably associated with the payer's desire to neutralize the pressure from the islands for special treatment within the formal local government finance system. The cost was low (0.4 per cent of total expenditure in Scottish local government), though the amounts were important for the recipient local governments. For some time SINA succeeded in removing island status from the annual budgetary debate. It was only when the mainland local governments with some island communities began to question the apparently favourable treatment of the three island local governments that the issue of SINA was reviewed (Scottish Parliament Local Government Committee, 2002). In 2001 SINA was extended to three other local governments with significant island populations, and the amounts calculated on a more formulaic basis (Scottish Executive, 2004).

It is sometimes the case that the payer holds objectives that it does not wish to make explicit, giving rise to tensions with the stated objectives of a funding formula. For example, Glennerster *et al.* (2000) comment at length on the baroque system of subsidies to the finance of local government housing in England, and claim that the national government may not have wanted the wide range of rent variations that would have arisen from the pure application of the formula. The method used to damp year-on-year changes in budgets was deployed to moderate the variations, and therefore served to obscure the logic underlying the mechanism (Glennerster *et al.*, 2000: 119). Indeed Glennerster *et al.* (2000) quote a ministry official who claims the payer could 'make music' with the budgetary allocations. They hypothesize that – based on the outcomes achieved – the payer's true objective of the housing subsidy grant was not the pursuit of equity or efficiency, but to minimize the total public expenditure on subsidized housing, net of any welfare payments made to tenants (Glennerster *et al.*, 2000: 127). This objective was not articulated explicitly.

In short, it usually requires only modest levels of ingenuity for a payer to be able to secure almost any desired distributional outcome, while nominally adhering to the use of formulae. Of course, the extent to which payers are prepared to use this freedom varies. And if a payer's choice brazenly contradicts technical consensus it runs the risk of exposure by the media or parliamentary scrutiny. However, debate on funding formulae will usually appear arcane. Public scrutiny therefore rarely leads to vigorous public debate or definitive judgements on the payer's choices.

8.2.1 Case study: implementation of funding formulae for English health care

The work on the English health care formulae described in Section 5.6.2 was the result of a long process of painstaking analysis by the study team and careful scrutiny by its advisory groups. It resulted in formulae that redistributed a large volume of NHS funds between health authorities. For example, Carr-Hill *et al.* (1997) estimate that in 1996/97, out of a total budget of £20,896 million allocated using the new formula, £776 million (3.7 per cent) was redistributed from low needs to high needs areas on the basis of the needs adjustments. This represented a net swing of £261 million from the previous national formula in favour of poorer localities, a figure that in some ways can be considered a measure of the benefits of the improved information and methodology deployed by the York team.

In order that the study team and its advisors could concentrate purely on technical issues, the bulk of the analytic work on developing the formulae was deliberately undertaken in ignorance of its likely redistributive effect. Implementation of the formulae was nevertheless always likely to result in a substantial shift in allocations away from wealthy areas towards more deprived areas. The former tend to return Conservative members of parliament, the latter Labour representatives. Thus, to the Conservative national government in power at that time, the results were politically uncomfortable. However, in contrast to its response to the preceding review of the funding formula, which it considered unacceptable and therefore amended, the national government accepted the findings and committed itself to implementing the results with effect from 1995.

Strictly speaking, the models developed by the York team indicated the need for *inpatient* services, which account for only 45 per cent of total health care expenditure. Therefore, the questions arise: in what proportions should the acute and psychiatric models be combined, and – in the absence of any empirical data – how should the non-inpatient services be treated? In the event, the national ministry broke down the national health care budget into three classes of programme: acute, psychiatric and 'other'. Acute inpatients and outpatients and a range of other services, such as maternity, were allocated using the acute model to adjust for health care needs, and they accounted for 64 per cent of the allocation. Psychiatric services, accounting for 12 per cent of the budget, were allocated according to the psychiatric model. The range of other services – which included community services and mental handicap services, and accounted for 24 per cent of expenditure, was allocated with no needs adjustment of any sort.

The decision to apply no needs adjustment to 24 per cent of services was a departure from the approach adopted in the Review of RAWP, which applied an index of acute inpatient need to most health care expenditure. Peacock and Smith (1995) sought to highlight the importance of the change. For example, using the data shown in Table 8.1, the combined index of relative needs in Central Manchester is calculated as

$$129.7 \times 0.64 + 208.1 \times 0.12 + 100.0 \times 0.24 = 132.0$$

To show the sensitivity of the results to the decision not to apply a needs weighting to 24 per cent of expenditure, Peacock and Smith calculate the measure of relative needs that results if the 24 per cent is instead allocated according to the York acute index. For Central Manchester, this 'full' formula is calculated as

$$129.7 \times 0.88 + 208.1 \times 0.12 = 139.1$$

Table 8.1 summarizes the results. Compared with the previous formula (a), the York acute index (b) distributed slightly more to needy areas, while the York psychiatric index (c) redistributed large sums towards high needs areas. The formula as implemented (d) diluted much of the impact of the York indices. If all expenditure were distributed on the basis of the York indices, high needs areas would receive more at the expense of low needs areas. Column (e) shows that if the acute model were used to allocate the 24 per cent, relative spending needs in Liverpool would increase by about 5 per cent. Those in Huntingdon and Mid Surrey would decrease by similar percentages. Thus the decision to apply no needs weighting to 24 per cent of expenditure – which was essentially a matter of judgement, given the lack of data on non-inpatient services, rather than technical choice – had the impact of diluting the redistributive influence of the new needs indices.

The unweighted 24 per cent policy decision received none of the intense analytic scrutiny that characterized the technical development of the formulae described in Section 5.6.2. Many commentators challenged the decision, and it received considerable media coverage at national and local level. Brennan and Carr-Hill (1996) argued that it is hard to justify, given the epidemiological evidence. This debate demonstrated a clear need to extend the methods developed in the inpatient sector to all aspects of health care. The national debate arising from the new formula also led the House of Commons Select Committee on Health to undertake an investigation into the resource allocation formula. The select committee is composed of members of parliament of all major political parties and is charged with scrutinizing the health policy of the national government. It sought evidence from the study team and a range of independent experts as well as the secretary of state for health. The unweighted 24 per cent was a particular source of concern to the committee, and, when questioned about the issue, the Secretary of State made an undertaking to introduce a needs weighting for all services (House of Commons Health Committee, 1995).

Subsequently, under the guidance of a Resource Allocation Group set up by the government, needs indices were steadily extended to virtually 100 per cent of all health care expenditure, with the result of skewing finances further towards high needs areas. It is noteworthy that the incoming Labour government

Table 8.1 Per capita needs as a percentage of the national average in English four health authorities

| Health authority | Percentage of national average | | | | |
	Previous needs index (a)	York acute index (b)	York psychiatric index (c)	Formula as implemented (d)	Formula with 100% needs weight (e)
Liverpool	114.7	121.8	146.0	119.7	124.7
Manchester	122.7	129.7	208.1	132.0	139.1
Huntingdon	89.0	86.7	63.4	87.1	83.9
Mid Surrey	89.9	82.2	73.6	85.4	81.2

Source: Peacock and Smith, 1995.

of 1997 sought to skew allocations even more strongly towards high needs areas by introducing a new equity criterion of 'contributing to the avoidable reduction of health inequalities'. This was discussed in detail in Chapter 4, and has the effect of directing health care finance specifically towards areas with high rates of premature mortality.

8.3 The payer's choices

The reason the payer enjoys such marked flexibility is that there are usually numerous judgements to be made in implementing a funding mechanism that transcend purely technical considerations. The payer's degrees of freedom include:

- the choice of analytic methods;
- the choice of what constitutes a 'legitimate' influence on spending need;
- the extent to which formula simplicity should be pursued at the expense of sensitivity to local needs;
- the extent to which known inadequacies in data are ignored, or the use of potentially useful data sources ruled out;
- the speed of implementation of a new formula.

These are considered in turn.

8.3.1 Analytic method

An informed payer will almost certainly wish to compare the distributional implications implied by alternative technical choices. One of the central roles of the 'exemplifications' of funding mechanisms is to demonstrate the implications of such choices. A particularly striking example was the review of finance to Scottish health authorities by Sir John Arbuthnott. The original proposals were based on an extensive statistical analysis of health care utilization within Scotland (Scottish Executive Health Department, 1999). However, commentary on the proposals was hostile, crystallized in the report of the parliamentary health committee, which highlighted the concerns summarized in Box 8.1.

The Scottish government appeared to accept at least some of these concerns. Sir John's final report retreated from the use of empirical statistical analysis, and instead recommended the use of an index of health care needs that embraced many generally accepted influences on health care needs, but which was not based on an empirical estimate of the link with health care expenditure (Scottish Executive Health Department, 2000).

This is not to say that empirical methods are always to be preferred. Sometimes the analytic or data complexities of deriving an empirical formula are a fundamental cause for concern. For example, from time to time the UK government has ruled out the use of regression methods to develop local government spending assessments, on the grounds that these may be unduly influenced by a

Box 8.1 Summary of Parliamentary Health Committee Report on Sir John Arbuthnott's Report

'We welcome Arbuthnott's attempts to address the imbalance in resource allocation in the NHS. And we acknowledge its efforts to take into account issues relating to remoteness, deprivation and gender when doing so.

'But while the committee recognises this substantial progress towards tackling inequality we have highlighted the need for further work to be done before the new formulae can be implemented with confidence.

'Our report details serious limitations with Arbuthnott's methodology and the formulae and data used to slice up the NHS cake in Scotland. Our particular concerns include:

- that the actual overall re-distribution of funds proposed by the report represents less than 2 per cent of the entire NHS budget and does not reflect adequately the real differences in health service needs
- the use of data on GP and community care services which does not adequately include Scotland's most deprived areas
- a lack of flexibility which fails to take account of the distinctive needs of many of our island communities
- that the use of only one year's data may contribute to inconsistencies in the way in which outwardly similar areas, such as the Borders and Dumfries & Galloway, are treated differently.

'Our recommendations include:

- in view of the ongoing work that still needs to be done, that the implementation of the Arbuthnott Report be postponed until further information and research is available
- that a progress report with a clear timetable for dealing with the inherent problems highlighted by the committee be issued to the Parliament by September 2000
- that the Executive establish a standing group to monitor and review the allocation formula to develop a fairer distribution over time, in a clear and open fashion.

'The committee does recognise the need to develop a simpler and fairer way to allocate NHS resources. The system should be based on clear aims and straightforward methods that will give the people of Scotland improved and fairer shares of their health service.

'But at the same time, we are determined that practical steps to reduce health inequalities and improve resource allocation, outwith the remit of this inquiry, should not be delayed.'

Source: Scottish Parliament (1999).

small number of high spending localities. As Chapter 5 explained, there are sometimes good technical reasons why this may be sensible. But equally the choice has at times appeared to reflect a desire to diminish the influence on grants-in-aid of certain classes of local government.

8.3.2 What is legitimate?

The designation of what constitute 'legitimate' risk adjustment factors is often a particularly sensitive issue for payers. A relatively uncontentious example was the decision by Stockholm County Council to ignore the statistically significant (but negative) coefficient of 'immigrant' status on health care expenditure, discussed in Section 4.5.1. There was consensus that this empirical finding may have been the result of poor access to health care among immigrant groups, and should not be replicated in the risk adjustment process.

In contrast, the finding described in Section 5.6.1 that population density had a statistically significant (and positive) effect on expenditure on children's social services presented the payer with a more finely balanced judgement to make. Did the effect result from systematically higher provision in urban areas, or from some unmeasured additional needs in urban areas? Although in such circumstances a payer may seek out expert judgement and invoke evidence from other sources, it is difficult to envisage the payer being entirely unaffected by the political consequences of including the contentious factor in the formula.

8.3.3 Simplicity or sensitivity?

A payer can make a formula steadily more intricate by choosing to introduce more variables as risk adjustment factors into a funding formula. If the formula is based on statistical methods, this will usually result in budgetary assessments that are closer to current spending than those based on more parsimonious models. As more variables are introduced, there is a greater chance that the specific 'quirks' of individual local governments can be captured by the statistical analysis. As discussed in Chapter 5, maximizing the statistical explanatory power of the funding formula should not in itself be an objective. Rather the task should be to capture legitimate causes of expenditure variation. Whether additional variables are legitimate influences on expenditure is a matter for case-by-case judgement over which the payer has ultimate control.

Indeed a feature of the political debates about funding formulae is a persistent tension between the technical accuracy of formulae (intended to promote efficiency and equity) and a desire for simplicity (intended to promote political accountability) (Sheldon, 1997; House of Commons Environment Committee, 1998). Politicians and the media frequently, and reasonably, bemoan the complexity of many funding mechanisms, and its adverse impact on the payer's accountability. Indeed, the ability of the payer to 'make music' with funding mechanisms attests to the accountability problem. At the same time, interest groups, politicians and localities also frequently complain that local 'special circumstances' are not accommodated within a funding mechanism. This lack of sensitivity to local spending needs usually implies a wish to search for more intricate formulae which would reflect the special circumstances more satisfactorily.

8.3.4 Choice of data sources

An implicit adjustment to a formula can be effected by the payer turning a blind eye to known inadequacies of a chosen formula. For example, capitation funding of UK general practitioners is based on the size of the 'list' of patients that are registered with them. Until recently, the mechanisms to ensure that the registration of patients changes when they die or move to another general practitioner were very unreliable and slow, and as a result there was historically a great deal of 'list inflation', particularly in inner city areas where there are large disadvantaged populations. This implied that, relative to the rest of the country, inner city general practitioners were probably receiving payments in excess of their entitlement.

However, this outcome suited the payer's purpose, as recruitment of general practitioners was in any case difficult in such areas, and any improvement in list counting would have entailed a shift in resources out of the inner cities. This situation was not addressed until the late 1990s, and necessitated the design of a new 'needs-based' risk adjusted capitation formula for general practitioners (Department of Health, 2003b). In the same vein, the Spanish national government chose not to introduce any risk adjustment into its regional health care funding mechanism, in spite of manifest variations in needs between the regions (Consejo de Politica Fiscal y Financiera, 1998).

A particularly important but rarely discussed freedom available to payers is the adjustment made for local price variations. Section 5.5 mentioned the arcane but extremely important Medicare county adjustment, which amends national payment rates according to local health care expenditure levels, thereby appearing to reward local providers for profligate delivery of health care as well as legitimate variations in input prices.

A more neutral stance would be to adjust for local price levels, independent of local health care expenditure, as attempted in English local government, where an 'area cost adjustment' is made on the basis of variations in input prices (principally wages) outside the public services. This methodology secures independence from the wages paid by local public services. However, there are numerous policy judgements that affect its impact on budgetary allocations. For example, should the price variation be modelled at the local government level (in which case statistical noise leads to implausible 'cliff edges' between adjacent jurisdictions), or at a regional level (in which case important intra-regional variations may be missed)? And what size should the chosen regions be?

McLean (2005: 143) highlights the intensely political issues surrounding implementation of the area cost adjustment. In particular, there are important judgements on the extent to which local governments as employers are at the mercy of local market conditions, or are able to pay according to national wage scales. And there are debates about the types of private sector workers that are comparable with public service workers, such as teachers, firefighters and nurses. The alternative exemplifications emerging from different technical choices give rise to large changes in expenditure allocations, and an independent review of the area cost adjustment has never been implemented in full (Elliott *et al.*, 1996).

8.3.5 Damping mechanisms

Many systems of formula funding have attached intricate damping mechanisms that seek to reduce the year-on-year changes in an organization's budget. Because of such mechanisms the original recommendations of the NHS Resource Allocation Working Party took 15 years to take full effect. In the same vein, Louis *et al.* (2003) describe widespread use of 'hold harmless' mechanisms in US federal formula funding, under which states are guaranteed a certain minimum budgetary allocation, regardless of the outcome of the funding formulae. Frequently, the hold harmless figure is 100 per cent of the current budget, suggesting that (in cash terms) no state loses finance from its historical expenditure levels as a result of the implementation of a formula. Such damping serves two principal purposes: reducing political turbulence and reducing local organizational problems associated with big changes in funding.

The English NHS uses a typical 'pace of change' policy to make damping principles operational. It retains an explicit objective of moving over time towards budgetary targets based purely on risk-adjusted capitation formulae. However, the pace of change mechanism places explicit rules on the minimum and maximum annual changes in actual budgets that local administrations can receive as they move towards those targets, implying an important legacy of historical expenditure. An example from 2005 is shown in Box 8.2. There is little analytic contribution towards the pace of change policy (indeed it is difficult to envisage what that contribution might comprise), and the policy is a frankly political choice made by government ministers.

Compared to the debate over the calculation of the capitation formulae, damping mechanisms are the subject of remarkably little controversy or debate. Because of the 'asymmetry of pain' between administrations that gain and lose from a new formula, they are often implemented with some sort of hold harmless provision to protect losers from budgetary loss. It is therefore much easier to effect a rapid pace of change when the global programme budget is increasing rapidly. It is correspondingly difficult to move towards capitation targets when increases in the global programme budget, or programme cuts are required. Yet paradoxically, as explained by Glennerster *et al.* (2000: 118), it is precisely under these circumstances that payers may find use of a formula most helpful, as it can help to reassure budget holders that the pain is being shared equitably.

A further apparently technical but highly influential detail on damping

Box 8.2 Pace of change policy in the English National Health Service, 2005

The national ministry makes annual budgetary allocations for health care to local health authorities known as Primary Care Trusts (PCTs). These budgets are built up from risk-adjusted capitation formulae applied to four sub-programmes, comprising hospital and community services (77 per cent), drug prescribing (13 per cent), primary care (9 per cent) and HIV/AIDS (1 per cent). After aggregation, these formulae yield a 'target' budget. The actual budgetary allocations for financial years 2006/07 and 2007/08 were then moderated according to the following 'pace of change' rules.

(a) average PCT growth is 9.2 per cent in 2006/07 and 9.4 per cent in 2007/08, (in line with the global budget set by the national government)
(b) no PCT is more than 3.5 per cent under target by the end of 2007/08
(c) no PCT receives less than 8.1 per cent growth over the two years
(d) no PCT moves further under target or further over target in relation to their 2006/07 opening position.

The resultant budgets must adhere in aggregate to the global budget for the NHS set by the national government.

Source: Department of Health (2005).

mechanisms can be the level of aggregation of local budgets to which damping is applied. If, as in the example in Box 8.2, the damping is applied to aggregate budgets, a local administration might be subject to quite a large loss on an individual programme, but not qualify for protection from damping because gains on other programmes cancel out this loss. If on the other hand each programme is damped, the administration enjoys protection for each programme on which it loses. One of the motivations for the Barnett formula described below was a desire to move away from what was effectively a programme-by-programme damping mechanism for public expenditure in Scotland towards a mechanism based only on aggregate national budgets.

Damping mechanisms can be implicit, rather than the explicit examples noted above. The needs-based formula for children's personal social services described in Chapter 5 implied large transfers of funds out of London (Carr-Hill *et al.*, 1999). In the event, these shifts were strongly dampened by a newly formulated input price adjustment. The authors question whether the national (Labour) government 'would have searched for a revised area cost adjustment with such vigour if the results of the needs analysis had not implied such a marked shift of resources' (Smith *et al.*, 2001).

8.4 Formula funding as negotiation

Although an all-powerful payer can often secure virtually any desired outcome from formula funding, it is more often the case that political consensus and compromise will be a central feature of the development of funding formulae. Within England, local and central government enter into intricate annual negotiations on grant allocations in which coalitions of local authorities seek formula changes that will act in their favour. Securing technical excellence in formula design is not usually a high priority. Indeed much of the research on local government funding formulae in England is commissioned not by the national government, but by local government interest groups, such as London authorities, metropolitan authorities and rural authorities, seeking to strengthen a partisan position. The formula outcome is determined by the national government in the light of the representations made by such interest groups. There is therefore not an ineluctable scientific logic to the choice of funding mechanism. Rather, the development of formulae is a sort of bargaining process in which the constituent parties seek a compromise on issues such as the nature of the funding formulae, the sources of data, the analytic methods to be used, and the legitimate indicators of spending needs to be deployed.

The importance of the political element of formula funding in the UK is highlighted by the regular national investigations of funding mechanisms (Audit Commission, 1993; House of Commons Select Committee on the Environment, 1994; House of Commons Health Committee, 1995; House of Commons Environment Committee, 1998). These investigations are often prompted by discontent with existing arrangements among certain interest groups, and highlight perceived weaknesses in existing formulae. However they rarely produce conclusive outcomes, and it is unusual to see a programme of research emerging from their deliberations. Indeed it is noteworthy that – in spite of the very large sums of public finance involved – the volume of UK research into formula funding is pitifully small, particularly in the local government sector.

A 2000 Green Paper proposed a reduction in the reliance on formulae as the basis for local government funding in England, in favour of allocating national grants according to the quality of local authority bids (Department of the Environment Transport and the Regions, 2000). However the consultation on the Green Paper indicated overwhelmingly that such a policy was likely to be unworkable, not least because of the perceived unfairness it would introduce (Office of the Deputy Prime Minister, 2002). The Government has therefore continued to base its grants to English local governments mainly on funding formulae. One interpretation of this decision is that it reduces political transaction costs compared to the alternative of assessing the merits of claims on a case by case basis.

Another attraction to the payer of funding formulae is that they constrain either politicians or bureaucrats in the budgeting process. For example, if a national government makes a commitment to allocate expenditure on a large programme of public services only through a formula, it precludes politicians from seeking to influence the budgeting process by directing targeted expenditure at particular localities or groups of localities. The only mechanism for such influence is through the choice of funding formula, which is a more difficult process for politicians and lobbyists to subvert, particularly if the formula is intended to be scientifically based. In the same way, a payer might circumscribe the freedom of its bureaucrats to manipulate the budgetary process, by insisting on the use of a specific formula, or at least requiring a particular process for the development of a formula.

8.4.1 Case study: allocations to the UK territories

One of the longest-standing examples of the use of a formula for allocating public service expenditure seeks to allocate government expenditure to the four 'territories' (or countries) of the United Kingdom – England, Wales, Scotland and Northern Ireland. This had its origins in 1886, when home rule for Ireland was a central political issue, and a 'unionist' national government was seeking to keep the United Kingdom intact (McLean, 2005). Goschen, the finance minister at that time, proposed a formula that assigned government expenditure to the (then) three territories of the United Kingdom of England and Wales, Scotland and Ireland in the proportions $80:11:9$, implying a strong redistribution of expenditure towards Ireland. As McLean comments, 'a rational Unionist politician needed a device for quiet redistribution: enough to alleviate grievance in the periphery but not to provoke resentment at the centre. Redistribution by formula did the trick'.

In various incarnations, the Goschen formula enjoyed extraordinary longevity, its basic principles remaining in place until 1978, in spite of massive changes in the relative size and needs of the populations of the UK territories. Indeed it is possible to argue that the attraction of the formula was that it served national government objectives by directing more resources to Ireland and Scotland, without reference to those countries' objective position relative to England. In particular there was a general expectation that Scottish expenditure on new public service programmes should be at least 11/80 of the expenditure in England and Wales, notwithstanding the steady population decline in Scotland relative to the rest of Britain.

Public service expenditure in Scotland became manifestly higher than that in comparable regions in England, and the Goschen principles became unsustainable. As a result, from 1978 a new formulaic approach was adopted, known as the 'Barnett' formula, in recognition of the Chief Secretary to the Treasury at the time (Heald, 1996). The principal objective of the formula was to seek some convergence of *per capita* spending levels on public services within the United Kingdom. It did so by applying the principle of equal *per capita* allocations across the territories on any annual *increases* in government expenditure. However, these principles were importantly not applied to the original expenditure levels. Therefore, even from a technical viewpoint, the Barnett formula was likely to result in painfully slow convergence towards equal *per capita* spending. Moreover, as McLean (2005) documents, it has rarely been applied with any vigour. He cites the example of a decision to persist with the use of an incorrect population estimate that was known to favour Scotland.

There is little scientific logic underlying the Barnett formula, or its predecessor. McLean and McMillan (2003) note that the Barnett formula appears particularly to favour Scotland and Northern Ireland, and argue that this reflects their relatively strong threat to the political integrity of the United Kingdom. The absence of science should not be surprising, and is not necessarily dysfunctional. Successive national governments have resorted to formulaic approaches in order to address profound political problems. The principal merits of the formulae have been in reducing political transaction costs in determining an annual financial allocation to the territories, by eliminating many of the excruciating budgetary negotiations that would take place in their absence (Heald, 1996). Under this interpretation, formula funding may be a cost-effective codification of a bargaining outcome, rather than a scientific expression of relative needs.

8.5 Concluding comments

The principal purpose of this book is to offer an analytic guide to the design of public service funding mechanisms, and I do not claim to offer a detailed theory of the politic economy of formula funding. Rather, this chapter has offered a brief commentary on the political context within which all funding mechanisms must operate. Formula funding is by its nature an intensely political undertaking, and those charged with its design should ensure that they have a firm understanding of the political context within which their work will be implemented.

This is not to say that technical excellence should be compromised by political expediency. However, debates on formulae funding are often clouded by a failure to separate technical and political judgements. Analysts developing formulae should in principle seek to be very clear about which choices lie in the technical domain and which are properly political in nature. However, the discussion has indicated that in practice the design of most funding formulae is a process not of ineluctable scientific logic, but requires instead numerous judgements that straddle the political and technical domains. In these circumstances, the principal requirement is that these choices are explained explicitly, in the form of a careful audit trail. Those responsible for implementing the formulae can then be properly held to account for their chosen mechanism.

9   Concluding comments

9.1 Introduction

Public services represent a major segment of most economies and are in many countries evolving extraordinarily rapidly. Under the influence of what has become known as the 'new' public management, governments are seeking to nurture improved responsiveness to users' needs, heightened attention to the outcomes secured, and improved efficiency. These trends are embodied in the adoption in many countries of instruments, such as 'performance budgeting', that seek to strengthen the traditionally weak linkage between funding and results found in the public sector (United States Government, 1993).

In pursuing this agenda, governments have implemented fundamental reforms to their public services (Osborne and Gaebler, 1992), such as:

* decentralizing powers and authority, alongside reduced reliance on direct central command;
* viewing public sector organizations as purchasers and regulators of services, rather than direct providers;
* introducing increased diversity and competition into the provision of services;
* seeking to empower users by improving information, enhancing provider choice and strengthening systems of redress;
* increasing efforts to measure and report performance, especially in difficult domains such as user outcomes and organizational efficiency.

Satisfactory methods of funding are an essential prerequisite for the success of many of these innovations, and the methods described in this book should therefore play a central role in the reform process.

Hitherto there has often been little discussion of how funding mechanisms should be designed in order to support public service reforms. For example, the principles of performance budgeting imply an increased interest in measuring explicitly public service outcomes, in the form of (say) educational attainment or health improvement. Yet there have been few concerted efforts to ensure that the level of funding for local governments is consistent with the performance standards they are expected to achieve.

This chapter draws together some of the major themes that have recurred throughout the book. I first highlight what in my view are the three most important unresolved issues in formula funding: linking the funding mechanism to the performance standards required of public service organizations; understanding the incentives inherent in formula funding; and correcting the information weaknesses in the funding mechanism. Section 9.5 then summarizes what I see to be the major priorities for any payer seeking to introduce or reform a formula funding system.

9.2 Linking with performance standards

This book has repeatedly noted the surprising lack of explicit connection between funding mechanisms and the performance standards that local organizations are expected to achieve. As early as the nineteenth century it was recognized that reimbursing schools by means of case payments was likely to be ineffective unless they were required to secure certain basic standards for their pupils (Foster *et al.*, 1980). Yet over 100 years later many payers continue to design payment mechanisms in isolation from standards. The link between performance standards and funding was discussed in detail in Chapter 4, which noted the variations between individuals in the expenditure required to achieve a given standard. Indeed, it may be infeasible to secure the standard at any level of expenditure for some individuals, if it is set too high.

Standards might be explicit, such as a requirement that further education students successfully complete their studies before a college receives the associated case payment. However, they are more often implicit in the performance measures on which organizations and managers are judged. For example, if pass rates in certain public examinations form the basis for school performance reports to the public, then the standard *de facto* becomes to ensure all pupils secure a pass in the relevant examinations.

The issue of standards is closely linked to the problem of cream skimming, another concern raised throughout the book. Organizations would have little incentive to cream skim if they were able with impunity to vary standards for users, or if performance were not monitored. The incentive to cream skim arises because of the need to adhere to some implicit or explicit standards, and an inadequacy of funding to secure those standards for some individuals. To persist with the education example, schools may seek to deter 'difficult' pupils because – without extra funding – they threaten a school's examination performance or truancy rates. Such performance records form the basis for managerial rewards and parental choice, which may in turn affect future managerial and organizational prospects.

Much may depend on the precise formulation of the performance measure. For example, the incentives for schools may change dramatically depending how examination success is measured. Consider three possibilities:

a   the proportion of pupils securing some grade threshold;
b   the average examination grade of all pupils;

c   the risk adjusted average grade (perhaps a measure of educational 'value added' over a certain period).

Under (a) the prime concern of the school is the effort required to secure the chosen examination threshold. The pupil case payment should then reflect that effort. Under (b) the school has an incentive to select pupils likely to secure the highest grades. The case payments should be graduated across the entire range of ability in order to counter that incentive. The incentives under (c) are more subtle, and reflect the ease with which the pupil's level of attainment at entry can be improved by the school's efforts.

The payer's objective will usually be to design a payment mechanism that places all organizations on a level playing field. That is, each organization is given the funds needed to secure a specified performance standard. Performance reporting and yardstick competition can then operate effectively, because any variations in achieved performance should be directly attributable to the actions of management rather than a shortage of funding or adverse environmental circumstances.

In the same way, a satisfactory funding mechanism would precisely counter any tendency for cream skimming. For example, if social health insurers are seen to discriminate against certain population groups, then the capitation payments associated with those groups should be increased until the incentive to cream skim disappears. Likewise, disadvantaged children could readily be made attractive to schools by increasing their case payments. Such refinements were the motivation underlying the development of DRGs in health care.

However, while easily stated in principle, there are countless difficulties encountered when seeking to make these principles operational. First, it is often difficult to secure independently verifiable indicators of an individual's disadvantage. In practice, as in the DRG system, the payer may rely on reports by service providers, with all the associated hazards. Second, payers often specify quite vague and multidimensional performance standards that may change quite regularly. And third, there is rarely good empirical evidence on how much expenditure a particular type of service user requires to secure any given service standard.

My view is that, rather than casting doubt on the feasibility of setting payment levels, these difficulties suggest an important, interesting and challenging research agenda. Without doubt, it will usually be the most disadvantaged members of society who lose out from inadequate risk adjustment and poorly designed formulae. There is therefore a strong case from a social justice perspective to pursue this issue with vigour.

9.3 Incentives under formula funding

The preceding chapters have noted the very strong incentives inherent in pure formula funding systems. Under capitation these include:

- reduced activity;
- preventative measures;

- low effort and technical inefficiency;
- quality skimping.

Under case payments they include:

- increased activity;
- cream skimming;
- increased technical efficiency;
- quality skimping;
- upcoding;
- data fraud.

Some of these are intended and virtuous. Others are unintended and adverse. In general, the payer will wish to reinforce the intended incentives and abate some of the stronger adverse incentives. To some extent this can be achieved by adjusting the payment mechanism. Possibilities include refining the risk adjustment mechanism (to reduce the gains from cream skimming) and using mixed payment systems (to moderate the stark activity incentives inherent in the pure systems).

However, the payer will usually also have to augment the payment mechanism with other regulatory instruments in order to ensure that desired outcomes are secured. In short, although a well-designed payment mechanism is a necessary condition for securing the payer's objectives, it is not on its own sufficient. This section summarizes some of the more important tools for ensuring the payment mechanism works as intended.

Under pure capitation, there is no direct incentive for local organizations to deliver services to any standard. There is therefore a fundamental need for the payer to put in place mechanisms to ensure that services are delivered at the required level and quality. These mechanisms might take a number of forms. For example, a frequently used but costly regulatory instrument is to undertake periodic inspection of local services. This is especially important for provider organizations, and is routinely found in schooling and health care, where it is often the case that only accredited organizations are permitted to provide public services.

Performance measurement is another widely used instrument for assuring service standards. By collecting and disseminating data on issues such as unit costs, access to services, processes and outcomes, payers can compare organizations, identify those where performance is anomalous, and put in place corrective action. Such data can often form the basis for managerial incentives and concerted organizational improvement efforts.

Many payers are experimenting specifically with *public* reporting of local performance data. Here the intention is to help citizens (as taxpayers) to hold their local services to account. Performance reporting is therefore likely to be especially effective where strong local democratic procedures are in place. However, its effectiveness depends heavily on the precise mode of dissemination. For example, researchers in health care have found low impact of dissemi-nation of individual performance scores where little attention is paid to how the data are presented to the public or their representatives (Mannion and Goddard, 2001). In contrast, aggregating performance data into a 'star rating', with exten-sive media coverage, has been highly influential in attracting public attention to NHS performance in England (Smith, 2002). The appropriate means of dissemi-nating performance data to managers, the media, the public and local governing boards is a promising area for future research.

Another mechanism for stimulating performance improvement is to offer users a choice of services within a local market of providers. The success of this approach depends heavily on ensuring real competition between providers, and giving users the means to make an informed choice. Performance data will therefore also play an important role in implementation. Citizens as service users are likely to require more detailed information than citizens as taxpayers, the nature and effectiveness of which is also an important research issue (Hibbard *et al.*, 2003).

The ultimate logic of the principle of provider choice is to offer users a voucher for the service to which they are entitled that can be used with any accredited provider. Systems such as DRG payments in health care and pupil case payments in schooling effectively become voucher systems when the user has a degree of choice over the provider. Important policy choices for the payer are then the range of providers from which a user may choose, and the extent to which users are able to 'top up' the case payment with their own private payment if the provider charges a fee in excess of the case payment. Formula funding has a fundamental role to play in voucher systems in setting the level of reimbursement for the provider.

User choice can also be applied to local purchasers. For example, a number of health care systems, such as Belgium, Germany, Israel, the Netherlands and Switzerland, offer citizens a choice of social health insurers (Saltman *et al.*, 2004). In the UK, the system of general practitioner fundholding offered patients a choice of GP purchasers (Glennerster *et al.*, 1994). In these systems, the use of a capitation payment (as a pseudo insurance premium) becomes the main funding mechanism, and securing an adequate capitation funding formula becomes a key determinant of the success of the policy.

Implementing managerial incentives alongside formula funding is one of the most effective approaches to correcting some of the adverse organizational incentives inherent in payment mechanisms. Managerial incentives can take many forms other than direct financial rewards, such as increased autonomy, personal advancement and prestige. For example, the systems of organizational ratings used in much of the English public sector (such as the NHS performance ratings and local government comprehensive performance assessments) are directed mainly at the prestige and career prospects of senior management. They have undoubtedly been successful in focusing the attention of managers on the national government's performance priorities, although of course poorly designed managerial incentives can in turn produce their own unintended con-sequences (Smith, 1995).

As Chapter 7 has demonstrated, it is possible to incorporate quality standards directly into the payment mechanism. This is certainly a promising development, and a rich domain for future research. However, the GP example is somewhat unusual because general practices are very small businesses in which the proprietors (the GPs) can directly reap the rewards from improved performance. It is less clear how this principle could be extended to other domains, such as local governments. To make financial allocations to such organizations conditional on performance risks exposing citizens to a double jeopardy – in one period they could experience poor quality services, and as a consequence their locality would secure lower central grants-in-aid in a future period. This is likely to offend most concepts of equity and natural justice. Rather, it is likely that the most promising innovations would be to direct rewards (and sanctions) for organizational performance at the *managers* of such organizations.

Finally, a central theme of this book has been the key role that information plays in all funding mechanisms, both to serve as a basis for calculating funding levels and as a means of checking on performance standards. More generally it is a crucial input into activities as diverse as inspection, user decisions and setting managerial rewards. Much of the information on which the public services rely emanates from the services themselves, and there is a clear danger that data will become corrupted as the stakes attached to them increase. Any threat to the perceived probity of the public services risks undermining confidence in those services, and popular support for them. Therefore, a key role for the payer is to decide on the nature and scope of independent data audit needed to counter any incentives for manipulation.

This section has sketched in only the briefest outline some of the additional mechanisms a payer may need to implement alongside formula funding. A full treatment is beyond the scope of this book. Rather, the intention has been to alert the policy maker of the need to consider how formula funding fits into the whole system of public service finance and delivery. Most of the initiatives, such as inspection, performance reporting, user choice, provider markets and managerial incentives are means of correcting the natural tendency of funding mechanisms to reduce service standards or (in the case of capitation) to ignore technical efficiency considerations. The payer has a formidable challenge in ensuring they fit together into a coherent design for the whole public service system.

9.4 Information for formula funding

The limitations of traditional information sources are an important constraint to the development of satisfactory funding mechanisms. The question therefore arises: is there scope for material improvements in the data on which funding formulae are based? The accelerating use of electronic user records certainly offers potential in this respect. Although primarily designed to secure more efficient and effective services for the user, developments such as electronic patient records also offer immense opportunities for increased use of individual level data as a basis for formulae, particularly case payments. In the medical field, the extraordinarily refined state of development of DRGs offers a glimpse of what can be achieved. The key requirement is that the data necessary for developing case payments are designed into the information system at an early stage, and that the data to be used for risk adjustment are recorded reliably and universally across all organizations in receipt of those payments.

Smith *et al.* (2001) also discuss the prospects for the more challenging domain of capitation payments. They suggest the possibility of a survey of public expenditure on individual citizens (or households) that permits quantification of the capitation expenditure weights for different population types. Designing and analysing such a survey will not be straightforward. Detailed examination of the significant personal characteristics associated with public expenditure (personal needs factors) is for capitation purposes futile if the prevalence of those factors in the general population cannot be measured with any confidence. The contingency table to be estimated by means of the survey is constrained by the population data held at the level of each recipient of funds. Thus, for example, if a capitation formula is required for distributing English NHS funds to local areas, current data restrictions mean that the only universally held individual level data available for such purposes are age, sex and post code of residence. So a finding that (say) smoking behaviour is a major influence on individual level health care expenditure is regrettably useless for capitation purposes at present as smoking status is not in general available in all local population registers. Moreover, even if it were available, such a characteristic is always vulnerable to errors in recording or fraud, and so may never be acceptable for capitation purposes.

However, if relevant population data are available, a capitation survey of expenditure on individuals becomes potentially useful, and should be designed to yield estimates of the expected expenditure requirements of citizens of each type over a given time period (say one year). The practical difficulty of tracking public service expenditure on an individual over an extended period should not be underestimated, and the cost of carrying out the survey must be a central consideration in deciding whether to pursue this methodology. However, developments in computer technology make such possibilities increasingly realistic. Diderichsen *et al.* (1997) have demonstrated the viability of such methods in Swedish health care, where there exist comprehensive computer-based records of every citizen's social circumstances and health care utilization.

A major benefit of the individual level approach is that it offers the potential for correcting for substitutions between services, along the lines sought by the Medicare HCC methods (Section 5.5). So for example, if there are two modes of treatment for a particular condition – say one based on inpatient care, the other on drug therapy – it does not matter which mode is used providing the associated expenditure consequences are recorded in the survey. The dependent variable in any analysis will then be total health care expenditure on the individual, and disaggregation into separate services becomes unnecessary so long as only a global budget calculation is required. More generally, the disaggregation of expenditure needs assessments into separate service headings might be obviated for multi-purpose local governments if it were possible to identify the individual's total consumption of all local government services.

On its own, a service use survey does not necessarily overcome all the limitations of an empirical approach to setting capitations. The capitation payment should reflect expected spending if some standard level of services were to be offered with some standard level of efficiency. There therefore remains a need to accommodate illegitimate influences on expenditure. Furthermore, it may prove infeasible to implement a survey that yields reliable estimates of expenditure requirements for each category of citizen. Under such circumstances, careful statistical modelling may be required to infer capitation payments for sparsely populated cells of the contingency table. And, by definition, unmet need cannot be captured by means of an empirical survey of utilization.

Good research into the determinants of public service utilization is generally sparse, and much would need to be done to establish the form that such a survey might take. For example, it may be the case that a standard unstratified sample may be unsatisfactory for many capitation purposes, particularly in (say) personal social services, where utilization is highly skewed to a relatively small number of heavy users. It may be that the survey would use a number of sources to generate results. For example, Van Vliet and Lamers (1998) have noted that the death of a citizen is a very strong indicator of heavy health care utilization, and it may therefore be interesting to combine a standard population survey of health care use with a special survey of those who had died in the previous year to derive capitation payments based (among other things) on survival status.

There are also challenges associated with estimating the costs of public service utilization, for which many important but arbitrary accounting choices may have to be made. For example, we found a wide range of local accounting procedures in use in the study of personal social services described in Section 5.6.2. Such variations do not necessarily have a large impact on the eventual capitation payments (sensitivity analysis indicated this was not a major issue). However, costing issues may become more important if data from a variety of services are to be combined, and a convincing methodology is almost certainly desirable in order to secure the credibility of the research.

In short, many issues need to be addressed before it will be possible to recommend the exact form that a service utilization survey might take, and the methods that might be used. Moreover, many types of survey are likely to be costly. However, it is often the case that vast sums of public money are distributed using formula funding methods, and investment in a more secure basis for distributing such resources may be a small price to pay for the increases in efficiency and equity it yields. Payers of all sorts should therefore consider the merits of an individual survey as a possible means of enhancing their empirical methodology for setting capitation payments.

9.5 Priorities for the future

Formula funding offers the payer great opportunities to introduce transparency, consistency, efficiency and fairness into public services. Indeed it is in many circumstances difficult to envisage any feasible alternative funding mechanism. The task for policy makers is therefore to determine the most effective mode of implementing formula funding.

Using only a moderate degree of ingenuity, a payer can often secure almost any desired distributional outcome from a funding formula. A fundamental question to address is therefore: What are the payer's objectives? Can they be articulated? And is the chosen formula consistent with them? The book has considered three broad categories of objective: efficiency, equity and political. These are often in conflict, and difficult to tease out. Yet, in the absence of clearly stated objectives it is all but impossible for analysts to develop satisfactory payment mechanisms.

For example, is it the case that payers are content with the manifest difficulty some disadvantaged citizens find with securing health insurance in countries with competitive insurance systems? If not, then they need to be able to articulate clearly the perceived inadequacies in the current outcomes, and the objectives for any revisions to the funding mechanism. Analysts can then consider appropriate adjustments to the capitation rates that promote the goal of ensuring that all citizens secure access to insurers in line with intentions. In short, payers need not feel that they are at the mercy of some conventional approach to calculating payment rates, but analysts need a clear statement of objectives in order to rectify inadequacies.

The challenge of integrating payment mechanisms with performance requirements is especially important (Section 9.2). If passive approaches to setting payment mechanisms are adopted, based on current spending patterns, the payer is implicitly signalling that the current pattern of performance is in line with intentions. If that is not the case, then the payer will need to consider adopting more radical approaches to setting payment levels, perhaps based on spending patterns in a subset of localities that are achieving desired outcomes, or (more likely) by experimenting with changes to payment rates based on a judgement (rather than empirical evidence) as to the expenditure levels that are needed to support changes in existing practice.

Moreover, a clear message from Section 9.3 is that payers must consider a 'whole system' approach towards the design of the public services. Funding mechanisms on their own will rarely secure all the payer's objectives. Indeed there may be many circumstances in which they act against some of those objectives. The payer must therefore always be alert to the need to design other instruments alongside funding formulae, such as performance reporting, data audit and managerial incentives. Likewise, the payer may need to consider whether new initiatives such as issuing guidelines on best professional practice, are consistent with current funding mechanisms. For example, it is not at all clear that the mass of new clinical guidelines and innovations in performance reporting in English health care are aligned with its new approach to hospital funding, based on DRG type payments.

Governments are experimenting with a wide range of new public service instruments designed to promote improved performance and efficiency, such as public performance reporting, vouchers for service users and competitive provider markets. Each of these relies crucially on satisfactory funding mechanisms. If local organizations are not funded fairly, then performance comparisons become meaningless. If the value of a voucher does not reflect expenditure needs, a user will find it difficult to secure the intended service. If the funding mechanism is inadequate, then competitive markets are unlikely to function efficiently.

In short, almost all such structural innovations require careful attention to the funding mechanism, and the payer needs to determine whether existing formulae are fit for purpose, and if not whether improvement is feasible. For example, Chapter 6 noted the large element of expenditure risk associated with health care for individual citizens in England, and the consequent difficulty of setting reliable budgets for general practitioner fundholders. This failing was in my view a crucial shortcoming of the fundholding scheme, leading to the potential for great inequity and risk avoidance behaviour on the part of GPs. Therefore, whatever the virtues of the policy, I would argue that a payer should be very cautious about implementing analogous fundholding schemes unless it is possible to develop appreciably better funding formulae than are currently feasible in English health care.

More generally, I believe there is much greater scope for more careful and systematic consideration of the magnitude and distribution of expenditure risk within the chosen public service system. Analysts should routinely prepare estimates of budgetary risk, allowing payers to determine whether the risk is concentrated in the right organizations within the system, and whether additional instruments are needed in order to counter any adverse consequences of risk averse behaviour. Such information could play an important part in the unresolved debates about the most appropriate 'level' of the system (individual, small provider, local government, region, nation) at which to direct certain payments.

The book has highlighted numerous new analytic opportunities. The development of new data sources offers immense possibilities, and may obviate the need for the some of the more complex techniques described in Chapter 5. However, there is still considerable scope for many analyses to take better account of illegitimate influences on service costs, most notably supply side variations in input prices and policy choices.

Furthermore, there is great scope for moving away from passive modelling of existing influences on expenditure towards the construction of 'optimal' payment mechanisms that seek to promote the payer's intentions more purposefully (Hauck *et al*, 2002; Glazer and McGuire, 2000). In particular, these might seek to reduce the poor level of services secured by some disadvantaged groups of the population. Yet, as Chapter 4 argues, optimal payment systems must usually be implemented alongside other mechanisms in order to induce the necessary changes in provider behaviour. Once again, careful design of the whole system will be needed.

Finally, there is often an important debate to be had about the correct balance between simplicity of the chosen formula and its sensitivity to variations in spending needs. The arguments for simplicity are that it leads to a transparent system of finance that promotes good local managerial decision making, and that it promotes the accountability of the governmental payer to the citizens who pay for the services through their tax contributions. In contrast, opaque or prolix formulae obscure the intended incentives, and make it difficult to report the basis for funding to citizens. Furthermore, frequent changes to formulae can leave all parties bewildered and can therefore be dysfunctional from both an efficiency and an accountability perspective.

However, complexity is an intrinsic feature of public services, and – as new data sources become available – it becomes feasible to model spending needs to increasing levels of accuracy. Furthermore, the increased refinement will often work to the benefit of disadvantaged groups, as it models reasons for expenditure variations that were hitherto not captured in the formula. To this end, there may therefore be powerful arguments for making formulae more complex. The role of the analyst is to make clear the reduction in sensitivity that results from moving from a complex formula to its simpler counterpart. Issues to be addressed might include who gains and who loses, and what the implications are for extra expenditure risk and the potential for adverse responses, such as cream skimming. It is then for the payer to decide whether the gains from simplicity outweigh the associated costs.

9.6 Conclusions

Although it had beginnings in the nineteenth century, it is only in recent years that formula funding has become a refined instrument of public service regulation. Satisfactory formula funding is made increasingly feasible by the rapid advances in data availability and analytic tools. Moreover, it is becoming an increasingly essential component of public service management. Not only does it promote equity and efficiency, but it is also an indispensable element of initiatives as diverse as decentralization, performance reporting, user vouchers and quasi-markets.

Although there are numerous successful examples of formula funding, this book has also suggested that in many circumstances payers have unrealistic expectations about what formula funding can achieve. I have argued that there is great scope for improving existing information sources and methodology. But not even the most carefully crafted formula will be sufficient to address all the payer's objectives. Rather, it will be a necessary and important component of the broader design of the public services. I believe passionately that – properly designed and delivered – those services are a major determinant of the wellbeing of citizens and form the foundations for a productive, just society. I hope this book has indicated some ways in which formula funding can contribute to that goal.

Technical appendix A

Some mathematics of risk pooling

This appendix presents some rudimentary mathematics of risk pooling. The main source is the material presented by Daykin *et al.* (1994). For most purposes it assumes random, independent arrival of claims, and that the claims arise from a homogeneous population of insured risks. These assumptions might be seriously over-restrictive in many public services. Claims may not be independent (sometimes arising, for example, from an epidemic). And the insured risks are most certainly not homogeneous. With suitable amendments these complications can be accommodated within the mathematical model presented here. However, they render the models less transparent, and so for the most part the treatment will be confined to the simplest situation.

A.1 Modelling the number of claims

First consider the number of claims against the risk pool. Assuming first that the expected number of claims in a period is n, and that they are randomly and independently distributed, they can be modelled as a Poisson process:

$$p_k(n) = e^{-n} \frac{n^k}{k!}$$

where p_k is the probability of observing k claims in the given period.

Note that the mean and variance of the Poisson distribution are: $\mu_n = n$ and $\sigma_n^2 = n$, and that the probabilities are readily calculated using the recursive equations:

$$p_0 = e^{-n}$$

$$p_k = \frac{n}{k} p_{k-1} = \frac{n^k}{k!} e^{-n}$$

As k and n get large, the central limit theorem implies that the cumulative Poisson distribution $F(k)$ – the probability that k or fewer claims are received – approximates the normal distribution $N(.)$, such that

$$F(k) \approx N\left(\frac{k-n)}{\sqrt{n}} \right)$$

Where this is not sufficiently accurate, a convenient approximation to the Poisson distribution is given by:

$$F(k) \approx N\left(\frac{3}{2}\left(k + \frac{5}{8}\right)^{2/3} n^{-1/6} - \frac{3}{2}\sqrt{n} + \frac{1}{24\sqrt{n}} \right)$$

The assumption of a pure Poisson process may be inappropriate – the parameter n may vary through time because of (a) long-term trends; (b) cyclical or seasonal variations. This is handled by adopting a mixed Poisson process, in which the parameter n is multiplied by a mixing variable q, with a pdf $h(q)$, such that $E(q) = 1$. The parameter q can be thought of as changing risk propensity, and effectively models the uncertainty in the parameter n. At any time when the mixing variable takes the value q, claims are distributed according to a Poisson process with mean nq, and the mixed Poisson probability p_k is now given by:

$$p_k = E(p_k(nq)) = \int_0^\infty e^{-nq}\frac{(nq)^k}{k!}h(q)dq$$

The key function of the mixing variable is to increase the variance to $\sigma_n^2 = n + n^2\sigma_q^2$ where σ_q^2 is the variance of the mixing variable q. The mean number of claims remains: $\mu_n = n$.

A.2 Modelling the size of claims

Suppose that the size of claims is independent of the number of claims, and are independently and identically distributed as a random variable Z. First define the probability that – given there are k claims in the chosen time period – the total claims against the risk pool are less than X:

$$S^{k*}(X) = \Pr\left\{\sum_{i=1}^{k} Z_i \leq X\right\}$$

Then the total claim X will be distributed according to the cumulative distribution function $F(.)$, where

$$F(X) = \sum_{i=0}^{\infty} p_k S^{k*}(X)$$

$F(X)$ is the probability that the claims will not exceed a value of X in total in the chosen time period. Note that for $k > 0$, $S^{k*}(.)$ satisfies the recursive equation:

$$S^{k*} = S * S^{(k-1)*}$$

The total claim distribution X is a compound distribution, referred to as a compound Poisson distribution when the claim numbers are Poisson distributed. Under the assumptions of independence noted above, the expected claim X is merely the product of the expected number of claims n and the expected size of each claim m:

$$E(X) = \mu_X = n.m$$

Further, in this Poisson case, the variance and skewness of X are given by:

$$\sigma_X^2 = n.a_2$$

$$\gamma_X = \frac{n.a_3}{(n.a_2)^{3/2}} = \frac{a_3}{a_2^{3/2}.\sqrt{n}}$$

where a_j is the jth moment of the distribution of Z about zero.

It is sometimes convenient to partition the variance as:

$$\sigma_X^2 = m^2 n + n.(a_2 - m^2)$$

The first term on the right hand side is the variance associated with the Poisson process (that is to variations in the number of claims), and the second term on the right hand side is the variance associated with the size of individual claims.

The total claim distribution X is referred to as a compound mixed Poisson distribution when the claim numbers are distributed as a mixed Poisson process. In the compound mixed Poisson case the variance and skewness are as follows:

$$\sigma_X^2 = n.a_2 + n^2 m^2 \sigma_q^2 = \sigma_0^2 + \mu_X^2 \sigma_q^2$$

$$\gamma_X = \frac{n.a_3 + 3n^2 m a_2 \sigma_q^2 + n^3 m^3 \gamma_q \sigma_q^3}{\sigma_X^3}$$

where $\sigma_0^2 = n.a_2$ is the variance in the compound Poisson case. Note that an additional term determined by the variance of the mixing variable is added to the expression for the variance. An alternative way of decomposing the variance of X is to write it as:

$$\sigma_X^2 = m^2 n + n(a_2 - m^2) + n^2 m^2 \sigma_q^2$$

The three components are:

a   the variance associated with the Poisson process (claim numbers only, with no claim size variation or mixing);

b   the variance associated with the individual claim sizes;

c   the variance associated with mixing.

The standard deviation of X is sometimes written:

$$\sigma_X = n.m.\sqrt{\frac{r_2}{n} + \sigma_q^2}$$

where $r_2 = (a_2/m^2)$

Note that r_2 is merely the square of the conventional coefficient of variation of Z, and can be thought of as an indication of the riskiness of the claim size distribution.

Then the coefficient of variation of the total claim size is given by:

$$\frac{\sigma_X}{\mu_X} = \sqrt{\frac{\sigma_0^2}{\mu_X^2} + \sigma_q^2} = \sqrt{\frac{r^2}{n} + \sigma_q^2}$$

Thus for small n the randomness associated with individual claims predominates, while as n increases the variation associated with the mixing element becomes more important.

A.3 Some elaborations

We have so far considered 'pure' insurance, in the sense that all claims of whatever size must be met by the risk pool. There are of course many arrangements such as reinsurance and copayments which might moderate this extreme case. These might include:

a *excluding large claims*: this entails modelling the distribution of S as a censored distribution $S_c(.)$ which takes the form $S_c(Z) = (S(Z)/S(C))$ for $Z < C$, the chosen cut-off.

b *limiting the size of all claims*: this entails modelling the distribution of S as a truncated distribution $S_t(.)$ which takes the form $S_t(Z) = S(Z)$ for $Z < T$, the chosen cut-off, and $S_t(Z) = 1$ for $Z \geq T$. If effected through a reinsurance contract, this arrangement is known as an excess of loss treaty.

c *cost sharing all claims*: this entails modelling the distribution of S as a distribution $S_r(.)$ which takes the form $S_r(Z) = S(Z/r)$ for all Z, where r is the proportion of the claims met by the risk pool.

d *limiting the aggregate of claims*: this is effectively a 'stop-loss' reinsurance arrangement under which the distribution function $F(X)$ for the total claim X is truncated at some limit M.

Each of these arrangements serves to reduce the risk exposure of the risk pool, and the analytic properties have been thoroughly explored in the insurance literature.

Sources: Kendall and Stuart, 1977; Daykin *et al.*, 1994.

Technical appendix B

Calculating measures of local health care supply

A fundamental need of the study described in Section 5.6.2 was to develop a measure of the *perceived availability* of various health care services to a particular small area. This measure should incorporate three elements: the inherent attractiveness of services; their proximity to the population of interest; and the effect of competing populations. The traditional method of treating such concepts is to develop a measure of the *accessibility* of the ward to health care services. This was achieved by using the ideas of spatial interaction modelling described by Wilson (1974).

The standard spatial interaction model is of the form:

$$T_{id} = gP_iS_df(c_{id}) \tag{B1}$$

where T_{id} is the number of interactions (say, hospital episodes per year) between residential zone i and destination d; P_i is some measure of the effective population of zone i; S_d is some measure of the size or attractiveness of destination d; c_{id} is some measure of distance (or time) between i and d; $f(.)$ is a distance decay or deterrence function; g is a gravitational constant.

Then the total number of interactions (say, hospital episodes) T_i generated by zone i per year is given by

$$T_i = gP_i\sum_d S_df(c_{id}) \tag{B2}$$

and the number of episodes T_d attracted to destination (hospital) d is

$$T_d = gS_d\sum_i P_if(c_{id}) \tag{B3}$$

Now in this study each hospital (destination) is limited in the number of patients it can treat. That is, the model is 'attraction constrained' (Batty, 1976: 39). It is therefore necessary to introduce a balancing factor B_d into the model for each destination d, so that (B1) is rewritten

$$T_{id} = gP_iB_dS_df(c_{id}) \tag{B4}$$

where

$$B_d = \frac{1}{\sum\limits_i P_i f(c_{id})} \qquad (B5)$$

Introduction of the factor B_d ensures that the influence of competing populations is properly modelled.

Then the accessibility A_i of zone i to hospital facilities can be given by the ratio of the predicted number of episodes in relation to population, which is represented by the expression

$$A_i = \left(\sum_d T_{id}\right)/P_i = \sum_d B_d S_d f(c_{id}) = \sum_d \left(\frac{S_d f(c_{id})}{\sum\limits_r P_r f(c_{rd})}\right) (B6)$$

Expression (B6) models the *relative* accessibility of residents in zone j to all hospital resources, given the availability of beds (S_d), the distance to the hospitals (c_{id}) and the competition from local populations. It is a *distance-weighted* form of the simple ratio 'beds per head'.

Thus in order to calculate the accessibility of residential zones, it is first necessary for each hospital to calculate the index B_d. Once the form of the deterrence function has been chosen, this is straightforward. Choice of measures for P_i and S_d is also straightforward: population and beds serve as reasonable proxies for demand (people) and supply (episodes). (Note that *demographic* determinants of utilization were treated elsewhere in this study, so that the population did not have to be weighted by need. The measure A_i is merely intended to give a measure of relative inpatient provision.) The measure of distance c_{id} should ideally be a measure of *perceived* distance, or possibly journey time. However, in this study the only available distance measures were straight line (or crow fly) distances, so these had to be used. A standard intrazonal cost was added to each distance.

Finally, possibly the most troublesome aspect of modelling is the choice of deterrence function $f(.)$. Scrutiny of the spatial location literature suggests a wide range of possible functional forms. Haggett *et al.*, 1977) describe two in widespread use:

$$f(c) = e^{-\beta c^\alpha}$$

$$f(c) = c^{-\beta} \qquad (B7)$$

where c is distance and α and b are parameters to be estimated.

The distance function can be calibrated using a gravity model of the sort described by Batty (1976), in which case the parameters α and β are chosen to maximize a suitable likelihood function. Because we had no information about hospital of treatment we could not calibrate a gravity model. The original Newtonian model of physical gravitation uses the second of the functional forms with $\beta = 2$ (the inverse square law). Unfortunately, in modelling social phenomena, there is no guarantee that such a neat result exists. As a result, it was necessary to appeal to previous studies and judgement to model deterrence.

Batty uses both functional forms for subregional modelling. Using the first, he sets $\alpha = 1$, and estimates β by an iterative process such that modelled mean trip length equals observed mean trip length. Values of between 0.1 and 0.3 are found. Using the second, values of β between 1.5 and 2.5 are found. In another study, Foot (1981) uses the first functional form with $\alpha = 1$ and $\beta = 0.2$. The relevance of these values to the current study is limited because of the very particular type of spatial interaction being modelled. Indeed, we might expect that – for different types of NHS referral – different types of deterrence might occur. The only directly relevant work is the study of London hospitals reported by Mayhew (1986). However, he gives no values for the deterrence function parameters. In general, relatively minor conditions might be expected to exhibit high elasticity with respect to distance (high values of β) while lower values of β might obtain for, say, regional specialties. Bearing in mind that we wished to arrive at a relatively broad brush measure of accessibility, it was unnecessary to model such subtleties.

Instead, accessibility was modelled using the following two deterrence functions:

$$f(d) = e^{-0.2c}$$

$$f(d) = c^{-2} \tag{B8}$$

The measures of accessibility implicit in these choices were examined to check that they were reasonable. It was eventually decided to use an inverse square deterrence function with intrazonal cost of ten kilometres.

Although the discussion in this appendix refers to NHS hospital accessibility, exactly the same methods were used to model the provision of family practitioner services and of private inpatient facilities. The only differences were in the measures S_d of the size or attractiveness of destination d. For family practitioners, the destination became a family practitioner surgery, and the size was the number of registered family practitioners. For private hospitals, the destination was the local authority ward, and the size was the number of visitors (presumed to be inpatients) in non-psychiatric hospitals on the 1991 census night.

References

Andersson, P., E. Varde and F. Diderichsen (2000). 'Modelling of resource allocation to health care authorities in Stockholm County'. *Health Care Management Science* 3(2), 141–150.

Arrow, K. (1963). 'Uncertainty and the welfare economics of medical care'. *American Economic Review* 53(5), 941–973.

Ash, A., R. Ellis, G. Pope, J. Ayanian, D. Bates, H. Burstin, L. Iezzoni, E. MacKay and W. Yu (2000). 'Using Diagnoses to Describe Populations and Predict Costs'. *Health Care Financing Review* 21(3), 7–28.

Ashworth, M., M. Jenkins, K. Burgess, H. Keynes, M. Wallace, D. Roberts and A. Majeed (2005). 'Which general practices have higher list inflation? An exploratory study'. *Family Practice* 22(5), 529–531.

Audit Commission (1993). *Passing the Bucks: The Impact of Standard Spending Assessments on Economy, Efficiency and Effectiveness*. London: HMSO.

Audit Commission (1996). *What the Doctor Ordered. A Study of GP Fundholders in England and Wales*. London: The Stationery Office.

Audit Commission (2003). *Improving School Buildings*. London: The Audit Commission.

Audit Commission (2005a). *Comprehensive Performance Assessment: The Harder Test*. London: The Audit Commission.

Audit Commission (2005b). *Financing Council Housing. A Report on the Impact of the National System of Finance on the Government's Objectives for Council Housing*. London: Audit Commission.

Audit Commission (2005c). *Governing Partnerships: Bridging the Accountability Gap*. London: Audit Commission.

Bachmann, M.O. and G. Bevan (1996). 'Determining the size of a total purchasing site to manage the financial risks of rare costly referrals: computer simulation model'. *British Medical Journal* 313(7064), 1054–1057.

Barnett, R.R., R. Levaggi and P. Smith (1991). 'Even some lump-sum grants can stimulate more than others'. *Environment and Planning C-Government and Policy* 9(3), 257–265.

Barrow, M. (1986). 'Central grants to local governments: a game theoretic approach'. *Environment and Planning C: Government and Policy* 4, 155–164.

Bartlett, W., J.A. Roberts and J. Le Grand (1998). *A Revolution in Social Policy: Quasi-market Reforms in the 1990s*. Bristol: The Policy Press.

Batty, M. (1976). *Urban Modelling: Algorithms, Calibrations, Predictions*. Cambridge: Cambridge University Press.

Baxter, K., M. Bachmann and G. Bevan (2000). 'Primary care groups: trade-offs in managing budgets and risk'. *Public Money and Management* 20(1), 53–62.

Bazzoli, G. (2004). 'Special issue. Paying for quality: evidence and a research agenda'. *Medical Care Research and Review* 61(3), 5S–150S.

Bebbington, A. and B. Davies (1983). 'Equity and efficiency in the allocation of personal social services'. *Journal of Social Policy* 12, 309–329.

Becker, D., D. Kessler and M. McClellan (2005). 'Detecting Medicare abuse'. *Journal of Health Economics* 24(1), 189–210.

Bennett, R. (1980). *The Geography of Public Finance*. London: Methuen.

Bennett, R. (1982). *Central Grants to Local Governments*. Cambridge: Cambridge University Press.

Besley, T. and S. Coate (2003). 'Centralized versus decentralized provision of local public goods: a political economy approach'. *Journal of Public Economics* 87(12), 2611–2637.

Biørn, E., T. Hagen, T. Iversen and J. Magnussen (2003). 'The effect of activity-based financing on hospital efficiency'. *Health Care Management Science* 6(4), 271–283.

Blundell, R. and F. Windmeijer (2000). 'Identifying demand for health resources using waiting times information'. *Health Economics* 9, 465–474.

Bojke, C., H. Gravelle and D. Wilkin (2001). 'Is bigger better for primary care groups and trusts?'. *British Medical Journal* 322(7286), 599–602.

Brennan, M. and R. A. Carr-Hill (1996). No need to weight community health programmes for resource allocation?'. Discussion paper 146. York: Centre for Health Economics.

Carr-Hill, R.A., G. Hardman, S. Martin, S. Peacock, T.A. Sheldon and P.C. Smith (1997). 'A new formula for distributing hospital funds in England'. *Interfaces* 27(1), 53–70.

Carr-Hill, R.A., N. Rice and P.C. Smith (1999). 'The determinants of expenditure on children's personal social services'. *British Journal of Social Work* 29(5), 679–706.

Carr-Hill, R.A., T.A. Sheldon, P. Smith, S. Martin, S. Peacock and G. Hardman (1994). 'Allocating resources to health authorities: development of methods for small area analysis of use of inpatient services'. *British Medical Journal* 309, 1046–1049.

Casalino, L., R. Gillies, S. Shortell, J. Schmittdiel, T. Bodenheimer, J. Robinson, T. Rundall, N. Oswald, H. Schauffler and M. Wang (2003). 'External incentives, information technology, and organized processes to improve health care quality for patients with chronic diseases'. *Journal of the American Medical Association* 289(4), 434–441.

Chalkley, M. and J. Malcomson (1998). 'Contracting for health services when patient demand does not reflect quality'. *Economic Journal* 17(1), 1–19.

Commission for Social Care Inspection (2004). *Direct Payments: What are the barriers?* London: Commission for Social Care Inspection.

Conrad, D.A. and J. Christianson (2004). 'Penetrating the "black box": financial incentives for improving the quality of physician services'. *Medical Care Research and Review* 61(3), 37S-68S.

Consejo de Politica Fiscal y Financiera (1998). 'Financiación de los servicios de sanidad en el periodo 1998–2001'. *Revista de Adminstración Sanitaria* 11(6), 125–151.

Culyer, A.J. (1995). 'Need – the idea won't do – but we still need it'. *Social Science and Medicine* 40(6), 727–730.

Culyer, A.J. and A. Wagstaff (1993). 'Equity and equality in health and health care'. *Journal of Health Economics* 12, 431–437.

Davies, H.T.O., S.M. Nutley and P.C. Smith (1999). 'What works? The role of evidence in public sector policy and practice'. *Public Money and Management* 19(1), 3–5.

Daykin, C., T. Pentikäinen and M. Pesonen (1994). *Practical Risk Theory for Actuaries*. London: Chapman and Hall.

Department for Education and Skills (2002). *Departmental Report 2002*. London: The Stationery Office.

Department of Health (2003a). *Investing in General Practice: The New GMS Contract*. London: Department of Health.

Department of Health (2003b). *Resource Allocation: Weighted Capitation Formula*. London: Department of Health.

Department of Health (2005). *2005–07 and 2007–08 PCT Revenue Allocations: A Short Guide*. London: Department of Health.

Department of Health and Social Security (1976). *Sharing Resources for Health in England: Report of the Resource Allocation Working Party*. London: HMSO.

Department of the Environment (1995). *Standard Spending Assessments: Guide to Methodology 1995/96*. London: Department of the Environment.

Department of the Environment Transport and the Regions (2000). *Modernizing Local Government Finance: A Green Paper*. London: The Stationery Office.

Dewatripont, M., I. Jewitt and J. Tirole (1997). 'The Economics of Career Concerns'. *Review of Economic Studies* 66(1), 183–217.

Diderichsen, F., E. Varde and M. Whitehead (1997). 'Resource allocation to health authorities: the quest for an equitable formula in Britain and Sweden'. *British Medical Journal* 315, 875–878.

Dranove, D., D. Kessler, M. McClellan and M. Satterthwaite (2003). 'Is more information better? The effects of "report cards" on health care providers'. *Journal of Political Economy* 111, 555–588.

Dudley, R., R. Miller, T. Korenbrot and H. Luft (1998). 'The impact of financial incentives on quality of health care'. *Milbank Quarterly* 76(4), 649–686.

Duncan, A. and P. Smith (1995). 'Modelling local government budgetary choices under expenditure limitation'. *Fiscal Studies* 16(4), 95–110.

Dusheiko, M., H. Gravelle, R. Jacobs and P. Smith (2005). 'The effects of budgets on doctor behaviour: evidence from a natural experiment'. *Journal of Health Economics* 25, 449–478.

Elliott, R., D. McDonald and R. MacIver (1996). *Review of the Area Cost Adjustment*. Aberdeen: University of Aberdeen.

Fishman, P.A. and D.K. Shay (1999). 'Development and estimation of a pediatric chronic disease score using automated pharmacy data'. *Medical Care* 37, 874–883.

Flowerdew, R., B. Francis and S. Lucas (1994). 'The Standard Spending Assessment As A Measure Of Spending Needs In Nonmetropolitan Districts'. *Environment and Planning C-Government and Policy* 12(1), 1–13.

Foot, D. (1981). *Operational Urban Models*. London: Methuen.

Foster, C., R. Jackman and M. Perlman (1980). *Local Government Finance in a Unitary State*. London: Allen & Unwin.

Francois, P. (2000). ' "Public Service motivation" as an argument for government provision'. *Journal of Public Economics* 78, 275–299.

Frey, B. (1997). 'A constitution for knaves crowds out civic virtues'. *Economic Journal* 107(443), 1043–1053.

Gibbons, S. (2004). 'The Costs of Urban Property Crime'. *Economic Journal* 114(499), 441–463.

Gibson, J. (1998). 'Political manipulation or feedback in English local authorities' standard spending assessments? The case of the abolition of the Inner London Education Authority'. *Public Administration* 76(4), 629–647.

Gilbert, G. and P. Picard (1996). 'Incentives and optimal size of local jurisdictions'. *European Economic Review* 40(1), 19–41.

Glazer, J. and T.G. McGuire (2000). 'Optimal risk adjustment in markets with adverse selection: an applicaton to managed care'. *American Economic Review* 90, 1055–1071.

Glazer, J. and A. Shmueli (1995). 'The physician's behavior and equity under a fund-holding contract'. *European Economic Review* 39, 781–785.

Glennerster, H., J. Hills and T. Travers (2000). *Paying for Health, Education, and Housing: How Does the Centre Pull the Purse Strings?* Oxford: Oxford University Press.

Glennerster, H., M. Matsaganis and P. Owens (1994). *Implementing GP Fundholding: Wild Card or Winning Hand?* Buckingham: Open University Press.

Glied, S. (2000). 'Managed care'. In J.P. Newhouse and A.J. Culyer (ed.) *Handbook of Health Economics*. Amsterdam: Elsevier.

Godfrey, L. (1988). *Misspecification Tests in Econometrics*. Cambridge: Cambridge University Press.

Goldstein, H. (1994). 'The use of regression analysis for resource allocation by central government'. *Environment and Planning C: Government and Policy* 12(1), 15–22.

Goldstein, H. (1995). *Multilevel Statistical Models*. London: Arnold.

Greene, W.H. (2000). *Econometric Analysis*. Upper Saddle River, New Jersey: Prentice-Hall, Inc.

Haggett, P., A.D. Cliff and A. Frey (1977). *Locational Models*. London: Edward Arnold.

Hale, R. and T. Travers (1993). *£36 Billion and Rising? A Study of Standard Spending Assessments (SSAs)*. London: Chartered Institute of Public Finance and Accountancy.

Hall, J., I. Preston and S. Smith (1996). *Alternatives to Current Regression Methods in the Calculation of Standard Spending Assessments*. London: Institute for Fiscal Studies.

Hamilton, B. (1983). 'The flypaper effect and other anomalies'. *Journal of Public Economics* 22, 343–362.

Hauck, K., R. Shaw and P. Smith (2002). 'Reducing avoidable inequalities in health: a new criterion for setting health care capitation payments'. *Health Economics* 11(8), 667–677.

Hausman, J.A. (1978). 'Specification tests in econometrics'. *Econometrics* 46, 1251–1271.

Heald, D. (1996). 'Formula-Controlled Territorial Public Expenditure in the United Kingdom'. *Public Finance/Finances Publique* 51(4/Suppl), 534–558.

Health Care Financing Administration (1998). Announcement of calendar year 1999 Medicare+Choice payment rates. Washington, Health Care Financing Administration.

Health Care Financing Administration (1999). Medicare+Choice Rates 2000: 45 day notice. Washington, Health Care Financing Administration.

Hibbard, J., J. Stockard and M. Tusler (2003). 'Does publicizing hospital performance stimulate quality improvement efforts?'. *Health Affairs* 22(3), 84–94.

Higher Education Funding Council for England (2002). *Funding Higher Education in England: How the HEFCE Allocates Its Funds*. Bristol: Higher Education Funding Council for England.

Hillman, A., M. Pauly and J. Kerstein (1989). 'How do financial incentives affect physicians' clinical decisions and the financial performance of health maintenance organizations?'. *New England Journal of Medicine* 321(2), 86–92.

Home Office (2003). *Police Monitors 2001/02*. London: Home Office.

House of Commons Environment Committee (1998). *Local Government Finance*. London: The Stationery Office.

House of Commons Health Committee (1995). *Public Expenditure/Resource Allocation*. London: HMSO.

House of Commons Select Committee on the Environment (1994). *Standard Spending Assessments*. London: HMSO.

Housing Corporation (2001). *Guide to the Allocation Process 2002/03*. London: The Housing Corporation.

Huby, M. (1995). 'Community care and the social fund'. *Social Work and Social Sciences Review* 6(1), 32–47.

Iezzoni, L.I., J.Z. Ayanian, D.W. Bates and H.R. Burstin (1998). 'Paying more fairly for Medicare capitated care'. *New England Journal of Medicine* 339(26), 1933–1937.

Institute of Medicine (2001). *Crossing the Quality Chasm: A New Health System for the 21st Century*. Washington: National Academy Press.

John, P. and H. Ward (2001). 'Political manipulation in a majoritarian democracy: central government target of public funds to English subnational government, in space and across time'. *British Journal of Politics and International Relations* 3(3), 308–339.

Kanavos, P. and U. Reinhardt (2003). 'Reference Pricing For Drugs: Is It Compatible With U.S. Health Care?'. *Health Affairs* 22(3), 16–30.

Keith-Lucas, B. (1980). *The Unreformed Local Government System*. London: Croom Helm.

Kendall, M. and A. Stuart (1977). *The Advanced Theory of Statistics*: Volume 1, *Distribution Theory*. London: Charles Griffin & Company.

King, D. (1984). *Fiscal Tiers: The Economics of Multi-level Government*. London: Allen & Unwin.

Kralewski, J., E. Rich, R. Feldman, B. Dowd, T. Bernhardt, C. Johnson and W. Gold (2000). 'The effects of medical group practice on physician payment methods on costs of care'. *Health Services Research* 35(3), 591–613.

Krueger, A.O. (1974). 'The political economy of the rent-seeking society'. *American Economic Review* 64, 291–303.

Laffont, J.-J. (2000). *Incentives and Political Economy*. Oxford: Oxford University Press.

Langenbrunner, J., E. Orosz, J. Kutzin and M. Wiley (2005). 'Purchasing and paying providers'. In J. Figueras, R. Robinson and E. Jakubowski (ed.) *Purchasing to Improve Health Systems Performance*. Maidenhead, Open University Press.

Le Grand, J. (2002). 'Knights, knaves or pawns? Human behaviour and social policy'. *Journal of Social Policy* 26(2), 149–169.

Le Grand, J. and W. Bartlett (eds) (1993). *Quasimarkets and Social Policy*. London: Macmillan.

Le Grand, J., N. Mays and J. Mulligan (eds) (1999). *Learning from the NHS Internal Market*. London: King's Fund Institute.

Learning and Skills Council (2004). *Funding Guidance for Further Education in 2004–05*. Coventry: Learning and Skills Council.

Leatherman, S., B. Berwick, D. Iles, L. Lewin, F. Davidoff, T. Nolan and M. Bisognano (2003). 'The business case for quality: case studies and an analysis'. *Health Affairs* 22(2), 17–30.

Leech, D. and E. Campos (2003). 'Is comprehensive education really free? A case study of the effects of secondary school admission policies on house prices in one local area'. *Journal of the Royal Statistical Society Series A-Statistics in Society* 166(1), 135–154.

Levaggi, R. and P. Smith (1994). 'On the Intergovernmental Fiscal Game'. *Public Finance – Finances Publiques* 49(1), 72–86.

Louis, T., T. Jabine and M. Gerstein (eds) (2003). *Statistical Issues in Allocating Funds by Formula: Panel on Formula Allocations*. Washington: The National Academies Press.

Mannion, R. and M. Goddard (2001). 'Impact of published clinical outcomes data: case study in NHS hospital trusts'. *British Medical Journal* 323, 260–263.

Mapelli, V. (1998). *L'allocazione delle risorse nel Servizio Sanitario Nazionale*. Rome: Commissione Tecnica per la Spesa Pubblica, Ministero del Tesoro.

Marshall, M., P. Shekelle, H. Davies and P. Smith (2003). 'Public reporting on quality: lessons from the United States and the United Kingdom'. *Health Affairs* 22(3), 134–148.

Martin, S., N. Rice and P. Smith (1998). 'Risk and the general practitioner budget holder'. *Social Science and Medicine* 47(10), 1547–1554.

Mayhew, L. (1986). *Urban Hospital Location*. London: Allen & Unwin.

Mays, N. and G. Bevan (1987). *Resource Allocation in the Health Service*. London: Bedford Square Press.

McGuire, T. (2000). 'Physician agency'. In J.P. Newhouse and A.J. Culyer (ed.) *Handbook of Health Economics*. Amsterdam: Elsevier.

McLean, I. (2004). 'Fiscal federalism in Australia'. *Public Administration* 82(1), 21–38.

McLean, I. (2005). *The Fiscal Crisis of the United Kingdom*. Basingstoke: Palgrave Macmillan.

McLean, I. and A. McMillan (2003). 'The distribution of public expenditure across the UK regions'. *Fiscal Studies* 24(1), 45–71.

MHA Associates and Operational Research in Health (1997). Study of costs of providing health services in rural areas. Resource Allocation Research Paper 14. London: Department of Health.

Milgrom, P. and J. Roberts (1992). *Economics, Organization and Management*. Englewood Cliffs: Prentice Hall.

Miller, R. and H. Luft (1994). 'Managed care plan performance since 1980: a literature analysis'. *Journal of the American Medical Association* 271, 1512–1519.

Monopolies and Mergers Commission (1996). *Severn Trent Plc and South West Water Plc: A Report on the Proposed Merger*. London: Monopolies and Mergers Commission.

Mooney, G., J. Hall, C. Donaldson and K. Gerard (1991). 'Utilisation as a measure of equity: Weighing heat?'. *Journal of Health Economics* 10, 475–480.

Mueller, D. (2003). *Public Choice III*. Cambridge: Cambridge University Press.

Natinal Foster Care Association (1998). *Survey of Allowances – June 1998*. London: NFCA.

Newhouse, J. (1994). 'Patients at risk: health reform and risk adjustment'. *Health Affairs* Spring (1), 135–146.

Newhouse, J.P. (1996). 'Reimbursing health plans and health providers: efficiency in production versus selection'. *Journal of Economic Literature* 34, 1236–1263.

Newhouse, J.P., W.G. Manning, E.B. Keeler and E.M. Sloss (1989). 'Adjusting capitation rates using objective health measures and prior utilization'. *Health Care Financing Review* 10(3), 41–54.

Niskanen, W. (1968). 'The peculiar economics of bureaucracy'. *American Economic Review* 58, 293–305.

Nove, A. (1980). *The Soviet Economic System*, 2nd edn. London: Allen & Unwin.

Oates, W. (1969). 'The effects of property taxes and local public spending on property values: an empirical study of tax capitalization and the Tiebout hypothesis'. *Journal of Political Economy* 77, 957–971.

Oates, W. (1999). 'An essay on fiscal federalism'. *Journal of Economic Literature* 37, 1120–1149.

Office of the Deputy Prime Minister (2002). *Strong Local Leadership: Quality Public Services*. London: The Stationery Office.

Office of the Deputy Prime Minister (2003). *Local Government Finance Report 2003/04*. London: Office of the Deputy Prime Minister.

Osborne, D. and T. Gaebler (1992). *Reinventing Government: How the Entrepreneurial Spirit is Transforming the Public Sector*. New York: Penguin Books.

Peacock, S. and P. Smith (1995). 'The resource allocation consequences of the new NHS needs formula'. In H.o.C.H. Committee (ed.) *Public Expenditure/Resource Allocation: Minutes of Evidence 22 June 1995*. London: The Stationery Office.

Pollack, H. and R. Zeckhauser (1996). 'Budgets as dynamic gatekeepers'. *Management Science* 42(5), 642–658.

Pope, G., J. Kautter, R. Ellis, A. Ash, J. Ayanian, L. Iezzoni, M. Ingber, J. Levy and J. Robst (2004). 'Risk adjustment of medicare capitation payments using the CMS-HCC model'. *Health Care Financing Review* 25(4), 119–141.

Prendergast, C. (1999). 'The provision of incentives in firms'. *Journal of Economic Literature* 37(1), 7–63.

PriceWaterhouseCoopers (2000). *Local Government Grant Distribution: An International Comparative Study*. London: PriceWaterhouseCoopers.

Ramsey, J.B. (1989). 'Tests for specification errors in classical linear least squares regression analysis'. *Journal of the Royal Statistical Society, Series B* 31, 350–371.

Revenue Grant Distribution Review Group (2000). *Improving Grant Distribution to Local Authorities*. London: Department of the Environment, Transport and the Regions.

Rice, N. and P. Smith (2001a). 'Capitation and risk adjustment in health care financing: an international progress report'. *The Milbank Quarterly* 79(1), 81–113.

Rice, N. and P.C. Smith (2001b). 'Ethics and geographical equity in health care'. *Journal of Medical Ethics* 27(4), 256–261.

Ross, K. and R. Levacic (eds) (1999). *Needs-based Resource Allocation in Education: Via Formula Funding of Schools*. Paria: UNESCO Publishing.

Royston, G.H.D., J.W. Hurst, E.G. Lister and P.A. Stewart (1992). 'Modelling the use of health services by populations of small areas to inform the allocation of central resources to larger regions'. *Socio-Economic Planning Sciences* 26(3), 169–180.

Saltman, R., R. Busse and J. Figueras (eds) (2004). *Social Health Insurance Systems in Western Europe*. Maidenhead: Open University Press.

Scott, A. (2001). 'Eliciting GPs' preferences for pecuniary and non-pecuniary job characteristics'. *Journal of Health Economics* 20(3), 329–347.

Scottish Executive (2001). *Grant-aided Expenditure 2001–02*. Edinburgh: Scottish Executive.

Scottish Executive (2004). *Local Government Finance Settlement: 2005–06, 2006–07 and 2007–08*. Edinburgh: Scottish Executive.

Scottish Executive Health Department (1999). *Fair Shares for All: Consultation Document*. Edinburgh: Scottish Executive Health Department.

Scottish Executive Health Department (2000). *Fair Shares for All: Final Report*. Edinburgh: Scottish Executive Health Department.

Scottish Parliament (1999). *Health Committee Calls for Further Work on Arbuthnott Report*, Press release CHEAL0018/1999. Edinburgh: Scottish Parliament.

Scottish Parliament Local Government Committee (2002). *Report on Inquiry into Local Government Finance*. Edinburgh: Scottish Parliament.

Seabright, P. (1996). 'Accountability and decentralisation in government: an incomplete contracts approach'. *European Economic Review* 40(1), 61–89.

Secretary of State for Social Security (2000). *Annual Report on the Social Fund 1999/2000*. London: The Stationery Office.

Sheldon, T. (1997). 'Formula fever: allocating resources in the NHS'. *British Medical Journal* 315, 964.

Sheldon, T. and R. Carr-Hill (1992). 'Resource allocation by regression in the National Health Service: a critique of the Resource Allocation Working Party's review'. *Journal of the Royal Statistical Society Series A-Statistics in Society* 155, 403–420.

Sheldon, T. and I. Watts (1993). 'Rurality and resource allocation in the UK'. *Health Policy* 26(1), 19–27.

Shleifer, A. (1985). 'A Theory of Yardstick Competition'. *Rand Journal of Economics* 16(3), 319–327.

Shmueli, A., N. Shamai, Y. Levi and M. Abraham (1998). 'In search of a national capitation formula: the Israeli experience'. In D. Chinitz and J. Cohen (ed.) *Governments and Health Systems: Implications of Different Involvements*. Chichester: Wiley.

Smith, P. (1995). 'On the unintended consequences of publishing performance data in the public sector'. *International Journal of Public Administration* 18(2/3), 277–310.

Smith, P. (1997). *Devolved Purchasing in Health Care: A Review of the Issues, Nuffield Occasional Papers, Health Economics Series Paper 2*. London: Nuffield Trust.

Smith, P. (2003). 'Formula funding of public services: an economic analysis'. *Oxford Review of Economic Policy* 19(2).

Smith, P. and N. York (2004). 'Quality incentives: the case of UK general practitioners'. *Health Affairs* 23, 112.

Smith, P., T.A. Sheldon, R.A. Carr-Hill, S. Martin, S. Peacock and G. Hardman (1994). 'Allocating resources to health authorities - results and policy implications of small-area analysis of use of inpatient services'. *British Medical Journal* 309(6961), 1050–1054.

Smith, P.C. (1999). 'Setting budgets for general practice in the new NHS'. *British Medical Journal* 318(7186), 776–779.

Smith, P.C. (2002). 'Performance management in British health care: Will it deliver?'. *Health Affairs* 21(3), 103–115.

Smith, P.C., N. Rice and R. Carr-Hill (2001). 'Capitation funding in the public sector'. *Journal of the Royal Statistical Society Series A – Statistics in Society* 164, 217–241.

Sommersguter-Reichmann, M. (2000). 'The impact of the Austrian hospital financing reform on hospital productivity: empirical evidence on efficiency and technology changes using a non-parametric input-based Malmquist approach'. *Health Care Management Science* 3(4), 309–321.

Spooner, A., A. Chapple and M. Roland (2001). 'What makes British general practitioners take part in a quality improvement scheme?'. *Journal of Health Services Research and Policy* 6(3), 145–150.

Steel, D. and D. Holt (1996). 'Analysing and adjusting aggregation effects: the ecological fallacy revisited'. *International Statistical Review* 64(1), 39–60.

Steuerle, C., V. Ooms, G. Peterson and R. Reischauer (eds) (2000). *Vouchers and the Provision of Public Services*. Washington: Brookings Institution Press.

Sutton, M. and P. Lock (2000). 'Regional differences in health care delivery: implications for a national resource allocation formula'. *Health Economics* 9(6), 547–559.

Sutton, M., H. Gravelle, S. Morris, A. Leyland, F. Windmeijer, C. Dibben and M. Muirhead (2002). *Allocation of Resources to English Areas: Individual and Small Area Determinants of Morbidity and Use of Healthcare Resources*. Edinburgh: ISD Consultancy Services.

Thomas, R.W. and E.S. Warren (1997). 'Evaluating the role of regression methods in the determination of Standard Spending Assessments'. *Environment and Planning C – Government and Policy* 15(1), 53–72.

Tiebout, C. (1956). 'A pure theory of local expenditure'. *Journal of Political Economy* 64(5), 416–424.

Tranmer, M. and D.G. Steel (1998). 'Using census data to investigate the causes of the ecological fallacy'. *Environment and Planning A* 30(5), 817–831.

United States Government (1993). *Government Performance Results Act*. Washington: US Government.

Van Barneveld, E.M., L.M. Lamers, R. Van Vliet and W. Van de Ven (1998). 'Mandatory pooling as a supplement to risk-adjusted capitation payments in a competitive health insurance market'. *Social Science and Medicine* 47(2), 223–232.

Van de Ven, W.P.M.M. and R. Ellis (2000). 'Risk adjustment in competitive health plan markets'. In J.P. Newhouse and A.J. Culyer (ed.) *Handbook of Health Economics*. Amsterdam: Elsevier.

Van Vliet, R.C.J.A. and L.M. Lamers (1998). 'The high costs of death: should health plans get higher payments when members die?'. *Medical Care* 36(10), 1451–1460.

Ward, H. and P. John (1999). 'Targeting benefits for electoral gain: constituency marginality and the distribution of grants to English local authorities'. *Political Studies* 47(1), 32–52.

West, A. and H. Pennell (2000). 'Publishing school examination results in England: incentives and consequences'. *Educational Studies* 26(4), 423–436.

Wilson, A.G. (1974). *Urban and Regional Models in Geography and Planning*. Cichester: Wiley.

Wilson, J.D. (1999). 'Theories of tax competition'. *National Tax Journal* 52(2), 269–304.

Wilson, R., R. Davies, A. Green, D. Owen and P. Elias (2002). *Spatial Variations in Labour Costs: Review of the Staff Market Forces Factor*. Coventry: Institute for Employment Research, University of Warwick.

Index

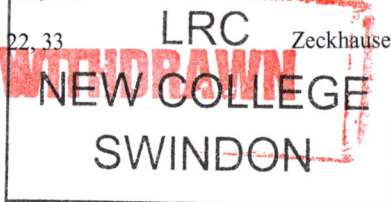